# The Six Sigma Path to Leadership

## Observations from the Trenches

Also available from ASQ Quality Press:

*Six Sigma for the Office: A Pocket Guide*
Roderick Munro

*Six Sigma for the Shop Floor: A Pocket Guide*
Roderick Munro

*Six Sigma Project Management: A Pocket Guide*
Jeffrey N. Lowenthall

*Customer Centered Six Sigma: Linking Customers, Process Improvement, and Financial Results*
Earl Naumann and Steven H. Hoisington

*The Six Sigma Journey from Art to Science*
Larry Walters

*Office Kaizen: Transforming Office Operations Into a Strategic Competitive Advantage*
William Lareau

*Defining and Analyzing a Business Process: A Six Sigma Pocket Guide*
Jeffrey N. Lowenthall

*Managing Change: Practical Strategies for Competitive Advantage*
Kari Tuominen

*Improving Performance through Statistical Thinking*
ASQ Statistics Division

To request a complimentary catalog of ASQ Quality Press publications, call 800-248-1946, or visit our website at http://qualitypress.asq.org.

# The Six Sigma Path to Leadership

## Observations from the Trenches

Dr. David H. Treichler
with Ronald D. Carmichael

ASQ Quality Press
Milwaukee, Wisconsin

American Society for Quality, Quality Press, Milwaukee 53203
© 2004 by David H. Treichler
All rights reserved. Published 2004
Printed in the United States of America

12  11  10  09  08  07  06  05  04  03     5  4  3  2  1

Library of Congress Cataloging-in-Publication Data

Treichler, David H. (David Howard), 1948-
  The Six Sigma path to leadership : observations from the trenches / by
David H. Treichler with Ronald D. Carmichael.-- 1st ed.
    p. cm.
Includes bibliographical references and index.
  ISBN 0-87389-615-7 (alk. paper)
  1. Leadership. 2. Teams in the workplace. 3. Organizational change.
4. Organizational learning. 5. Organizational effectiveness. 6. Six sigma
(Quality control standard). 7. Sarbanes Oxley Compliance. 8. Strategic
Roadmapping. 9. Capability migration mapping.

HD57.7.T74 2004
658.4'092—dc22

                                            2003024329

ISBN  0-87389-615-7

Publisher: William A. Tony
Acquisitions Editor: Annemieke Hytinen
Project Editor: Paul O'Mara
Production Administrator: Randy Benson
Special Marketing Representative: David Luth

ASQ Mission: The American Society for Quality advances individual, organizational, and
community excellence worldwide through learning, quality improvement, and knowledge exchange.

Attention Bookstores, Wholesalers, Schools and Corporations: ASQ Quality Press books,
videotapes, audiotapes, and software are available at quantity discounts with bulk purchases for
business, educational, or instructional use. For information, please contact ASQ Quality Press at
800-248-1946, or write to ASQ Quality Press, P.O. Box 3005, Milwaukee, WI 53201-3005.

To place orders or to request a free copy of the ASQ Quality Press Publications Catalog, including
ASQ membership information, call 800-248-1946. Visit our Web site at www.asq.org or
http://qualitypress.asq.org.

∞  Printed on acid-free paper

Quality Press
600 N. Plankinton Avenue
Milwaukee, Wisconsin 53203
Call toll free 800-248-1946
Fax 414-272-1734
www.asq.org
http://qualitypress.asq.org
http://standardsgroup.asq.org
E-mail: authors@asq.org

*To Harold J. Kammerer,*

*who taught me never to give up.*

# Table of Contents

# CD Contents

# Preface

SIX SIGMA LEADERS TEACH THE LEADERS OF THE FUTURE.

This book was inspired by the musings of a couple of Six Sigma Black Belts (practitioners) who went on to become Six Sigma business leaders and defenders of the faith. What follows is a collection of articles written (and tools developed) during the author's own journey from novice to leader. As such, the book provides more than a few lessons about applying Six Sigma from the very practitioners who have "been there and done that." But the book is written for anyone, from senior management to curious novice, with the intent to encourage and assist everyone, wherever they may be in their own Six Sigma journey.

The Six Sigma path is, and will be, different for every reader. Because of this, the author has sought to present information that is true – in general – for most organizations, as well as very specific tales that he and other Six Sigma practitioners have encountered in "the trenches" of their own organizations. Some are the kinds of stories that can only be found by sitting down with a Black Belt over a beer.

This book does not devote space to the use of standard Six Sigma tools, techniques, and methodologies. More than a few books and journal articles have already been written that thoroughly cover those topics. What this book does contain are a few tools, developed by the author over the course of his own journey, that have been used repeatedly in different Six Sigma organizations. These tools are simply samples the reader can use as a springboard to develop tools to meet his or her own specific needs in the quest to gather, evaluate, and analyze data in support of fact-based decisions.

The tales of transformation in this book are focused on knowledge-based applications because there are, at this time, few documented examples for those companies that are seeking to integrate Six Sigma into their knowledge-based processes and strategic applications. There are, however, many well-documented examples of Six Sigma as it is applied to manufacturing. These are readily available in other sources. But even beyond knowledge-based applications, the stories presented in this book illustrate how to apply Six Sigma across the organization to leverage significant performance improvement.

As a Six Sigma leader/professional, the reader has an important role in teaching others how to establish and manage a Six Sigma organization. This doesn't necessarily mean creating a cadre of Green Belts and Black Belts, but rather acting as a role model of one that uses Six Sigma tools and methodologies to establish the facts of any situation. Developing tools to gather, validate, and interpret relevant data is essential to the reader's knowledge of the particular situation. Becoming a mentor to help others develop similar tools for themselves is also an important part of the teaching and learning process that is essential to leadership.

An avid advocate of personal growth, the author has deliberately attempted to document the growth experienced during his own Six Sigma journey. This book is not a Six Sigma "self-help" book, nor does it contain defined and rigid training program requirements on what it takes to do Six Sigma right. (The author does have strong views about Six Sigma training and has devoted a significant portion of a chapter to the subject of training, but it is not the main focus of the book.) Rather, what follows is a collection of observations designed to inspire and spark the reader's imagination about what Six Sigma *could be*, what the people who engage in this profession *could know* and be able to do, and what the reader *could find helpful* if engaged in Design for Six Sigma, global applications of Six Sigma, supply chain opportunities, software applications, knowledge-based organization applications, and, finally, the leadership of their entire organization, not just a Six Sigma cadre within the organization.

The author is always looking for data to continuously improve the relevance and applicability of the book, and the reader can play a big role in assisting this effort. As questions or suggestions on how to make subsequent editions of this book more relevant to the reader's needs arise, please e-mail them to the author's attention to authors@asq.org.

As in every effort, there are individuals without whom the end product would be substantially less valuable to all concerned. As such, special thanks are due to many individuals who have extended the author's understandings of Six Sigma.

There are many who have contributed to the author's knowledge and understandings of Six Sigma and change management. It is not possible to give proper credit to them all in this space and all Six Sigma leaders and practitioners have and will encounter such people in their own journeys. However, three individuals were essential to the final preparation of this book and are essential to the continued development of the author's ideas and understandings of Six Sigma and communication of the lessons learned along the way.

Gwen Berthiez is an organizational development/organization effectiveness consultant with Raytheon Company in Tucson, Arizona. She is also a former manager of the Academy for Excellence in Russelsheim, Germany, which provides automotive sales and after-sales training, serving General Motors Europe's dealer network in 22 countries globally. Gwen participated in many of the early efforts recounted in the Tactical

Transformation section and provided a technical edit of this work, which has added substantially to the clarity and meaningfulness of the final product.

Rick and Rita Cronise of Cronise Communications in Victor, New York, provide outstanding technical editing and document preparation, and consistently provide creative insights and recommendations that make for a much more interesting final product. They worked their usual magic on this project.

Three individuals who provided invaluable insight into the Design for Six Sigma efforts across many firms are:

- Donald L Deptowicz, director of innovation and continuous improvement methodologies for Delphi Automotive. Previously he led efforts in aerothermal design, engine components for the F119 Engine, and managed the Product Center Engineering at Pratt and Whitney. Immediately prior to joining Delphi, he also led Design for Six Sigma efforts at Allied Signal.

- Phil Lardiere, CEO of the Pendleton Group located in Seneca, South Carolina. Phil held senior leadership positions at Reynolds Aluminum, Johnson Controls, Allied Signal, and Magna Corporation. He has consulted with top firms in the automotive, pharmaceutical, chemical, electronics, and financial industries.

- Gene Wiggs, a Master Black Belt for General Electric Aircraft Engines in Cincinnati, Ohio.

Four individuals contributed either concepts or drafts of concepts that have been incorporated in sections of this work:

- Dr. John Lewis, an R6Sigma (Raytheon Six Sigma) expert for the Information and Intelligence Systems Division of Raytheon Company in Garland, Texas, and the former president and general manager of Raytheon Training Italia, S.r.l. in Rome, Italy. John was an early reviewer of the Design for Six Sigma chapter and was involved in the development of some of the concepts further defined in the Tales of Transformation section.

- Dr. Antone Kusmanoff, a senior design engineer for the L-3 Communications Aircraft Integration Systems Division in Greenville, Texas. Antone is the primary author of the account reprinted in the chapter on supply chain and also contributed to the chapter on early customer engagement.

- Jim LaMantia and Audrey Kostrzewa, Master Experts with Raytheon Intelligence and Information Systems added concepts and elements to the Strategic Roadmapping section which related to Core Value/Core Purpose analysis.

A major focus of this book has been on the lessons learned so that the reader may gain from the experiences of others. Each of the individuals named and many hundreds of others have contributed to the lessons reflected herein. It is sincerely hoped that recording and sharing these lessons will leverage the effectiveness of practitioners and leaders who lead, or intend to lead, Six Sigma companies and organizations.

# Introduction

SIX SIGMA IS A JOURNEY OF LEADERSHIP DEVELOPMENT.

Six Sigma is a long journey. However, it is one of the most rewarding journeys that an individual or company may elect to take. Six Sigma is many things, but foremost it is a data-driven leadership approach using specific tools and methodologies that lead to fact-based decision-making. The focus is on performance throughout the organization. The resulting culture of leaders is one that does not tolerate waste or inefficiency. It is very creative in its approach to doing business, and it offers solutions that exceed the customer's requirements and expectations.

The concept of a culture of leaders may seem strange at first glance. Yet one of the things that Six Sigma does is empower individuals throughout the organization to develop individual leadership skills and capabilities. This is accomplished through projects that teach them to gather data, analyze them, and, as a part of a team, determine the best course of action for the company to follow to enhance performance.

Six Sigma is a broad tent. There are applications for Six Sigma in nearly every function of an organization. Specific chapters look at product design, software development, supply chain and knowledge businesses, as well as all of the support functions present in any business or nonbusiness enterprise, including government.

The leverage that Six Sigma brings to an organization is startling to those who have not experienced truly effective performance improvement efforts in the past. It is not without issues, however, nor is it simple or easy to implement. In the last section various issues are analyzed and recommendations are provided on approaches and concepts advanced. The conclusion to this book provides specific recommendations to rapidly realize performance improvements from a Six Sigma effort.

The sum of this effort is to provide a different look at Six Sigma, one that is more grounded than the typical. The author's personal journey in pursuit of performance excellence and accelerated results is reflected in each chapter. As with life in general, his path to the present has been neither linear nor sequential. It has not been confined to one industry or even one continent. This has all resulted in an enriched experience and a better understanding of humankind.

Likewise, it is the author's sincere hope that each and every business leader, Six Sigma Black Belt, Master Black Belt, and Champion has the opportunity to experience the rich variety that exists in the world. Working with people from different domains and cultures has led to the realization that at the end of the day they all have the same goal, which is to help their organization perform better today than it did yesterday. In that regard, we are all brothers and sisters regardless of where we perform our work. And to that end, Six Sigma gives us a common vocabulary in which to exchange our ideas, knowledge, and experience along with a tool set and methodology that helps each of us make sense of the world around us.

# Section A

# Quantum Leadership

EVERY INDIVIDUAL WHO EMBRACES SIX SIGMA HAS A TREMENDOUS OPPORTUNITY TO DEVELOP THE KIND OF LEADERSHIP SKILLS THAT CAN HELP ANY ORGANIZATION SUCCESSFULLY WEATHER THE STORMS OF RAPIDLY CHANGING COMPETITIVE ENVIRONMENTS.

The chapters in this section focus on those aspects of the Six Sigma experience that make it a fertile training ground for the leadership of the future. The author has previously shared these insights with senior leadership teams in major global companies.

*Chapter 1: Six Sigma as Leadership* describes how it takes an exceptional leader, a Quantum Leader, to meet the challenges of a highly competitive, rapid-fire future. Six Sigma deployment develops and sharpens critical leadership skills such as working in partnership with people at all levels of the organization, hearing the voice of the customer, collecting data and analyzing needs, scoping projects, structuring tasks for success, consulting, providing leadership to project teams, consistently meeting objectives, and striving for continuous improvement in all areas. All of these skills can be directly transferred to leading an organization, from a small not-for-profit group to a massive multinational corporation.

The Leadership Teams in many organizations still regard leadership development as a by-product of the Six Sigma experience. This chapter recommends that it become a primary focus.

*Chapter 2: The Quick and the Dead: The Role of Quantum Leaders* differentiates between Change Agents and Quantum Leaders, which are defined as those who actually accelerate change and achieve substantially greater results as an end product. This chapter compares and contrasts Quantum Leaders and Change Agents in detail to help the reader to discern the difference.

*Chapter 3: The Performance Roadmap* builds on the concepts of The Quick and the Dead, with a "map" of specific organizational actions that leverage results and enable the Six Sigma leader to achieve dramatically improved results.

*Chapter 4: Building the Quantum Leader Strategic Roadmap* details an approach building a "map" that integrates not only the plan sufficiency and detailed planning for implementation, but also checks the back against the criteria deemed necessary to ensure that it is consistent with the core values of the organization.

Without a roadmap it is almost impossible for a visionary leader to achieve even pedestrian results. This chapter moves the discussion to the Leadership Team. It results in a well-understood and shared set of goals focused on the essential results to achieve the desired future state. Quantum Leaders need a plan in order to know where they are taking the organization. Six Sigma plays a major role in developing this plan.

# 1

# Six Sigma as Leadership

SIX SIGMA IS A MODEL FOR LEADERSHIP TRAINING AND PROVIDES
EXPERIENCE IN HOW TO ACHIEVE RESULTS THROUGH TEAMS.

## QUANTUM RESULTS

Leaders are expected to get results. Yet only a few leaders are able to achieve what the author refers to as Quantum results, or the ability to take an organization to dramatically higher levels of performance.

What makes these few leaders different from the others? They have the ability to look beyond the clutter in every decision and dispassionately pierce to the facts of the matter. They are successful because they are not side tracked by personal or nonobjective concerns or issues; instead, they focus on what will obtain business results.

## QUANTUM LEADERSHIP

A Quantum Leader is most often someone in a leadership role within an organization, someone who personally employs the tools, methods, and skills of Six Sigma in his or her decision-making and holds others in the organization accountable for using them as well. Simply put, a Quantum Leader blends his or her experience, data-driven decisions, and people skills to inspire others to dig deeper and reach higher.

Business results often reflect a Quantum Leader's data-driven decisions, particularly when they directly influence the decisions of the business Leadership Team and those business leaders at the highest levels of the organization who bear final responsibility for the performance of the organization.

When the Leadership Team as a group uses Six Sigma to manage the organization, the operating results far outperform those organizations where their counterparts believe in business as usual.

## THE LEADERSHIP APPROACH TO DOING BUSINESS

At a recent conference, the author asked several practicing Six Sigma Black Belts to define exactly what Six Sigma meant to them. In less than two minutes, responses jumped from "Six Sigma is 3.14 defects per million opportunities," at one extreme, to "Six Sigma is a culture," at the other extreme.

While both responses are technically correct, the author's view is that Six Sigma is an essential and foundational leadership approach to doing business.

Six Sigma drives the total organization – inclusive of all job descriptions and ranks of employees from engineering, marketing, Information Technology, finance, and facilities, to manufacturing – to make dispassionate decisions based on objective data that have been systematically and planfully gathered and analyzed.

## THE TYPICAL APPROACH TO DOING BUSINESS

Data-driven decision-making is dependent upon good and plentiful data. However, in many organizations most decisions are made without the ability to gather such data. In many instances only partial or suggestive data at best are available, and in some instances, no data can be obtained, and yet a decision must be made.

The author has observed that in most instances more and different data are available than the decision-makers seek, or take the time to obtain. This may be a result of time constraints, lack of data collection and methodology skills, or a fatal flaw – the sheer lack of foresight tempered and forged by patience. Data can be obtained that most individuals do not pursue and this contributes to the subjective or intuitive basis for many, if not most, business decisions.

At the contra position to this are those organizations where analysis paralysis blocks any important decisions from being made. This is often a trait of very large organizations where authority and responsibility are diffused. In this case more and more data are collected, or an analysis is endlessly reworked. For whatever reason, the analysis does not effectively reveal the facts of the matter. Clearly in this situation, the Leadership Team hesitates to come to any decision because they do not trust that the analysis reveals the facts of the matter.

After observing Leadership Teams in a variety of firms and disciplines, it becomes evident that companies with the worst operating results are those in which Leadership Team membership is based on longevity or personal relationships with the in-crowd or "circle of friends" within the organization. Perhaps they reason that longevity begets wisdom, thus bestowing upon these members the ability to draw upon their vast experiences to make appropriate decisions. However, this approach to business decision-making often leads to disaster. Longevity alone as a basis for selecting decision-makers relies on instincts born of past successes and failures to indiscriminately and unpredictably determine what might cause future successes or failures.

## SIX SIGMA AS THE LEADERSHIP CRITERION

Six Sigma teaches and trains leaders how to obtain, validate, and analyze the data upon which decisions can be made. But the Six Sigma methods are not foolproof. The author has observed instances of decisions, based on data provided using Six Sigma methods, that have still led to unexpected or suboptimal results. This is usually because the wrong questions were asked.

Asking the right questions depends on having the right experience for the situation coupled with the appropriate/proper application of Six Sigma tools and methods.

Teams usually conduct Six Sigma projects. The power of the Six Sigma approach lies in the team's aggregate experience to achieve balanced and accurate data design, development, and collection. It is the team's aggregate experience that also creates the multifaceted perceptual screen used to validate subsequent results.

## BEYOND POLITICS

Data come in different types. There are formal data that are collected, analyzed, and used to create the facts that lead to optimal results. The other data are informal and generally the result of personal interpretation of experience, observation, or imparted wisdom.

All too often, informal data brought to the entire Six Sigma team by its members are weighted differently from the hard data obtained by the team using standard Six Sigma tools. The danger of data weighting becomes apparent when informal data are used to justify actions diametrically opposed to those indicated by the hard data findings because of *political realities*.

The two most frequently occurring *political realities* that are used to influence/dominate the course of a decision are either that upper management will not accept the fact-based recommendation, or no budget exists to undertake the effort, so why advance it? And – of course – no one with career ambitions wants to become the ill-fated messenger. These two ambivalent circumstances negatively influence the essential long-term changes that must result from deployment of an organization wide Six Sigma program. However, the perceptions of the Leadership Team members about the organization they lead and the roles of those being groomed as future company leaders determine the limits to the change that will occur.

Clearly, if the Leadership Team wishes to make data-driven decisions, they must remove the *fear factor* that exists in every organization. Every leader must convincingly communicate to all of his or her employees that political considerations will not be invoked to amend data-driven and properly analyzed team recommendations. Resource contention may force prioritization of activity, but contrary decisions should not be undertaken. Management must prove to employees that it does not shoot messengers. Management must reward teams that do their homework, conduct fact-based data collection, and achieve impartial analyses that influence key decisions.

## INVESTING IN THE FUTURE

When organizations begin to understand the bottom-line impact of Six Sigma activity there is a tendency to train and deploy vast legions of Black Belts and Green Belts with a mandate to go forth and immediately save immense sums of money.

Many companies get out ahead of themselves, playing the numbers game (based on predicted savings). At some point management comes to the realization that they are facing a negative cash flow for a period of time as employees are released from regular work to participate in or lead analysis or projects that will eventually lead to the predicted savings.

The Leadership Team must be educated (or educate itself) about this lag time during the early phases of a Six Sigma business analysis or project, and prepare for the temporary degradation that precedes the upswing in performance. Once the Leadership Team understands and anticipates this temporary decrease in productivity, launching any change activity will be more effective.

Resource deployment is always a contentious factor during the early phases of a Six Sigma project. Selection or deferral of various projects may either motivate or subvert rapid deployment and the subsequent results that are achieved.

Starting small and growing a Six Sigma activity/initiative from realized savings is the most rational approach. Leadership's role is to evaluate, prioritize, schedule, and budget the work to be done, while maintaining employee motivation for projects waiting their turn in the pipeline.

Realized savings raises the question of measurement of those savings. Not only must the firm or organization have metrics in place to measure performance improvement, but it must also have predetermined criteria with which to measure actual cost savings realized for a Six Sigma effort/project. Cost savings are hard to accomplish and must be worked together between the financial organization and the Six Sigma community with the backing and support of the Leadership Team.

It is leadership and leadership alone that open the doors for a view into an organization's finances. At best cost savings are hard to achieve without building a bureaucratic function to simultaneously track results and establish objectivity and validate the data. The cost savings issues are explored in greater depth throughout this work.

## LEADERSHIP: FROM CONCEPT TO REALITY

Six Sigma as leadership is the theme of this book. However, leading by Six Sigma application is not the whole story, nor the automatic prescription for leadership success.

In meetings of Six Sigma Black Belts and upper management where the upper management itself is not employing Six Sigma, the concept of Six Sigma *as* leadership seems to permeate the room, more as an implication than as an expressed statement. The Six Sigma community has been given the responsibility to obtain results that upper management is seeking, but without the independence or authority to take proactive steps without checking back.

For example, a company that prides itself on its superior engineering capabilities made a significant investment over time to tailor applications of Six Sigma and then train, deploy, and support a large cadre of Black Belts and Green Belts. Large savings from this effort were reported, however, gentle probing made it clear that the firm did not employ Design for Six Sigma, which is the application of Six Sigma tools, methods, and skill sets that yield results in the design phase of product development.

Instead, the design community was investing heavily in finding ways to improve schedules and avoid huge expenditures, but only at the end of large complex projects. The problem: projects were already far behind the original schedules and way over the initial budgets. The design community received much recognition for their *end of project heroics*, yet what they really accomplished was to continue to add sandbags after the flood had wiped out the town.

Nonetheless, the engineering design community successfully convinced upper management that they were doing just fine without embracing the Six Sigma culture that was growing around them. Management was not aware of the extent to which the schedule and cost overruns they had been so busy fixing could have been avoided altogether through the application of Design for Six Sigma. Without Design for Six Sigma, the engineering design community continued to introduce new variability into the factory at the very same time as the Six Sigma community worked to eliminate variability from the products currently under production. Thus, the organization as a whole did not realize the full extent of the cost and performance benefits from Six Sigma that they were capable of achieving. *When deployed at the inception of a project, Six Sigma can be the exact antithesis of end of project heroics.*

Another company the author interviewed undertook to grow a Six Sigma Leadership Team and prepared to pervasively embrace Six Sigma throughout the firm. A Six Sigma culture was created over time by steeping the entire workforce in the Six Sigma data-driven decision-making ethic. Growing up in a Six Sigma culture makes it the way things are naturally done – the only way of conducting business. Emerging leaders gain their experience using Six Sigma tools and methodologies, and the skills they develop become the basis for their decision-making.

Most firms do not have the luxury of measuring their progress over decades. Changing a culture in a short period of time (relatively speaking) is only accomplished when the Leadership Team understands Six Sigma, gains experience in the actual application of Six Sigma principles and disciplines to solve business problems, supports each other, and establishes the multifaceted perceptual screens that give an integrated balance to the data and facts obtained for each and every situation.

Leadership Teams must do more than just *get it*. They must live it. They must lead by example, demonstrating to all employees, customers, suppliers, and the general public that business is conducted one way and one way only – through fact-based decision-making.

Companies that grow to dominate their industries do the best job of making decisions based on the most factual data and most complete picture of any situation they are facing. When a whole organization is knowledgeable about Six Sigma tools, skill sets, and methodologies, all employees are empowered to obtain data and present a more complete factual picture up the chain of command to their leadership for decision-making. This is the organization most likely to succeed where others fail or achieve lesser results.

In the final analysis it is all a matter of leadership. Leadership cannot *get it* at the conceptual or intellectual level. That is mere lip service to Six Sigma. Instead, leadership must live Six Sigma, lead by Six Sigma, and infuse Six Sigma into every business decision. Leadership must lead the way by providing training, resources, and opportunities for practicing and employing Six Sigma. And leadership must then reinforce to every constituent of their organization precisely how Six Sigma data-driven decision-making has net the company the success it currently enjoys.

## THE MAKING OF THE QUANTUM LEADER

Leadership grounding in Six Sigma methodology, followed by Black Belt and Master Black Belt experience, provides a very fertile training ground for senior leadership development. For those readers aspiring to senior leadership roles, the next chapter addresses the fundamental difference between a Quantum Leader and a Change Agent and examines the pivotal role of the Quantum Leader as one who achieves dramatic short- and long-term improvements in performance. Corporate boards are increasingly seeking Quantum Leaders to assume senior leadership roles.

Finally, a single individual can make a difference in any organization with the right circumstances, training, opportunity, resources, and support. As experience is gained the individual becomes more effective at whatever he or she may undertake. Six Sigma is no different. For Leadership Teams, and others who aspire to become Quantum Leaders, it is clear that individuals are more successful when they live and lead by the Six Sigma approach.

## SUMMARY

Leaders are expected to get results. Yet only a few leaders are able to achieve what the author refers to as Quantum results, or the ability to take an organization to dramatically higher levels of performance.

What makes these few leaders different from the others? They have the ability to look beyond all of the clutter in every decision and dispassionately pierce to the facts of the matter. They are successful because they are not side tracked by personal or nonobjective concerns or issues; instead, they focus on what will obtain business results.

This chapter defined a Quantum Leader as someone in a leadership role within an organization, someone who personally employs the tools, methods, and skills of Six Sigma in his or her decision-making and holds others in the organization accountable for using them as well.

Leadership grounding in Six Sigma methodology, followed by Black Belt and Master Black Belt experience, provides a very fertile training ground for senior leadership development.

# 2

# The Quick and the Dead—
# The Role of Quantum Leaders

LEADERS OBTAIN DRAMATIC IMPROVEMENTS IN PERFORMANCE WHEN THEY
REALIZE THAT IT TAKES MORE THAN JUST BEING A CHANGE AGENT.

## CHANGE AGENT SYNOPSIS

The theoretical role of the Change Agent in modern organizations is well documented. However, organizations face increasingly rapid changes as a result of technology, competition, and customer expectation. The relentless and ever-increasing pace of change results in Change Agents discovering that their incremental solutions to pressing problems are too little, too late. Thus, organizations are increasingly in search of Quantum Leaders, those individuals capable of rapid and sustained organizational change. The success of the Quantum Leader can be attributed to a difference in focus, priorities, and behavior. This chapter, based on the author's experience with both Change Agents and Quantum Leaders, provides a characterization of each. It compares and contrasts the two roles and discusses the increasing need for Quantum Leadership in organizations if they are to survive and thrive.

## RIGHT CHANGE, RIGHT TIME

Survival is a matter of change. Growth and prosperity are factors of how fast and adept an organization and its individuals are at anticipating and making the right changes at the right time. The ability to anticipate and lead the right change at the right time is not a matter of luck, nor is it a matter of following a prescribed set of step-by-step instructions or a well-prepared script. And, it cannot be taught in business school. Instead, growth and prosperity result from leadership that:

- Studies the marketplace and environment.

- Envisions an alternative future.

- Maps a course that leads to that future state.

- Builds a consensus around the vision and the course.

- Creates the capability to create that future.

- Plunges ahead without hesitation or regret.

- Learns from mistakes and rapidly implements lessons learned.

- Engages external organizations as if they were internal.

- Learns continuously and teaches others.

- Perpetuates forward momentum.

Visionary leaders are not content to maintain the status quo because they recognize that remaining static provides a target for the competition and ultimately leads to customer dissatisfaction. Organizations that continually introduce new products and product enhancements, or that acquire or start up new lines of business and champion innovation, are much more difficult to deal with in the competitive marketplace.

## CHANGE AGENTS

The traditional role of the Change Agent is itself changing because incremental improvement is no longer sufficient in an era of accelerating innovation in technology and communication. Change Agents are expected to introduce quantum change into organizations that are not prepared or structured to manage that kind of change.

To help the reader to understand the dilemma, the traditional role of the Change Agent in most organizations is outlined. Specifically, Change Agents:

- Do it faster, cheaper, better.

- Attack the symptoms of status quo.

- Target incremental change.

- Focus on process improvement.

- Pursue a top-down approach.

- Work in isolation.

- Are managed by the organization.

*The main focus is on process-based incremental change.*

## Do it faster, cheaper, better

Since the days of Frederick Taylor the primary concern of industrial organizations has been to find means and methods of reducing cycle-times, reducing content to eliminate cost, and making a better product for a lower (or worst case, the same) cost as the current market entries. Over the years organizations have translated this obsession to all processes and roles. However, it has been difficult to obtain consistent improvement in nonautomated processes for two reasons:

First, the Hawthorne Effect showed that employees under the microscope could, without exception, outperform the typical rates of activity without fundamentally changing anything that they would do normally. However, as soon as the attention was removed performance would return to the typical rates.

Second, most organizations do a poor job of measuring average daily outputs. Metrics are threatening to individuals because they reveal how much room for improvement exists.

The faster, cheaper, better method breaks down when attention is removed from the process actors, as they usually return to the typical level of activity. This is because the change is not embedded in the culture and daily expectations when the attention is focused elsewhere.

## Attack the symptoms of status quo

Change Agents respond to the problem of the moment, attacking issues identified as most painful for the organization to deal with. However, organizations are adept at developing "workarounds" that somehow become institutionalized. The reason "workarounds" become institutionalized is that organizations evolve solutions over time and follow the pain of the moment. Thus, the attention is on the immediate problem and not on fixing one that was addressed previously and is under control, even if that solution is not performing at optimal levels.

It takes a great deal of energy to fix the root cause of the problem. Most people will find a temporary solution that takes the problem off the radar screen until either increased volume or a nonstandard requirement collides with the system insufficiency. These temporary solutions are the result, most often, of default processes. Processes, other than on a manufacturing line, are seldom systematically engineered for flow, continuity, and minimization. Change and variation are introduced into the system or process flow every time there is turnover.

For instance, a new person on the job sees what the predecessor did, but does not develop an understanding or appreciation for what the other contributors to that process must do to complete the whole cycle. Thus, without knowing the effects of his or her actions, the new person modifies the task to expand or enhance the enjoyable parts and reduce or minimize the parts that are least attractive or interesting. This results in discontinuities, rework, and new workarounds when the downstream people find that they no longer receive their inputs in the same format, form, or including the content necessary to perform their functions.

## Target incremental change

Change Agents focus on the immediate problem and seek means of resolving it. If it is possible to improve the flow at a given point, or reduce the cycle time, or simply put the program back on schedule, they have achieved their immediate objective. Since there are usually so many points of pain within the organization, any improvement is usually seen as good enough and the Change Agent is off to address the next point of pain.

Change Agents often fear doing more than incremental changes to a process or system. Minor changes are easier to introduce into a system or workgroup. They may not be embraced long term, but they do have an immediate impact, and management is pleased by the improvements that the Change Agent is able to demonstrate. Major change is more unpredictable and much harder to implement in an established organization. Thus, Change Agents seek to make serial improvements that build over time to a larger solution. However, the integration of single-point efforts is and remains a major issue.

Improvement projects cannot take place in a vacuum. They have major impacts across the organization, often times unseen until the improvement activity is put into effect. This is the reason that most improvement teams are cross-functional in nature, aimed at ensuring that someone from other affected organizations participates in the redesign activity and can provide input on probable impacts. This allows the team to avoid handing problems downstream to other organizations rather than fixing them the first time.

One organization, for example, employs a strategy team to participate in all project reviews and also to receive and analyze all business analysis reports. The strategy team is responsible for the coordination across the organization of all efforts and for ensuring that the work done in one area does not contradict the work done in another. Coordination is essential, particularly as the organization grows larger. Management provides the enterprise vision through the strategy team.

## Focus on process improvement

There is a strong belief among Change Agents that the most effective means of achieving improvement is to change the "official" process that employees are supposed to follow. The expectation is that if all processes can be improved then there will be an improvement in the work actually performed.

The problem of incremental process improvement is that it reinforces the status quo. The focus is not how to achieve quantum change, but to make the process more responsive to the current set of requirements. Process improvement is generally retrospectively enabled (closing the barn door after the horse escapes) rather than prospectively charged (employing creative ways to achieve the same goal quicker, better, and cheaper before anything negative has happened).

Six Sigma practitioners work in teams that are prospectively charged with the responsibility to find a way to achieve the same goal quicker, better, and cheaper, at least annually. In the early stages, low-hanging fruit permits easily achievable gains. However, over time, realizing gains becomes progressively more difficult requiring more and more radical changes to achieve results. This only results from mature teams, willing to take risks and be open with each other about what they do all day.

## Pursue a top-down approach

Change Agents are empowered by the leadership to undertake their activities. Generally there is a growing realization that the current operating results are not sufficient. Attempts through the usual means are made to improve results. Only when these attempts fail to bear fruit does the organization seek out Change Agents to go forth and do battle with the bureaucracy. At this point management is looking for any improvements that can be achieved. However, management is not yet in a place where they will seek anything other than incremental changes. They know that the firm is not performing to its potential; however, the leadership has a stake in maintaining the status quo.

Leadership Teams are usually a product of the current system. In many cases they created the current organization and have invested themselves in making it work. For this reason they believe that their survival is tied to maintaining what they have put into place. Thus, Change Agents usually work on a short leash. Incremental change is permissible; quantum change is unpredictable and usually leads to unfamiliar business models and results.

Former Premier Gorbachev induced quantum change in the former Soviet Union and lost control as a result. This is the fear of Leadership Teams in many organizations.

## Work in isolation

Change Agents work in isolation. They are generally not a part of the organization that is to be changed. The theory is that someone who is in the organization is less willing to make substantial change because he or she has to live with it afterward. The theory further states that someone within the system is a product of the system and has already put into place the workarounds necessary to get the work done, no matter how inefficient they may be.

Change Agents generally are asked to form a team in the workgroup to analyze and recommend changes, but as change leaders rather than subject-matter experts, they are a lone voice in the wilderness, working with a reluctant group at best. Since change is pushed down, resistance is high and overcome only through a coercive implication.

## Are managed by the organization

Since Change Agents are generally put into place by the leadership of the organization, their boundaries (length of their leash) are set up front and the expectations clearly articulated. They are given budgets, access, and direction. They are expected to produce results within pre-authorized limitations. The actions taken are generally linked to the current annual operating plan and are expected to be short term in focus and immediate in impact. Current alignment is the focus of actions taken and drives the scope and nature of the work to be performed.

One major problem is that the impetus for change is not at the level of the individuals actually performing the work. The view of the situation is very different depending on where in the organization one resides. Operating pain as seen on a profit and loss statement may not be at all visible to the worker who is trying to assemble the product to a drawing that has the wrong dimensions. It is necessary to integrate the levels of understanding through the various layers, as well as across the functional areas of the organization, to establish the current reality before effective and sustainable change can be introduced.

# QUANTUM LEADERS

The Quantum Leader envisions the desired future state and accelerates change within the organization, creating a leapfrog effect that launches the organization toward the Vision. This section further describes how Quantum Leaders:

- Communicate and build consensus on the Vision.
- Change the measurements.
- Perform "blood" transfusions.
- Engage people who make the organization uncomfortable.
- Find the doers and liberate them.
- Manage the status quo people.
- Put change in context.
- Are lightning rods.
- Just do it.
- Don't linger – they move on.

They lead change through interpreting data and modeling behavior.

## Communicate and build a consensus on the Vision

Quantum Leaders may either be promoted from within where they have built a solid coalition, like a Jack Welch at General Electric, or are brought in from another company where they have built support for an alternative Vision for the organization, such as a Dan Burnham at Raytheon.

Initial efforts are centered on talking with a wide cross-section of the organization. The Vision may be technically correct for the industry, but the Quantum Leader must understand the cultural support and resistance to expect, assess how to implement it, and create a plan to build consensus regarding the Vision until it becomes one with the culture. This is not an easy task, but most employees are willing to give a leader who seeks out their individual perspectives, opinions, and suggestions, the benefit of the doubt. However, the new direction must be clearly explained.

Clarity and simplicity are the keys to success. A clear Vision with high impact inspires trust and engenders support.

## Change the measurements

What gets measured and rewarded is what gets done. *Corollary: If the measurements don't change, neither do the results.*

The Quantum Leader changes what is measured so that the metrics support the envisioned future state. But changing the measurements alone does not effect change until those who are to be rewarded for a change in performance understand exactly how the measures will be interpreted and exactly what behaviors and results are desired.

The Quantum Leader aligns the measurements and rewarded results with the overall goals and expectations of the organization. To be successful, this alignment must be consistent all the way to the top. If, for example, rapid decision-making is a desired performance, then those who accomplish rapid decisions must be clearly rewarded while those arriving at decisions more slowly are either not rewarded or provided a significantly differentiated reward.

## Perform "blood" transfusions

Quantum Leaders put systems and people in place who will make a difference in performance, generally bringing up individuals from lower levels or from outside the organization and placing them into positions of influence and power. Job rotation transfuses the "blood" of the organization and prevents rigor mortis from setting in.

If institutional memory is important, then it is important to retain those with this memory. However, if these veterans are resistant to change, placing them into new positions provides them with an opportunity to start fresh and be "green" once more where they are coaxed to grow and adapt to the change. If they choose to remain resistant to change, then they are encouraged to step aside to make way for others who are adaptable and able to perform the functions required.

## Engage people who make the organization uncomfortable

In most organizations there is a second tier of "leaders." These people are part of a "circle of friends," and they are often charged with leading initiatives in the organization. They can be counted on to produce just what management is looking for, and no more. They are able to maintain the status quo while leading "change initiatives."

The Quantum Leader avoids involvement in such events and instead seeks to stretch the organization beyond the status quo by engaging individuals who have been outside the "circle of friends" because they are the ones most capable of changing the results. They are the ones with alternate ways of approaching the market or organizational problems, and they offer a different understanding of the reality of the business. Their ideas, observations, and approaches can open up new thinking. Dialogues with them often result in finding a better way and totally different means of achieving the results desired.

The search for a new and better way may mean giving up markets or product niches in favor of emerging markets and niches. Or it may mean moving into totally new markets as General Electric did when it aggressively pursued the services markets to grow revenues. People who were only comfortable in building things were not ready to get their arms around the "soft" services businesses because it was hard to measure the product that was delivered. It was a different mindset. And that, in a nutshell, is exactly what the people who make the organization uncomfortable do. They introduce a different mindset.

## Find the doers and liberate them

Every organization has a wealth of talent at the lower levels of management and below. These individuals are less wedded to the past history of the organization, and are willing to do what is necessary to build and ensure their place in the future of the organization.

The Quantum Leader nurtures these people, bringing them along as fast as they are ready for responsibility and turning them loose to make mistakes, while learning as rapidly as possible. If people are not provided early leadership opportunities, their development is restricted and slowed. Their overall contributions to the organization are also slowed.

The Quantum Leader exploits the talent of the organization and seeks to create flexible, broadly anchored individuals who work throughout the organization and learn the impact of a decision in one area upon the operations in another. The goal is to develop a broad base of enterprise-focused individual leaders who understand the Vision and how it is capable of transforming the organization.

## Manage the status quo people

When change within an organization accelerates there will always be early adopters of the new way. There will be others who sit on the fence watching and waiting to see how the change is going to work and what effect it will have on them and their future. Those who cling to the status quo often find that they are being bypassed by the early adopters who are moving up the organization more rapidly than they are. The former "circle of friends" composed of those who used to control things, now frequently find themselves as bystanders to the new approach to doing business.

This later group must be appropriately managed or they will use their influence to create roadblocks to the change. The Quantum Leader never underestimates the power of entrenched individuals, and actively engages them in the process, not as leaders, but as substantial contributors who are held accountable for their results and whose progress is examined and published for the whole organization to see.

## Put change in context

Quantum Leaders link all of the changes that are being recommended and deployed to the Vision. Changes are carefully evaluated and the results are broadly and clearly displayed throughout the workplace so that every employee can see the improvement that is or is not being achieved.

Quantum Leaders frequently bring in outside evaluation and standards firms to collect a baseline of the company and act as an impartial party to validate successes and help to evaluate the reasons behind performance that falls below expectations. Their reports are widely disseminated and the Quantum Leader meets with all employees to communicate the findings. Further meetings are held and plans for future performance are constructed. The plans are openly discussed with employees so everyone in the organization understands and has an opportunity to provide input to what is happening. Everyone then knows the origins of the plans, what their role is in the actions to be taken, and what the expected results are. Once the plans are implemented, the progress toward achieving the desired results is again widely disseminated and displayed for all employees.

## Are lightning rods

Resistance causes friction. Friction causes heat. The Quantum Leader devises plans and methods that channel the heat in constructive ways rather than dissipating it throughout the organization. A leader of any type cannot be effective when every action is questioned and there is neither trust nor faith in that individual by the workforce, investors, or customers. The Quantum Leader seeks to attract and convert heat into potential energy and apply that energy to actions that add value to the company. One means of channeling the energy is to create forums where the proposed change (source of heat) is explored in-depth by a representative cross section of the organization. The discussion continues until it can be understood, accepted, and clearly explained to others along with the metrics for improvement. If the forum approach proves ineffective, the Quantum Leader creates a remedial plan that will implement the change with the least resistance and take the organization to the expected place. The Quantum Leader takes responsibility and acts with the authority given to him or her at the earliest point in time.

## Just do it

Inertia can defeat even the best-intentioned individual. There is always an immediate crisis that must be managed. There is always a reason to put off introducing change into a system that is not performing, including fear of making things worse. However, Quantum Leaders know that the result of not moving quickly is the probability of being overtaken by the competition (if they haven't already) and loss of markets to those firms that are moving in new directions and making change a daily event. The old adage that "the only thing that is constant is change" must be updated to say, "the only thing that is constant is ever-increasing rapid change."

Quantum Leaders know that time is never on their side, whether they are a market leader or market laggard. Even a wrong decision at least takes them to a new place where new leverage can be created. But a slow decision, or worse – no decision, leaves the firm vulnerable to organizations that have adopted rapid, data-driven decision-making as their way of life.

## Don't linger—they move on

Quantum Leaders do not wait for results, but immediately move on to the next level of effort, building upon each success and leveraging every positive result. Plans are adjusted on the fly. Core and essential actions are the bible of everyday existence. What can be done beyond is a plus. Action is taken on all fronts simultaneously. Results may not be uniform, but energy and drive take the organization to levels that far exceed where they were at the beginning of every day.

Quantum Leaders are energetic and surround themselves with people who have the same Vision, the same high level of energy, and the same drive to make things better today than they were yesterday while simultaneously envisioning and planning how to make things better tomorrow than they are today.

Quantum Leaders seek out and develop those individuals who will manage efforts to completion, and ensure that adequate metrics and reporting structures are in place and operating before shifting focus to other efforts. Quantum Leaders know it is essential to plan the management of all efforts completely and as a team. The approach is not to hand off or delegate, but rather to allow new leads to rise to take responsibility and ensure that the entire team effort is focused, integrated, and ongoing. This allows the Quantum Leader to develop new Quantum Leaders and at the same time leverage the resources of the entire team.

## DIFFERENT APPROACHES TO CHANGE

*Change Agents and Quantum Leaders have different*
*approaches to change.*

| Change Agents | Quantum Leaders |
|---|---|
| Come up with better processes/products/services | Continually invent more effective organizations |
| Aim for growth | Aim for dexterity |
| Cut costs | Explode the organization and change the business model |
| Work from the top down | Work from where they are |
| Focus on tools | Focus on people |
| Collect data and perform analyses | Use data to lead change |
| Consult | Lead empowered teams |
| Package projects and transition them | Model behavior |
| Do what they know | Research constantly |
| Follow the leaders in their industry | Become industry leaders by going outside their own industry for data and models to emulate |

## Quantum Leaders focus on creating organizational capacity/capability

**Change Agents come up with better processes/products/services while Quantum Leaders continually invent more effective organizations.**

This is an essential difference. Both the Quantum Leader and the Change Agent want to put the most innovative and competitive products and services into the marketplace. The difference is that the Quantum Leader leapfrogs the trap of fixing ineffective processes/product/services by inventing a more effective/capable organization and nurturing a culture that places great value on high-quality, innovative, and competitive products. Once quality becomes the cultural ethic, everyone in the organization takes ownership over his or her part to make innovative and competitive products, thus actions flow from the bottom up rather than the top down. Measurements and rewards support this cultural ethic of quality and evolve over time to sustain it. The Quantum Leader holds the Vision and brings the resources to bear to make it a reality.

## Quantum Leaders aim for dexterity

**Change Agents aim for growth while Quantum Leaders aim for dexterity.**

All too often organizations are seen as commodities that can be added to or removed from an investment portfolio. Thus, the focus is to harvest the crop today and not worry about the crop for next year because that may well be someone else's problem.

Long-term growth occurs through successive quarters of growth. However, optimizing for the short term often negates long-term growth. Decisions that bring immediate results rob the organization of the investments necessary to achieve results in the long term.

The Quantum Leader creates the ability for the organization to rapidly adjust to changing conditions, technology, customers, and product demands and opportunities. In any given quarter this may not optimize results. In fact, it may actually cause an early deterioration in the results from established products to bring on new revenue streams earlier. This may be the result of new products or services or simply enhancements, or it may be the investment into new markets and niches altogether. The effect is to create a balance within the firm. This balance is the ability to move rapidly in the direction of opportunity, like a tennis player who leaps back to center court in anticipation of the next return.

## Quantum Leaders explode the organization

**Change Agents cut costs while Quantum Leaders explode the organization and change the business model.**

Cutting costs indicates that the product line is maturing and that competition has entered the market, eroding margins. It is an inevitable indication that the firm is trying to milk a revenue stream that is on the downhill slope. When products are new they command high margins and the organizational response is to rapidly (and often inefficiently) create processes and systems to respond to meeting the current and anticipated demand. Seldom is any attempt made to rationalize the processes and systems. Orders are in the house and the management focus is on how to meet the demand right then. Default processes and systems characterize the organization at this stage.

Quantum Leaders are not satisfied to milk the current revenue stream but look to leverage the strengths of the organization and either outsource, partner, or invest in weaknesses to make the product flow at the pull of the customer.

Quantum Leaders require their managers to make their areas efficient and responsive, but cost cutting is not the sole focus because it saps the will to be efficient. Measures are aligned to provide visibility and rewards to those areas that contribute to overall profitability.

Quantum Leaders encourage their managers to have an enterprise view, and to limit point optimization that reduces overall system efficiency and capability. Rewards are instead based on what the individual is able to control, which includes any "system optimization" that is within their control.

## Quantum Leaders work from where they are

**Change Agents work from the top down while Quantum Leaders work from where they are.**

Management typically sends a Change Agent off to address the most recurring points of pain. Change Agents are proficient at fixing the immediate problem, but generally do not attack workarounds since they are usually meeting the current needs. For this reason, there is little pressure to change. However, most Change Agents, unless they seek to replace large numbers of employees, tend to go slowly with the changes they induce in order to gain acceptance as they progress.

A Quantum Leader does not need to be the senior-most executive in a business. Anyone can be a Quantum Leader as long as the Leadership Team understands and endorses the efforts of this individual. It is imperative for Quantum Leaders to have this understanding with their Leadership Teams and the ability to openly discuss plans, actions, and results.

Quantum Leaders effect change where they are and reach out to involve their peers and superiors in their activities. Remember that Quantum Leaders communicate and build a consensus about the Vision. That Vision may be for the department, the work team, or a time-limited program. Change starts small and is spread one individual at a time. The person who starts the change may be the lowest-ranking individual in the firm, the highest, or anyone in between.

What sets Quantum Leaders apart is their ability to communicate a Vision and convince others to share that Vision and work toward achieving the pictured end-state. The ideal scene is to have an organization that contains only Quantum Leaders who work together to create and execute integrated Visions that optimize customer-driven flexibility and performance.

## Quantum Leaders focus on people

**Change Agents are focused on tools while Quantum Leaders are focused on people.**

Change Agents want to demonstrate how to use a specific tool or tool set to bring about the desired performance. They know what must be done to "fix" the situation, and they have been trained to use certain tool sets. For them, that is the shortest path to results.

Quantum Leaders understand that performance is the result of thousands or hundreds of thousands of individual decisions made by individuals each day. These decisions:

- Determine whether the products meet specifications.

- Cause a customer to be satisfied or dissatisfied.

- Choose short-term goals at the expense of the long-run performance of the organization.

Quantum Leaders cannot possibly review or make all of those decisions by themselves. That is why it is so important for them to create and build a consensus about the Vision, build an organization of values, create aligned capability, and delegate authority and responsibility early and often.

## Quantum Leaders use data to lead change

**Change Agents collect and display data while Quantum Leaders use data to lead change.**

Change Agents spend a great deal of time creating tools to collect data and running statistical tools to organize and display the data. These data are usually analyzed and interpreted by someone in the responsible organization.

Quantum Leaders enable the mechanical process by which data are transformed into information. They create the means by which the data are regularly collected and reported and transformed into knowledge that is shared across the organization. This knowledge becomes the basis for evaluating alternative futures and decision-making.

# QUANTUM LEADERS LEAD EMPOWERED TEAMS

**Change Agents consult while Quantum Leaders lead empowered teams.**

The Change Agent attempts to bring lessons learned in similar situations to those teams that will be responsible for implementation. While this knowledge is important to a clear understanding of what has been effective in the past, it cannot be entirely applicable without modification. As a consultant, the Change Agent finds that he or she cannot prescribe the actions to be taken, but must prompt the teams to find their own way with some advice.

Quantum Leaders, on the other hand, not only take responsibility for making change occur, but are directly involved in organizing, directing, and personally taking the actions necessary to enable others to do their part.

Quantum Leaders give authority with responsibility and accept no excuses for failure to take requisite actions. They not only frequently ask for status reports, but they largely and publicly reward those who are first to complete their activities. The status of the Quantum Leader's actions is posted along with those of everyone else to demonstrate that the Quantum Leader values these activities and is willing to place these implementation actions above other responsibilities. The hard chargers who quickly achieve their objectives and put into place metric capture and reporting systems to make progress visible, and who encourage continued effectivity, are those who are tapped by the Quantum Leader for more responsible assignments.

## Quantum Leaders model behavior

**Change Agents package projects and transition them while Quantum Leaders model behavior.**

Change Agents are usually external to the organization undergoing change. Therefore, they lead the discovery process and then hand over responsibility to members of the organization to effect the necessary changes. This has become the favored approach since members of the organization have the relationships and standing to effect the change.

Quantum Leaders are the first to stand up and volunteer to take on the necessary tasks to implement a change. The Quantum Leaders are also the first to complete those tasks and report back to the team, even though their tasks are often the hardest to complete. The strength of modeling behavior is that it demonstrates what is expected. It results in earning the respect of the members of the organization because the Quantum Leader is willing to do anything any other employee is asked to do. Thus, there is no separation of responsibility. Every employee can see what is expected and knows that the Quantum Leader not only talks the talk, but also walks the walk.

## Quantum Leaders research constantly

**Change Agents do what they know while Quantum Leaders research constantly.**

Ironically, Change Agents become so familiar with their tools and strategies and processes that they become resistant to changing the approach they use in effecting change within their organizations.

Quantum Leaders constantly ask questions and search for data and knowledge to give the most complete picture possible of the situations that are being faced on a daily basis. They do not assume that what they did yesterday is what will be most effective today. New data are examined as frequently as possible to look for trends and changes in trends.

Early detection of change raises numerous questions: What is different? Why is the result different today than yesterday? What are the causal factors? What are the environmental influences and what effect are they having on the situation? Has the customer changed a requirement? When new technology comes into the marketplace, what effect will the change have on product requirements and functionality? What will new functionality require for existing products and will it cause a ripple effect in terms of new equipment required, new skills, and/or new materials? Is it a major redesign? Is someone already in the market with the new product and, if so, how long will it take for a competing product to be introduced by this firm? Will leapfrog technology be available or will it merely be a catch-up effort that will pick up the crumbs left over by late adapters?

Quantum Leaders have inquiring minds and continually seek answers to the questions that drive corporate decisions. And, they look for people in their organizations who are innately curious, asking questions, and carefully listening to the answers. Those who respond to questions with data from independent research are noted and brought to the attention of personnel to be quickly moved to positions of greater responsibility if they demonstrate the ability to get results.

## Quantum Leaders go outside for models to emulate

**Change Agents use examples from within the organization while Quantum Leaders go outside the organization (and even the industry) for data and models to emulate.**

Change Agents play "follow the leader." In many cases market leaders become the poster boys of those firms seeking the same status. The problem with this approach is that successful models come from environments that were different than those currently in existence. Product enhancements that once captured marketshare are no longer sufficient to capture marketshare now.

Quantum Leaders look for the best ideas from whatever source they can find. With a different context to deal with, Quantum Leaders look toward the emerging firms for models. Their success may not yet be established; however, they are dealing with a context that is closer to that which the firm is currently going to navigate. Organizations in different industries are often the model firms, based on their excellence in specific areas that apply to the firm but may not be directly transferable. For example, a firm in the entertainment industry or hospitality industry may be the best in the world for customer service. A durable goods manufacturer may find that they can emulate some of the behaviors of those organizations to help increase repeat sales through rapid handling of customer complaints. While this may not have been a focus in the past, it may well be an opportunity. It is easier to adapt a successful model from another context than to invent a whole new model and do all the development required. Thus, outside models can leverage results and accelerate realization of those results.

The Quantum Leader also leverages external relationships. It is not enough to simply look outside for models and data. Having personal relationships and being involved in helping to solve problems in outside organizations stimulates comparisons and adaptation in new and different contexts. The involvement and relationships also helps the leader to identify resources that would not be visible to the organization were the leader not interacting in those external environments.

## THE QUANTUM LEADER IN TURBULENT TIMES

Quantum Leaders think strategically, plan tactically, and execute flawlessly. This is the key to their success.

Quantum Leaders are masters of speed. They are able to quickly diagnose the major difficulties of the firm and have the connections to bring in external resources when necessary. They complement and challenge any internal candidates with the potential to lead in spite of rapidly changing environments.

One of the greatest organizational challenges facing Quantum Leaders is the entrenched "circle of friends" that have long influenced or even dominated decision-making within the organization. Before a Quantum Leader can be truly effective, the Leadership Team of the organization needs to take decisive action to move or remove those in this "circle of friends" and entrust the authority and responsibility to act to those who are being developed to lead the organization into the future.

Quantum Leaders know that in order to achieve quantum improvements in organizational performance they must focus on establishing flexible, customer-driven, and responsive organizations that are capable of meeting rapidly changing requirements and have the capacity to respond faster than the competition. But most firms reinforce and maintain the status quo. Those firms that have gotten into deep trouble are the first to look for Quantum Leaders, only to find that few, if any, exist within their organization. The reason is simple: those with the potential to grow into Quantum Leaders are rarely given an opportunity to exercise their skills within the firm when times are good. For that reason, Quantum Leaders are most often found in organizations that are in turnaround, and desperate management brought them in.

Organizations need to grow their own Quantum Leaders if they expect to survive and thrive in turbulent times.

## SUMMARY

Growth and prosperity result from leadership that:

- Studies the marketplace and environment.

- Envisions an alternative future.

- Maps a course that leads to that future state.

- Builds a consensus around the Vision and the course.
- Creates the capability to create that future.
- Plunges ahead without hesitation or regret.
- Learns from mistakes and rapidly implements lessons learned.
- Engages external organizations as if they were internal.
- Learns continuously and teaches others.
- Perpetuates forward momentum.

There are significant differences between Change Agents and Quantum Leaders: Specifically, Change Agents:

- Do it faster, cheaper, better.
- Attack the symptoms of status quo.
- Target incremental change.
- Focus on process improvement.
- Pursue a top-down approach.
- Work in isolation.
- Are managed by the organization.

The main focus is on process-based incremental change. In comparison, Quantum Leaders:

- Communicate and build consensus on the Vision.
- Change the measurements.
- Perform "blood" transfusions.
- Engage people who make the organization uncomfortable.
- Find the doers and liberate them.
- Manage the status quo people.
- Put change in context.
- Are lightning rods.
- Just do it.
- Don't linger – they move on.

They lead change through interpreting data and modeling behavior.

# 3

# The Roadmap to Performance

THE APPLICATION OF SPECIFIC TOOLS AND METHODOLOGIES ON A CONSISTENT
BASIS IS THE PATH THAT LEADS TO DRAMATIC PERFORMANCE IMPROVEMENT.

## A DIFFERENT ROAD

The previous chapter described in detail how the road to quantum improvement is not
dotted with Change Agents filling holes and patching processes. Rather, quantum
improvement sometimes requires a whole new road to be built.

Given that, this chapter outlines both a roadmap of techniques and a blueprint for
building that new road leading to quantum improvement in performance and results.

## PERFORMANCE AND RESULTS

Quantum Leaders seek quantum improvement in the performance and results achieved
by the organization. But the dual focus on performance and results can only be achieved
if the Six Sigma efforts are initiated early in the life of programs, products, or service
delivery and applied continually throughout the lifecycle.

Achieving improvement at this level requires constant and consistent application of
Six Sigma methodology, with concerted efforts by everyone in the organization to
uncover opportunities and then flawlessly exploit those opportunities. Diligence and
dedication are essential.

Quantum Leaders need expertise (or empowered team members with skill) in
aligning the right assets to the available opportunities. For any organization to
achieve maximum effect from the investment it is making, three vital skill sets essential for its leaders (including Black Belts and Green Belts) are Quality Function

Deployment (QFD), Design for Six Sigma (DFSS) and Critical Chain Scheduling/ Program Management.

These tools affect the three greatest points for leveraging results on a program. QFD, or derivations thereof, is a method of determining exactly how the solution the company is to offer meets the exact requirements of that customer. DFSS is a probabilistic design approach that uses statistical modeling to determine failure points and ensure that the design exceeds design standards set by the customer. Critical chain is a method that stands program management on its ear by removing the normal buffers in a program and forcing program actors to work as efficiently as possible without counting on buffer time to save projects that run over. (This is a simplified explanation of these tool sets, and the author suggests the reader explore the various sources available in the Bibliography for more information).

## The road to program performance

Quantum Leaders continually evaluate and align measurement to desired performance, adjusting the "people mix" to accelerate results. Throughout the program execution, the Quantum Leader constantly evaluates the data on performance, adjusting the measures to ensure that they are driving the desired behaviors and not just using "default metrics" that are similar to those that have always been used. In addition, the Quantum Leader constantly evaluates the performance of the people on the program and questions whether the people in any given position are as effective as needed to achieve quantum levels of improvement.

## Aligning people and measures

As necessary, the Quantum Leader performs "blood transfusions," introducing new leaders, new energy, and new focus to find different solutions to the business problems confronting the organization. The refrain, "If you always do what you always did, you'll always get what you always got" is the underlying motive to introduce new blood into the system. Default processes do not lead to quantum gains in performance. Successful approaches will get the same or slightly better results than last time, but will not get quantum improvements.

Rapid gains are made when something new is introduced into the system. This is why many organizations rotate people across assignments, to introduce change into the system. Many organizations also do not believe its' important for a manager to be an expert in the area to be managed. The concept is that the individual will not get trapped into doing things the way they have always been done. The uninitiated will ask questions that those who are a part of the system will not ask. The nonexpert will be much more challenging of the individuals in the organization, trying to make sure that the employee understands her or his job responsibilities, and in trying to understand them, will help the individual begin to think outside of the box.

The downside to this approach is that more variation will be introduced into the system, since the manager may not be as focused on certain compliance issues or requirements as someone who has more familiarity with the position. The compromise seems to be to pair an outsider with a technically strong insider to make sure that essential issues are addressed as both struggle to induce and manage change within the organization.

# THE RIGHT TOOL AT THE RIGHT TIME

A Quantum Leader applies just the right Six Sigma tools and methods at each phase of a program lifecycle (see Figure 3.1). At each step in the process, the goal is to continue to build value:

- Business development phase—Define value

- Business capture/Proposal phase—Increase value

- Program commencement phase—Secure value

- Program execution phase—Protect and grow value

- Program closeout phase—Extract value

## Business development phase

*Define Value* **by creating a QFD document with the customer and major suppliers.**

In nearly every late program intervention the author has been involved with, whether it be a manufacturing, software, or service-based environment, one consistent root cause of poor program performance has been the lack of a clear understanding of the customer's requirements.

Often, the engineering community will state that the customer doesn't know the specifics of what they want, or the customer changes the requirements as the effort evolves. Observers within the organization may comment that there is a certain level of professional arrogance on the part of the engineering community. Having developed a high level of domain knowledge, engineers are tempted to believe that they know what the customer wants better than the customer does. This leads to a need for the Six Sigma Black and Green Belts to engage the program office, engineering, and customer representatives in an exercise to clearly and precisely define the requirements and the approach to satisfying them.

When this happens the Six Sigma community must discriminate between those requirements that are essential to meet and those that are nice to have. At the end of the process, everyone must be clear on what the customer wants within certain price parameters and the limits of those price sensitivities.

QFD is an intense activity to gather (hear, understand, and collect) data to represent the *voice of the customer*, to confirm the requirements, and determine the functionality necessary to fulfill those requirements. QFD may involve the customer only in defining the requirements, leaving the fulfillment phase to the engineering community after the customer has departed; however, this approach is unnecessarily limiting. By involving

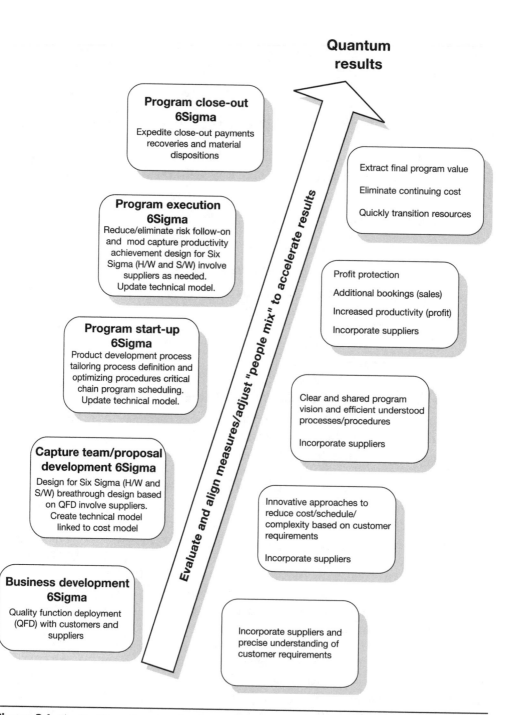

**Figure 3.1** The Six Sigma Quantum Leader roadmap.

the customer and major suppliers in the entire effort it is possible and even probable that the final product will be more closely aligned to the specifications, expectations, and requirements of the customer. Involving the major suppliers throughout the process ensures that supplier capabilities are aligned with the initial design concept. The final objective is a delighted customer. Providing exactly what the customer wants at the best possible price leads to customer delight. QFD is the best tool available to determine exactly and clearly what the customer wants.

## Business capture/Proposal phase

*Increase Value* **with a completed QFD as the basis for DFSS conceptual design during proposal development.**

Various studies have shown that the point of accelerated diminishing returns affecting program performance is before the design moves from concept to detail. The many companies that have utilized Design for Manufacture (DFM) or Design for Assembly (DFA) have found that they regularly reduce costs, complexity and variation in final product integrity through early structured DFM and DFA activity. In instances where the author used a DFM-type activity on software development, substantial complexity was eliminated, a uniform and consistent approach to the development problem was agreed upon, and both cycle-time and cost were substantially reduced as a result.

Applying a DFSS approach to the requirements definition at the conceptual and detailed design stages builds bridges between the design and the manufacturing/integration groups. For software, interfaces can be expedited when all developers and hardware engineers work together in a concerted DFSS effort to define requirements and discuss conceptual approaches to meeting those requirements early in the proposal development stage. New and unanticipated problems may be avoided at integration. Software design for Six Sigma activity is just as effective in reducing rework and expediting hardware/software integration, reducing overall cost and schedule.

On the hardware side, elegant engineering solutions may be difficult to manufacture. Some engineering optimization can occur if the design and manufacturing engineering groups get together before finalization of the conceptual design and a frank discussion is held about how the design engineer "sees" the solution in a DFSS activity. The manufacturing engineers are able to ask questions about the design in terms of the limitations of manufacturing capabilities within their organization. By simplifying the design and ensuring that the manufacturing operations have the equipment and skill sets to build the product as envisioned, a great deal of scrap, rework, and waste are eliminated.

DFSS activity also has a positive impact on overall manufacturability and/or integration and reducing final product cost. At this stage it is relatively inexpensive to change the design. Once detailed design has been completed the cost increases substantially. When the product is in production, the cost increases even more rapidly because of the need to replace tooling, fixtures, or other elements of production that have been called out specifically in the design documents.

Because of this, value can be significantly increased by completing the QFD and DFSS analyses that are then used as the basis for the technical solution section of the proposal or business capture mechanism. It is important to have all team members review and agree to the DFSS results and inputs prior to moving to the next phase.

## Program commencement phase

*Secure Value* **by communicating and embedding the Vision, defining optimal processes and procedures, and implementing Critical Chain-based scheduling.**

When a program or business project has been won, it is necessary to eliminate the default processes and build custom processes that take advantage of the strengths and skill sets of those performing the processes. This leads to Six Sigma process/procedure definition and optimization.

At the same time application of Critical Chain Scheduling/Program Management is required to pass on to the next phase. Critical chain removes the traditional buffers in program schedules and moves the buffers to the end of the schedule. This approach forces those who are engaged in performing the process to complete their tasks as soon as possible. This is different than having them complete tasks at the point in time that the schedule permits. The lesson learned from critical chain theory is that work will fill the available time to perform it regardless of what that time allowance might be.

One of the most important actions taken by a Quantum Leader is to communicate and obtain buy-in to the Vision from the program staff. Questions must be answered up front. What is the expected end-state? What are the anticipated results of the efforts to be undertaken? How will those who are seeking to change performance know when they have successfully achieved their objectives? All of this is difficult to understand if a Vision has not been developed, shared, and accepted by all individuals contributing to the anticipated results.

At the same time the Vision is shared and embraced by the staff, the Six Sigma Black Belts and Green Belts work with the teams to defeat the "default process and procedure syndrome." Most programs have many experienced individuals. Rather than proceeding to build a team approach to the work to be done, experienced individuals tend to do things the way they have always been done; sometimes in the very same manner they may have been taught when they first joined the organization. The problem with default processes is that they occur in isolation, removed from the needs of the customer, other process stakeholders, or the organization as a whole.

The concept of securing value is that processes and procedures are mutually understood, mutually executed, and used to support efficient, cost-effective activity that in turn supports the customer value delivery. To this end, critical chain scheduling is seen as an advantageous approach to program execution in that it drives behaviors that support maximizing customer value delivery. It drives behaviors that minimize cost, applies resources at the points in time when they are most effective, and responds to the actual needs of the program execution rather than expectations imposed from the outside that are not driven by the intrinsic nature of the program effort.

## Program execution phase

*Protect and Grow Value* **by using Six Sigma tools to mitigate risk, capture opportunity, and improve organizational or program performance.**

Expert application of Six Sigma tools is essential to reduce and eliminate program risk (profit protection); capture follow-on orders and engineering change opportunities (bookings and sales); and achieve productivity improvement (bottom-line profit). This includes for example, things such as executing the program according to critical chain scheduling and program management, employing DFSS to resolve design issues or address design opportunities, and updating a QFD with the customer and/or suppliers to expedite rapid resolution of program risk.

Protecting and growing value during program execution is a result of risk minimization, opportunity capture, and productivity improvement. Six Sigma Black Belts and Green Belts have a major role to play in optimizing program performance. Six Sigma tools and methods address risk mitigation. DFSS activity is a method of rapidly determining a course of action when a design, whether hardware or software, does not meet customer expectations for quality, functionality, cost, or schedule.

Six Sigma tools and methods are successful in reducing program risk through application of Design of Experiments to understand causal relationships and predict outcomes. Reality trees, cause-and-effect diagrams, and failure modes and effects analysis are all used effectively to visually display and analyze data to spot trends and understand relationships. When used appropriately, these tool and methods provide the program with the ability to make well-informed, fact-based decisions while avoiding increased variability.

These same tools are effective when paired with brainstorming, creative decision-making, affinitization, prioritization, and other specialized tools and methods for developing effective proposals. Implementing DFSS activities can also lead to new and more cost-effective approaches to solving a customer problem and increasing value leading to new business, whether follow-on business opportunities or engineering changes. These DFSS activities often include the customer and suppliers, leading to optimal solution sets.

Six Sigma tools are effective in determining research and development investments that may have the greatest potential for capturing additional business and solving a customer problem, whether through a QFD or DFSS activity. Productivity improvements are the natural result of most Six Sigma efforts. However, it is important to realize that when a program manager is trained in Six Sigma tools and methods and charged with the responsibility to manage the program risk and business capture in addition to productivity improvement, quantum results can be achieved in program performance.

This also assumes that the program managers who undergo Six Sigma training and certification are high-performing individuals to begin with and have substantial program-related experience. When armed with the tools and methods of Six Sigma their effectiveness and program impact are greatly magnified. They also become an investment in the future of the company in that when they take over programs as lead program manager, they already are effective in driving high performance and results.

## Program closeout phase

*Extract Value* **by rapidly transitioning assets and accelerating payments at program closeout.**

Prior to the final review, program assets must be transitioned and/or dispositioned. There is a need to rapidly act on the program closeout to reduce cost to the customer, extract value of assets that will no longer be required, and redeploy personnel and retained assets to other productive uses.

The key to extracting value is to rapidly redeploy or disposition assets from the program. This permits a rapid final billing to the customer and minimizes the carrying efforts necessary to wind down the effort and receive final payments.

While time and material programs permit increased sales when people continue to manage low value and low priority efforts at closeout, the work is not challenging or desirable to the engineers and support personnel working the effort. It is not conducive to increasing skills, knowledge, or experience that enhances the career of the individual. It is also common that the incentives for rapid closeout are not in place. Space costs are not always allocated to a program, so there is no incentive to move out of facilities. Non-dispositioned assets may remain in storage for years, ensuring not only that there is a carrying cost, but also that any value the assets may have had at one time is no longer available for recovery.

A Quantum Leader is effective in ensuring that all Six Sigma tools and methods are used to rapidly transition and disposition program assets to permit accelerated closeout payments and full utilization of human and physical assets.

# IMPLEMENTING THE SIX SIGMA PROGRAM PERFORMANCE ROADMAP

**Build Six Sigma into all business development activity.**

Train Green Belts and Program Managers in and use QFD.

**Bid with DFSS embedded into all proposals.**

- Train in and use DFSS (both hardware and software).

- Train in and use critical chain scheduling and program management.

**Select high-performing Six Sigma Black Belts to become Program Managers.**

Program Six Sigma Black Belts lead a balanced program performance improvement activity and report on risk reduction, program opportunity capture, and productivity performance.

**Balance the "people mix" according to ongoing measures to accelerate results.**

Bestow Six Sigma Black Belts with major program management responsibility and authority upon successful completion of assignments.

## SUMMARY

The purpose of this chapter was to examine how the Quantum Leader integrates Six Sigma with capabilities and focus to achieve quantum gains in program performance and results. This roadmap is intended to begin a discussion about the application of tools and methods in furtherance of the reader's corporate goals and expectations.

# 4

# Building the Quantum Leadership Strategic Roadmap

SUCCESSFUL FIRMS CREATE A VISION OF A DESIRED FUTURE STATE THAT CONSTITUTES THE STRATEGIC POSITIONING OF THE FIRM AND A ROADMAP TO ACHIEVE IT.

Quantum Leaders need a plan in order to know where they are taking the organization. One often-heard criticism of strategic positioning and similar efforts is that the implementation of the strategies that have been identified, and realization of the expected benefits, often do not come about. It is one thing to identify what the firm should do and quite another to actually do it. Successful efforts begin with the Leadership Team and include a well-defined concerted effort on the part of that team to lead the way. This means that the members of the Leadership Team must have their own skin in the game and their own reputations on the line. Six Sigma can play a major role in developing this kind of implementation plan.

## SIX SIGMA: THE KEY TO IMPLEMENTING STRATEGIC POSITIONING

Once strategic positioning tasks have been identified, implementation is often the weakest point in the process. This is because most strategic positioning efforts do not include planning for implementation as part of the original activity. Instead, planning for implementation tasks are delegated to others not part of the decision-making process. Frequently, the press of day-to-day activity overwhelms the planning effort. When this happens, the activity is either not conducted at all, or is minimized so as not to realize the anticipated benefits. To address this weakness of many such efforts, Task Statements of Work and an implementation-tracking tool can be successfully employed.

One approach that has been successful is to conduct a Six Sigma Blitz with the Leadership Team focused on the following process (see Figure 4.1).

The devil is always in the details and the details of each step in the process follow.

# ASSIGN PREREADINGS

The Leadership Team begins the roadmap process by examining ground that has already been covered. This is done by assigning prereadings on how organizations transform themselves and studies of firms that have successfully achieved high levels of continuing success. Many books and articles are available to provide a conceptual understanding of how some firms progress from a current state to a desired state and the level of effort and commitment required to achieve this. At the beginning of the first day each Leadership Team member describes the key take away he or she found in the prereadings. A brief period is set for each member to discuss his or her findings.

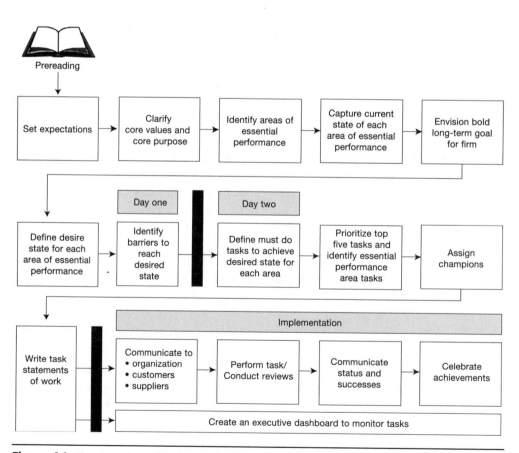

**Figure 4.1** The strategic positioning roadmap – process flow.

# SET EXPECTATIONS

This stage in the process sets the expectations of the Leadership Team and gets everyone on the same page. Activities include a discussion of the agenda, the expected outcomes, and a brief set of comments from the key members of the Leadership Team about their commitment to the process and the activities that will come out of this effort.

# CLARIFY THE CORE VALUES

Every organization has a set of core values. However, Leadership Teams often do not clarify these on a regular basis. This is particularly true when:

- New members join the team.
- Mergers, acquisitions, or divestitures change the nature and/or organization of the firm.
- There are substantial changes in the markets.
- There are substantial changes in customers that cause the Leadership Team to rethink what is important as they assume the task of changing directions.

Coming to understand the core values of the organization is important because they are the bedrock of the organization's culture. In order to change the organization's performance, actions taken must be consistent with the core values so the members of the organization will embrace the changes that are sought.

# CLARIFY THE CORE PURPOSE

The standard line of why a firm exists is to increase shareholder value. However, this may be accomplished in a variety of ways. Having a discussion of the purpose of the firm focuses the discussion of the future state that is desired.

For example, if the purpose of the firm is to solve technically challenging problems in innovative and cost-effective ways, then the space in which the firm works toward for the future state is fairly wide.

However, if the core purpose is to solve technically challenging *education* problems in innovative and cost-effective ways, then the space in which the future state will exist is narrowed. In *this* case, a purpose of providing below-market satellite launch services would probably be outside the scope of the envisioned activity that would be embraced by the Leadership Team and the members of the organization.

# IDENTIFY AREAS OF ESSENTIAL PERFORMANCE

Each firm has several areas that are so important to the performance of the firm that they should be considered areas of essential performance.

The previous example of the firm's purpose being to solve technically challenging *education* problems in innovative and cost effective ways, areas of essential performance could include, but not be limited to:

- People

- Technology

- Financial performance

These three are essential. People with the right skills and experience mix must be employed by the firm, to solve problems. The technology must be resident within the firm, and the people capable of managing and developing that technology must also be present if technical solutions are the desired outcome. Financial performance is understood from two points of view. First, the firm must understand financial performance in order to create cost-effective solutions. Second, the firm must perform financially if it is to survive and continue to provide the cost-effective technical solutions that it deems to be its core purpose.

# CAPTURE THE CURRENT STATE OF EACH AREA

The current state should encompass both the problems that the firm encounters in executing its strategy and the basic areas of strength that the firm exploits. Leadership Teams tend to focus on the problem areas. Since they know they are looking toward a future state, they reason that it is just the inverse of the problems currently encountered. For this reason, the statement of the current state must address both the problems *and* the strengths to ensure that the future state is built off of the strengths that exist and not just "wishful thinking."

# ENVISION A BOLD LONG-TERM GOAL

Next, it is vital to envision a long-term desired state that the Leadership Team wishes to see the firm achieve. This should be the mother of all stretch goals – something so bold that the team should almost be embarrassed to set it as the overall goal. However, a bold goal is exactly what is needed to galvanize the Leadership Team and the team members of the organization into action.

If everyone is focused on the same long-term goal, expectations come into alignment. Everyone has a clear direction. It is much easier to create and share a vision around which the entire organization rallies. To some extent this is like the individual who has a dream to achieve greatness. If one is not bold enough to dream, then one cannot take the steps to make it come true.

# DEFINE THE DESIRED STATE FOR EACH AREA

Once the bold, long-term goal has been envisioned, the desired state for each area of essential performance can be defined. This desired state represents what the collective Leadership Team wishes to achieve within a set period of time, and they are essential steps toward the long-term goal. While the desired state may be a dramatic change over what exists today, it will normally only take the firm a fraction of the way to the bold long-term goal.

The desired state needs to be built from the strengths that the firm possesses today. Unless the strategy is to acquire a market leader in a particular business segment, the desired state needs to have a strong foundation in place today; otherwise, it is doubtful that it could be achieved within three-to-five years (or the time frame envisioned by the Leadership Team). Any desired state must have a running start if it is to be achieved within a reasonable time frame.

## Create a statement of the desired state

Once the desired state is defined, it is necessary to record a concise statement for each area of essential performance that captures and crystallizes in a measurable way where the firm's Leadership Team expects to be at the end of the designated period. This crisp statement becomes the focal point for all activity undertaken to reach the goal. The more succinctly stated and measurable this desired state, the greater the ability to achieve it. A refrain often heard (or at least observed) in companies is, *"what gets measured gets action; what gets rewarded gets achieved."* With these two thoughts in mind, it is clear that if the statement of the desired state is clearly worded, measurable, and easily communicated with an appropriate reward system in place, then the probability of achievement is substantially enhanced.

# IDENTIFY BARRIERS FOR EACH AREA

If there were no barriers in the areas of essential performance, the firm would have already achieved the desired state in most cases. When identifying these barriers it is crucial to be brutal and honest. Often, the most obvious barriers are not the real barriers. Getting to the root cause of barriers for each area of essential performance is absolutely necessary to achieve the transformation to the desired state. Once the barriers are identified, then the Task Statements of Work are used to specify how the identified barriers will be overcome. If the tactical solution is not evident in the assigned tasks, the firm will suboptimize the effort and increase the risk that the desired state will not be achieved.

For example, suppose the rate of research and development invested by a competitor is the identified barrier to achieving a no. 1 sales position in a given market. The task assigned is to increase research and development spending to equal that competitor. The Leadership Team should question whether this task would achieve the desired state, especially if this is the only task identified to achieve that state. The Leadership Team needs to look at the products that are in development. How do they stack up against the known strengths of the competitors' products and how do they map to the customers' preferences and requirements? Simplistic solutions seldom take the firm to the desired state.

## IDENTIFY SPECIFIC ACTIONS TO ACHIEVE THE DESIRED STATE

The next step is to develop a set of specific actions or tasks that absolutely must be accomplished in order for the firm to achieve the levels of desired essential performance for each identified area. These specific actions come from brainstorming the opportunities to overcome each barrier identified and achieve the desired state. While individual tasks may accomplish both objectives, the concept at this stage is to capture all ideas, regardless of merit or practicality. An absurd idea, spoken aloud, may be the catalyst for another participant to identify a more practical approach that meets one or more of the objectives. And the idea that actually solves a problem or meets the objective may not have been brainstormed had the absurd idea not been voiced. Once the ideas are written down, other techniques are applied to generate solutions to the barriers or identify specific actions and tasks required to achieve the desire state.

For example, individual ideas can be affinitized into similar subject areas. While the techniques may differ in the affinitization groups, the core idea underlying them is the same. At this stage, any ideas that are not practical or feasible are weeded out and the groupings of ideas are whittled down to the practical, doable action sets that may have multiple facets, but all address the same barrier or element of the desired state.

## PRIORITIZE THE TOP-FIVE TASKS

Once the opportunity set (identified in the previous step) is affinitized and reduced to the practical actions that lead to achievement of the desired state, the participants are asked to prioritize the task groups according to their importance in achieving the desired state (see Figure 4.2).

Whittling down the ideas that have been generated requires the coordinated efforts of many individuals and groups within the firm. However, according to the well-known 80/20 rule, 20 percent of the actions achieve 80 percent of the solution. In this case, the top-five list is an attempt to identify that 20 percent, give them focused attention with adequate resources, and ensure that these actions are completed expeditiously. Once the most visible (top-five) actions are completed, the barriers and

| Votes | EPA | Task No. | Top-Five Projects | Percent Complete | Status Plan |
|-------|-----|----------|-------------------|-----------------|-------------|
| 26 | MG | **G 1** | **Develop/disseminate roadmap as part of strategic plan Champion: Steve J** | **48.00%** | **31.00%** |
| | | G 1.1 | Identify the elements of investment | 100.00% | 80.00% |
| | | G 1.2 | Acquire new talent for new markets | 20.00% | 0.00% |
| | | G 1.3 | Commit to training for domain experts | 20.00% | 0.00% |
| | | G 1.4 | Growth organization design | 50.00% | 50.00% |
| | | G 1.5 | Implement growth metrics | 50.00% | 25.00% |
| 20 | Peo | **E 1** | **Develop necessary skill sets Champion: Al S** | **37.50%** | **68.75%** |
| | | E 1.1 | Determine key skill requirements per forecasts | 100.00% | 50.00% |
| | | E 1.2 | Incentivize people upgrade skill sets | 0.00% | 100.00% |
| | | E 1.3 | Identify training providers | 50.00% | 25.00% |
| | | E 1.4 | Establish training rotation assignments | 0.00% | 100.00% |
| 19 | MG | **G 2** | **Clarify roles and responsibilities across organization Champion: Walter S** | **25.00%** | **100.00%** |
| | | G 2.1 | Product line business development vs. corporate | **50.00%** | **100.00%** |
| | | G 2.2 | Performance metrics – define, deploy, analyze, and change | **0.00%** | **100.00%** |
| 17 | MG | **G 3** | **Upgrade key technology Champion: Sara S** | **25.00%** | **100.00%** |
| | | G 3.1 | Define customer requirements/expectations | 25.00% | 100.00% |
| | | G 3.2 | Evaluate and select from among current and projected offerings | 25.00% | 100.00% |
| 12 | Peo | **E 2** | **Align incentives and rewards with with business objectives Champion: Sandra S** | **25.00%** | **100.00%** |
| | | E 2.1 | Evaluate areas of under performance | 100.00% | 100.00% |
| | | E 2.2 | Evaluate five-year history of incentives and rewards | 0.00% | 100.00% |
| | | E 2.3 | Model the financial impact of alignment | 0.00% | 100.00% |
| | | E 2.4 | Obtain board approval and communicate | 0.00% | 100.00% |

**Figure 4.2** Executive dashboard – top-five.

resistance to other actions necessary for a complete change generally get swept up in the momentum of change.

# IDENTIFY OTHER TASKS BY ESSENTIAL AREAS

Apart from the top-five, it is important to create another set of tasks that also need to be accomplished to ensure the success in reaching the desired states. The remaining tasks should be identified with an essential performance area and an assessment conducted regarding sufficiency (see Figure 4.3).

| Votes | Task No. | Essential Performance Area | Percent Complete Status | |
|---|---|---|---|---|
| | | **Customer Champion: Willie S** | **11.00%** | **83.33%** |
| 3 | C 1 | Train business development in CRM | 33.00% | 50.00% |
| 0 | C 2 | Deploy CRM tools | 0.00% | 100.00% |
| 0 | C 3 | Establish CRM metrics and reporting | 0.00% | 100.00% |
| | | **People Champion: Timmy T** | **12.00%** | **85.00%** |
| 9 | E 3 | Exceed plan for personnel staffing by 10% in sales | 25.00% | 100.00% |
| 0 | E 4 | Accelerate deployment of approved quality of work-life programs | 25.00% | 100.00% |
| 0 | E 5 | Develop process to assess engineer performance | 10.00% | 25.00% |
| 0 | E 6 | Implement new career development guidelines | 0.00% | 100.00% |
| 0 | E 7 | Develop metrics on employee development | 0.00% | 100.00% |
| | | **Managed Growth Champion: Jimmy C** | **37.40%** | **67.00%** |
| 9 | G 4 | Devote Leadership Team time to growth | 37.00% | 10.00% |
| 5 | G 5 | Facilitate organizational cross communication | 25.00% | 75.00% |
| 2 | G 6 | Focus on goal deployment and follow through | 100.00% | 100.00% |
| 2 | G 7 | Increase job rotation and cross training across sites | 0.00% | 100.00% |
| 1 | G 8 | Increase teaming with outside firms to extend capabilities and enhance positions in growth markets | 25.00% | 50.00% |

**Figure 4.3** Executive dashboard – essential performance areas.

At this point the solution set should be evaluated against the core purpose, core values, desired states identified for each essential performance area, and the bold long-term goal. Once these alignments are confirmed, the solution set should be further evaluated to determine whether in the judgment of the Leadership Team as a whole the actions identified would achieve both the desired states and the bold long-term goal. If the answer is no, then the Leadership Team must specifically identify alternate actions or tasks that will make the solution set sufficient to reach both sets of objectives.

## ASSIGN A CHAMPION FOR EACH SET

Once the remaining tasks are grouped into areas of essential performance, a Champion is identified for each area. This individual will be held responsible for seeing that the remaining actions in her or his area of oversight are accomplished even though they may be actions taken by other members of the Leadership Team. This Champion will be the individual responsible for reporting progress in the reviews to be conducted throughout the implementation phase.

## WRITE THE TASK STATEMENTS OF WORK

The most critical action taken to ensure that the roadmap can be followed is to create a Task Statement of Work for each task (see Figure 4.4). This is often the detailed planning done by the Champion for each area of essential performance. The major transformation

| | Descriptions | | Task Lead | Due date | Status |
|---|---|---|---|---|---|
| Project Description | Managed Growth | | Jimmy C | | |
| Issue to be addressed | | | | | |
| TASK | G 4 | Focus leadership attention to growth | Walter L | | |
| Notes | | Leadership set aside time each day to talk with/meet new customers/prospects<br>VPs engage in technology strategy/investments<br>VPs network in external organizations/ trade groups<br>Leadership Team participates and drives performance reviews | | | |
| Sub-Tasks | G 4.5 | Create metrics to assess how much additional Leadership Team time is spent on growth | Suzanne S | | |
| | G 4.6 | Organize monthly reviews by growth areas to focus on common issues | Moira K | | |
| TASK | G 5 | Accelerate communication | Donald R | | |
| | G 5.1 | Set up town hall meetings at each site to brief employees of performance, growth, and status of change efforts | Alice M | | |
| Sub-Tasks | G 5.2 | Conduct team building exercises and events for Leadership Team | Joanie O | | |
| | G 5.3 | Key personnel exchange program among product lines and sites | Walter L | | |
| | G 5.4 | Deploy enhanced collaborative work tools across sites and engineering groups | Eric G | | |
| TASK | G 6 | Focus on leadership skills development | Steve J | | |
| TASK | G 7 | Key personnel job rotation | Timmy T | | |
| | G 7.1 | Transfer and cross train domain experience | Albert E | | |
| | G 7.2 | Rotate business development assignments of key personnel between sites | Jackie C | | |
| Sub-Tasks | G 7.3 | Move leadership across sites to understand cultural differences and break down barriers to collaboration | Jimmy C | | |
| | G 7.4 | Accelerate movement of work across sites – set goals measure and incentivize<br>Increase joint cross PL objectives | Albert E<br>Cathy K | | |
| TASK | G 8 | Increase teaming with outside firms | Jackie C | | |

| | | | Phone | e-mail |
|---|---|---|---|---|
| Team members and contact info | 1 | Jimmy C | 123-456-7899 | JimC@ |
| | 2 | Suzanne S | 123-456-7898 | SuzS@ |
| | 3 | Moira K | 123-456-7897 | MoiK@ |
| | 4 | Donald R | 123-456-7896 | DonR@ |
| | 5 | Alice M | 123-456-7895 | AliM@ |
| | 6 | Joanie O | 123-456-7894 | JoaO@ |
| | 7 | Walter L | 123-456-7893 | WalL@ |
| | 8 | Eric G | 123-456-7892 | EriG@ |
| | 9 | Steve J | 123-456-7891 | SteJ@ |
| | 10 | Jackie C | 123-456-7890 | JacC@ |
| | 11 | Cathy K | 123-456-7889 | CatS@ |

**Figure 4.4** Task statement of work – Essential performance area: growth.   *Continued*

*Continued*

| Resources required | 1 | e-room web server |
|---|---|---|
| | 2 | Policy rewrite and publication |
| | 3 | Relocation funding |
| | 4 | Travel for town hall meetings |
| | 5 | Outside membership funding |

| | |
|---|---|
| Incremental implementation cost | $32,750 |
| Milestones (if any) | See above |
| Specific improvement expected | Increasing sales by 50% over three years |
| Evaluation criteria/metrics | Varies by task, see above |
| Improvement owner (reporting) | Jimmy C |
| Approving authority | Robert K |
| Target date for completion | December 31, 2XXX |
| Actual date of completion | TBD |

**Figure 4.4** Task statement of work – Essential performance area: growth.

that takes place at this stage is committing to paper the specific tasks to be undertaken with assigning task leads, teams, and due dates. At the same time, the resources required to complete the actions are identified and the expected results stated. When the task statements are rolled up together the Leadership Team is able to see the work plan for realizing the desired states and achieving the bold long-term goal. It is at this point that the concepts turn into an understandable roadmap, with the challenges identified and the commitment that is required to achieve the desired state. Ideally, at this point, the whole Leadership Team reviews the task statements. If any Champion does not believe that she or he is capable of accomplishing the assigned tasks, those tasks are reevaluated and modified or a new Champion is assigned.

## CREATE AN EXECUTIVE DASHBOARD TO MONITOR PROGRESS

The executive dashboard is a tool to manage the implementation of the tasks. The purpose of the dashboard is to provide a summary of the status of each major task. Subtasks are not identified on the dashboard. Instead, they are specified on the individual task statements, and, thus, the individual responsible for overall management of the effort has the ability to drill down to the status on each subtask, as necessary.

This dashboard and the integrated task statements can be Web-enabled for very large projects with many subtasks and large implementation teams. This allows the task leads to periodically update the status of their tasks and have it roll into the dashboard. Any Leadership Team member may view the dashboard to obtain the current status of the major tasks.

# COMMUNICATE TO THE ORGANIZATION, CUSTOMERS, AND SUPPLIERS

It is vital to communicate the effort to the organization, customers, and suppliers. The team members of the organization will be expected to work within the framework of any and all changes in the organization structure, procedures, or processes that result from the tasks undertaken by the Leadership Team. It is important for them to understand what is happening, why it is happening, what the desired states represent, and how the desired states will impact them. They should embrace the bold, long-term goal. If team members do not identify with this long-term goal, then their lack of support will complicate the task of the Champions and their teams.

There is also a need to differentiate the communications according to the audience. Suppliers and customers need to be part of the audience for communications regarding the roadmap and the implications of it. However, the firm must recognize that suppliers and customers are in constant contact with competitors. Therefore, the communications must be tailored to ensure that competition-sensitive information is not provided to external parties. For this reason the message must be tailored to fit the needs of each audience without compromising competition-sensitive aspects of the roadmap.

# CONDUCT REVIEWS

Conduct periodic reviews of the progress. An overall Implementation Manager should be identified. This person should be a member of the Leadership Team in order to have the standing to be able to encourage the Champions to achieve their tasks. This person also reviews the progress of each task and identifies any new barriers that may arise or unexpected complications. If additional resources are required for any reason this person works with the Task Leads and Champions to ensure that they are provided and strategies for overcoming new barriers identified and worked.

As a whole, the Leadership Team needs to review the progress and discuss issues around the implementation that may require cross-organizational cooperation or dedication of additional resources.

# COMMUNICATE STATUS

The organization's team members, customers, and suppliers need to be provided with progress reports after the reviews. Only if movement is identified will the key supporters needed to ensure that the final goals are reached continue to pay attention to the effort and change their own behaviors as needed to achieve that final desired state. One of the main reasons for the failure of change efforts is that those who are expected to change do not see a continuing reason to do so and revert back to previous approaches to doing business because it is not evident that anyone cares.

# CELEBRATE ACHIEVEMENT

As the tasks that move the firm to the desired states in each essential performance area are completed, they should be celebrated. This is to reinforce the permanence of the changes to the desired state, which is a reinforcement of the effectiveness of the team efforts and the commitment of the Leadership Team to the new way of doing business.

# SUMMARY

The roadmap to strategic positioning is an evolved process. The key elements that Six Sigma brings are not only a rapid facilitated process of identifying common strategies and approaches, but also detailed simultaneous planning of the tasks required to successfully traverse the road mapped. Following are examples of tools to help in this implementation phase of strategic positioning:

- Top-five executive dashboard
- Areas of essential performance executive dashboard
- Task statement of work

# Section B

# The Change Accelerator

ACCELERATOR: A DEVICE USED TO PRODUCE HIGH-ENERGY, HIGH-SPEED CHARGED PARTICLES USED IN HIGH-ENERGY NUCLEAR PHYSICS, SYNCHROTRON RADIATION RESEARCH ... AND CERTAIN SIX SIGMA METHODOLOGIES.

The key to transforming any organization is a methodology that achieves rapid results. The author partnered with Ron Carmichael, a very experienced and highly creative Black Belt, to modify and evolve the rapid-execution workshop format that is equally applicable to both business analysis and project execution initiatives.

This section explores the workshop format and other rapid-execution Six Sigma techniques/approaches that Ron and other highly skilled Six Sigma practitioners have successfully used to accelerate change in organizations.

*Chapter 5: Jumpstarting Six Sigma* offers kick-in-the-pants ideas to start up Six Sigma efforts or to keep them going during the time lag before real results drive the organization to adopt Six Sigma as the way the company chooses to conduct business on a daily basis.

*Chapter 6: Eliminating Default Processes* explains the origins and effects of default processes. These are processes that evolve without direction as a result of changing personnel or being applied to new situations without being adequately tailored to the new situation. The main focus on this chapter is to offer recommendations for eliminating or appropriately adapting these default processes to match the current requirements.

*Chapter 7: Six Sigma Phases* introduces Six Sigma as a methodology to create an innovative environment and a means to bring about organizationwide cultural change.

*Chapter 8: Performance Improvement Workshops* explores the steps and methods used to accelerate understanding of root causes and the opportunities available to improve results. It gives a nuts-and-bolts look at how a workshop format, in and of itself, can be an effective method to save cost and time. Both thrusts, cost and time savings, integrally dovetail with the Six Sigma philosophy.

*Chapter 9: Accelerated Needs Analysis Workshops* discusses the application of Six Sigma project workshops to accelerate needs analysis. This particular chapter is focused on the acceleration of what the company's workforce needs to learn to be more capable, knowledgeable, and skillful in performing their assigned tasks.

*Chapter 10: Sarbanes Oxley Section 404 Internal Controls Assessment Deployment* details how Six Sigma is a highly efficient and effective means to deploy such an assessment system. Quantum Leaders must lead ethically. They must ensure that the organization provides accurate information to investors. With recent public examples where this leadership responsibility was flaunted, Congress imposed a set of requirements on publicly traded firms to annually assess the internal financial controls of the organization. This chapter thoroughly examines these requirements and how Six Sigma can be used to meet or even exceed them.

*Chapter 11: Software Innovation Workshops* examines how to "find money left on the table," which is another area where Six Sigma has much to offer in the way of performance improvement, yet few have experience in successfully leading such efforts.

*Chapter 12: Design for Six Sigma* explores issues regarding the lessons learned in embedding DFSS into the fabric and culture of several major market leaders.

The last three chapters deal with training and educational application of Six Sigma to expand the thinking of Six Sigma practitioners about what is possible, and how Six Sigma can be the integrating force to accelerate change across the entire organization.

*Chapter 13: Black Belt and Green Belt Preparation* raises questions about how these key players are currently trained, offering alternatives that make deployment more effective and that achieve quicker results. The approaches discussed build the competencies and skills required of future leaders who should be groomed and selected from Six Sigma Black and Green Belt ranks. These recommendations dovetail with those in the strategic planning and governance chapters in the Tales of Transformation section.

*Chapter 14: Beyond the Black Belt* examines management, mentoring, and succession issues that occupy the spare moments between the Black Belt's daily battles and ways to avoid bureaucratic pitfalls inherent in rapidly changing organizations.

*Chapter 15: Six Sigma as an Integrating Force* concludes this section on change acceleration with a discussion about leading organizational integration. Whether that integration is a result of a corporate business unit acquisition or simply the integration of new members into evolving or established work groups, Six Sigma speeds the integration process by providing a common language and philosophy as a bridge to understanding and conceptualizing the work to be performed.

# 5

# Jumpstarting Six Sigma

SUCCESS BREEDS SUCCESS. IN ORDER TO ACCELERATE OR JUMPSTART RESULTS IT IS IMPORTANT TO PICK BATTLES WISELY AND TAKE ACTION TO ENSURE EARLY AND OFTEN THE SUCCESS OF INITIAL PROJECTS.

While applicable to everyone, this chapter is especially dedicated to those who wish to introduce Six Sigma activities within their organization but are having trouble getting started, or to those who have already started Six Sigma activities but are finding their efforts in delivering anticipated results to be lagging.

## THE IGNITION AND THE KEY

When a revolutionary way of conducting business is introduced, the typical reaction is fear or resistance, or, for many, simply ignoring it, hoping that it will go away. Political revolutions may happen overnight, but revolutionary change never seems to happen that way in established businesses.

Every change movement has early adopters, open resisters, and everyone else who sits on the fence waiting to see if the movement will build support and move forward or fail and go away. The key to success is success.

## DISCERNING POSITIVE AND NEGATIVE POWER

It goes without saying that jumpstarting a Six Sigma effort requires top-down alignment and support. Setting targets for improvement and immediately and publicly rewarding those who have achieved those targets brings the rest of the organization into alignment behind the leadership.

To achieve accelerated success, the leadership of the organization must "walk the talk" and actually use the Six Sigma tools to demonstrate not only their understanding of them, but also their commitment to use them to manage the organization. One way to do this is to develop a strategic or operating plan using Six Sigma tools. This demonstrates how effective they are in reaching rapid consensus on thorny topics and issues, while simultaneously clarifying and aligning the whole team on the direction the leadership has selected to pursue.

When priorities are set in the planning stages, leadership communicates to the company what is important. If Six Sigma activity is an afterthought or something that is not being used by the senior leadership, then it becomes an afterthought to those who are following the leadership, which is generally everyone else in the organization.

Public rewards are essential for sustained involvement and support for any activity, whether it is Six Sigma or not. Wildly successful companies are the ones that reward and celebrate early and often.

# THE PROCEDURE: HOW TO JUMPSTART SIX SIGMA EFFORTS

The following steps describe how to jumpstart Six Sigma activities from the point of identifying potential projects to the point of delivering final results to management. Some activities are concurrent. Depending on the project, many of the steps may become recurrent.

1. Planning
   - Identify project (objective/goals)
   - Preparation checklist
   - Identify participants
   - Design plan format

2. Work Preparation (collect documentation)
   - Collect materials
   - Arrange room (logistics - lunches)
   - Notify participants

3. Current Reality – Data Collection (current processes)
   - Organizational context
   - Current metrics
   - Current results

4. Undesirable Effects

- Evaluate/validate data

- Identify undesirable effects of current reality based on data obtained

- Identify root causes of current results

- Identify/analyze complexity drivers

5. Idea Generation (brainstorming)

- Creative thinking – possible solutions/opportunities to improve results

6. Feasibility/Evaluation (affinitize ideas into actions)

- Cost savings/investment

- Select/prioritize

- Assign actions

7. Develop Task Plans

- Task Statements of Work to define and detail specific actions and actors

- Roles and responsibilities

- New process map and metrics

8. Implementation

- Management approval/authorization/budget

- Authorize and empower project teams

- Training/tracking closure

While it is necessary to conduct the data collection and analysis steps before moving into the issue and idea generation steps, it is sometimes necessary to go back and collect more data as the result of these steps or when the undesirable effects are defined and the true scope of the task becomes more evident. The same is true when the final task list and Task Statements of Work are developed. It is not uncommon to loop through the steps two or three times before completing a given project.

## ACCELERATION TO TRANSFORMATION

Jumpstarting Six Sigma requires the Six Sigma team to think small, act fast, and move on. The team must find meaningful ways to achieve rapid results to build a core of support for more ambitious activity. The preferred approach is to gain early successes through tactical transformations or singular, highly visible, opportunities for achieving rapid results. It helps to have at least a few key people who are early adopters.

The initial assessment needs to be quick – no more than a day or two, which should be sufficient time to understand the data and make initial recommendations, as long as the data are captured and validated prior to the initial assessment. This also permits the Six Sigma team to identify and prepare experts for possible involvement during the business assessment, as necessary.

To accelerate the process, the business assessment activities need to be accomplished within three days. Projects coming out of the assessments need to be few in number, inexpensive to accomplish, and produce results in less than 30 days. To achieve this kind of rapid implementation, the specific actions need to be thoroughly planned and agreed upon during the three-day business assessment with funding and authorization to proceed provided at that time.

As soon as the approval to proceed is granted, the Six Sigma team needs to focus on preparing for the prescribed projects by creating and ensuring that data capture instruments are validated before use, building relationships with potential early adopters, and providing key people with clearly defined roles and opportunities to showcase their abilities and leadership in the project execution. The Six Sigma team must also prearrange ways to celebrate and provide recognition for the key people who participate in the activities.

The Six Sigma activities must be project managed to ensure that unexpected barriers are rapidly resolved to keep all of the projects moving toward rapid completion.

Whenever a target project is completed, it is time to celebrate. Project participants are thanked and recognized for their efforts. The larger organization is invited to share in the celebration to foster understanding and support for the Six Sigma activities. By participating in the celebration, senior leadership reaffirms their support for the Six Sigma activities and demonstrates their commitment to following through. In this way, the senior leadership communicates and reinforces the Vision of a Six Sigma company and the importance that each employee has in building Six Sigma into their individual jobs as well as their organization's way of doing business.

## REVVING THE ENGINE OF CHANGE

Many Six Sigma projects are handicapped by analysis paralysis. With the focus on data-driven decisions, many projects find themselves held captive to gathering additional data or trying to find just the right solution. In some instances management is reluctant to expend funds on something that is seen as addressing the symptoms and not the root cause.

To be successful, Six Sigma teams must keep management focused on continual as well as continuous improvement. Keeping the momentum up means moving forward on any solution that is 80 percent complete, as long as it can be initiated quickly and inexpensively, knowing that there will inevitably be a second round to work on the remaining 20 percent.

The company wants improvement. Shareholders and customers want to enjoy the benefits of improvement. Companies caught in a holding pattern for a total solution often find that the cost of the total solution is beyond reach in one effort. In these cases, the competition may step in and gain favor with the customer because they are taking smaller but consistent steps and showing continual improvement.

Consolidation of gains is important. Employees who are asked to change their processes and work behaviors need time to accept and work with the changes before they are able to articulate the benefits. This leads to the concept of iterative cycles rather than a single sustained effort. That does not mean that the Six Sigma team should take periodic breathers to let the organization catch up, but rather that Six Sigma efforts should move across different parts of the organization to allow those who have completed their business analysis, undertaken several projects, and implemented them fully to have time to become comfortable with the changes in their work lives.

Once employees have had time to master one small step toward improvement in their work processes, making more small changes will more easily be accepted and accomplished.

Training and deploying Green Belts who have a command of basic Six Sigma tools and have a conceptual understanding of Six Sigma principles also leverages the results and accelerates the accomplishments. Use of Green Belts minimizes the learning curve and the need to get comfortable with the type of analysis that Six Sigma requires.

Taking "small bites of the elephant" allows rapid and repeated success, whereas trying to swallow the whole problem in a single effort makes for a long drawn-out set of projects. When efforts drag on and do not come to a rapid conclusion, those involved have a tendency to lose interest. When something takes too much time or requires an investment beyond what the individual is able to manage in the daily routine, the probability of the dramatic results associated with successful Six Sigma projects decreases dramatically.

## EXPERTS ON CALL: ROADSIDE ASSISTANCE

In large companies, in particular, there is a tendency to create teams of Black Belts that move from project to project as a means of leveraging the value realized from the investment in training and business analysis/projects conducted. While this may seem to make good business sense, it actually causes these firms to under realize or even completely miss some of the possible benefits that Six Sigma can bring about.

In an analysis of a division of one large aerospace manufacturer it became startlingly clear that the company was spending most of its money on program execution. The customer paid for products to be delivered according to established schedules. Materials and labor were run routinely through the programs. But in that particular division, as is true of many organizations, there was no one person within the division responsible for Six Sigma activity. Instead, whenever a need was identified, someone was requested from a pool of Black Belts to come in and help, much like calling for roadside assistance. The periodic Six Sigma project may have temporarily solved a major problem, but without a conscious and consolidated effort at planning and coordinating Six Sigma activities, it was hit or miss at best – much like keeping jumper cables in the car without taking the time to recharge, or even replace, the battery.

# THROWING AWAY THE JUMPER CABLES

An alternative approach that ensures the maximum return on the Six Sigma investment is to assign and train one person on the program to be the Six Sigma manager. There are three areas where this individual is able to wring the maximum value out of the program.

First, the Six Sigma Manager participates in all program-related capture activity and employs Six Sigma in conducting various assessments such as the QFD on the conceptual design level in preparing the bid. This ensures that there are opportunities to propose innovative technical solutions that may prove to be more cost effective than or technically superior to competing bids. This is one way to maximize backlog on the program and ensure program continuity.

The second area of responsibility is in resolving issues related to schedule and cost. The Six Sigma Manager conducts business analyses and manages individual Six Sigma projects as necessary to ensure that the program remains on schedule and within budget. Keeping programs within budget and schedule protects profits, providing an advantage in the capture of new business or any modifications or add-ons that the customer seeks from time to time.

The third area is in productivity improvement, which is traditionally considered the domain of Six Sigma. Productivity improvements bring about an increase in profits realized by saving the company money that would have been wasted in unproductive activities or processes.

The Six Sigma Manager learns how to keep programs on schedule and under budget while wringing substantial productivity improvements out as the program progresses. The Six Sigma Manager understands how to focus the program on customer needs and wants through the data capture process. Thus, this assignment is a tremendous training ground for future Program Managers who would continue to manage through Six Sigma when they make the transition to the new role. At the same time the company has demonstrated a commitment to leveraging program results through the investment made in Six Sigma.

# ACCELERATING TO QUANTUM RESULTS

Achieving quantum results starts at the top. Whether jumpstarting or accelerating results, it is essential for senior leaders in the organization to "walk the talk" by demonstrating that they themselves are managing using Six Sigma.

However, few senior leaders are Black Belts. Because they are expected to understand Six Sigma and somehow make the transition to managing through Six Sigma, it is essential for them to have a mentor capable of helping them learn how to manage using Six Sigma and act as their conscience in spreading the Six Sigma Vision. Most often a mentor is a Six Sigma Master Black Belt or a Champion who is, by definition, the most experienced individual in the company at orchestrating performance improvement not already serving as a senior leader.

Often, Six Sigma Black Belts have an active role in mentoring mid-level leaders, although some firms also reserve this as a Master or Champion function.

With the assistance of the Six Sigma mentor, senior leaders can clarify, crystallize, and communicate their Vision and then navigate the entire enterprise toward making that Vision a reality.

## SUMMARY

Some companies understand that Six Sigma is actually an emerging leadership subculture within the firm. They realize that the future leadership will come from this group of individuals. As a result they provide the opportunities for Six Sigma to be effectively deployed and supported to gain results.

As a training ground for future leadership one effective approach is to assign Black Belts to programs to manage three areas: business acquisition, which ensures continuing income and profits; schedule and cost, which protects planned profitability; and productivity improvement, which adds profits through reductions in planned cost.

Those companies that do not understand the leadership development aspect of Six Sigma make it another add-on that they hope will make customers believe that their company is serious about being a market leader. Unfortunately, add-on Six Sigma demonstrates that they do not understand what it takes to either retain that leadership if they currently enjoy it, or to achieve that position in the future if they do not.

# 6

# Eliminating Default Processes

BUREAUCRACY IS EVERYWHERE AND BUREAUCRACY IS NOWHERE.

## BUREAUCRACY IS PERVASIVE

Bureaucracy happens when processes take on a life of their own, making it difficult to get anything done. When the flow of work stagnates, it is very difficult to pinpoint any single cause that would eliminate the problem. At the surface it may look like apathetic individuals who are creating the bureaucracy. However, the stinging tentacles of bureaucracy can trap and paralyze even the most dynamic and gung-ho people in the organization.

Some organizations solve the problem by changing all of the people involved, expecting that new faces will find a way to prevail. But this is the equivalent of cutting the tops off of a particularly vicious patch of weeds rather than pulling them up from the roots. Even with new people involved, the processes that were in place remain and, eventually, the bureaucracy grows back, sometimes even stronger than before.

Why is it that some processes prevent progress while others promote progress? The answer is *default processes*. These are processes that have been left to "grow wild" over time, sometimes through many generations of workers.

## DEFAULT PROCESSES: THE NEW PERSON SYNDROME

The single greatest cause of default processes is employee turnover without proper training. Even a process that was properly defined and well established in the beginning changes when a new person takes over those responsibilities. The new person has a different personality. Some people are organized; others are not. Some easily establish relationships. Others see everyone as a threat. Some people follow up on every detail. Others work best on the big picture issues and leave the details to others. The diversity of personality types, preferences, and individual strengths causes differences in how processes are managed from one person to another.

When someone leaves a position, the next person usually receives very little training or guidance in how to perform the work. An overview is given and then the new person is expected to learn on the job.

It takes time and effort to show someone all that they need to know to perform the required tasks, especially when the process is complex with many variables. Most supervisors are too busy to take the time, or not knowledgeable enough about the job themselves, to thoroughly train new people. But someone is always around who can answer questions, so most supervisors assume that the new people will pick up what they need to do as they go.

Complicating this on-the-job training scenario is the structure of most organizations. Processes are rarely self-contained. They have roots and tentacles, which reach out and touch different parts of the company. In most instances, someone within the firm does something that triggers the default process. He or she performs a task that is antecedent to a specific task in the default process for which the new person is responsible. If that antecedent task is not accomplished expeditiously and correctly, the new person may not know enough to realize that it is missing or incorrect. Even if the new person realizes that something needs to be done about the missing task, the "crisis of the moment" may delay follow-up on the task even further.

When the new person finally gets to the task, if she or he finds that everything is not present to complete it in one step, or a manageable series of steps, it may get sidetracked again. In this way, a single unfinished task may smolder at the bottom of the new person's "in basket" until it becomes hot enough to alert the legions of crisis managers, who finally descend to put out the fire.

In our example, the hand-off from the upstream process is critical to the success of this step. If the person performing the prior task has done everything correctly and sent it on ready for the next step, it should flow right through. Most transactions happen just this way. But when something is missing, incorrect, or miscommunicated, it can consume as much as 80 percent of the task performer's time. Beyond that, when people are new to a position, they don't know what they don't know. Hence, important questions never get asked. This increases the likelihood of error exponentially.

When people rely on each other for parts of a process, their working relationships determine – to a large extent – the success of their hand-offs, much like runners in a relay race. Success also depends on understanding enough about the upstream and downstream tasks to know what is critical for each individual to do to successfully complete them.

Clearly, when someone new enters a process stream, relationships are changed and there is substantial probability that, at least for a while, the process as a whole will operate less efficiently. However, even if individuals do not change positions, the positions themselves may change due to shifts in organizational requirements, markets, regulations, laws, or common practices. These changes may be reactive (made immediately) to try to address the current understanding of a changed requirement without really knowing what needs to be done. Such reactive changes are unlikely to be either effective or efficient.

All of these factors feed into the default process syndrome. Changes in people, changes in external environments, changes in products and services, and changes in internal priorities, perceptions, and practices may induce a change or need for a change in a process. In almost every case, a default process is highly inefficient for the organization and the customers of the organization.

## FIXING THE DEFAULT PROCESS

One Six Sigma team developed a toolset that has proven remarkably effective in breaking bureaucracy and fixing those change-resistant processes that never seem to work for the company or its customers. It is based on the application of several tools within a two to three day cross-functional workshop.

Their process is successful in resolving performance issues across the organization, whether in finance, marketing, procurement, or in the design, development, and production areas. Six Sigma project workshops are as effective for organizations that provide services as they are for those delivering products.

While developing the toolset, the Six Sigma team determined that it needed an enterprise outlook on processes to be successful. Nearly every workshop identified process elements that were either upstream or external to the process that was "under the microscope" as being the most significant cause of process difficulties. Endless loops seemed to be a recurrent theme whenever information or approvals were required from external organizations. These endless loops were lovingly known as "black holes" because they sucked in and prevented all attempts at progress despite the most earnest efforts to reach and collaborate with any counterparts on the "other side."

One technique that was employed by the Six Sigma team to bring about organizational change was to assemble a cross-functional team to take a "time out." This forced everyone to take an objective look at the process efficiency, which was prerequisite to being able to effectively recommend or incorporate changing requirements, from whatever source. Cross-functional teams, which included customers, and – if appropriate – vendors or suppliers, had the ability to take such an objective look at the process.

Because they were identified so often as causes of process difficulties, representatives from upstream and downstream processes were included on any team that conducted analyses or recommended solutions. This helped all of the participants to move beyond "ownership" and into collaborative working relationships. It also helped participants to break out of the "It's always been done that way" syndrome. The key point is that it may have always been done that way, but something has changed. It may have been a new person, a new product, a new customer, a new internal requirement, or something in the environment in which the firm operated that forced the need for change.

# RESEQUENCING AND SIMPLIFYING

When processes grow "wild" of their own accord, steps are not always done at the optimal point. A step may occur at a point where it takes several hours to perform. After closer examination, the cross-functional team may discover that by having an upstream person include this step at the beginning of what he or she does, it might take only a few minutes.

Seldom are work processes reviewed or discussed in any detail by those involved. But a simple change like having the right person do a step at the right time to minimize the effort can reap tremendous returns in productivity.

These types of efficiencies can be achieved only when all of the players talk to each other about what they do and what the issues are about how they do their work. The integrated cross-functional teams are able to discover these types of savings when they analyze the process together and discuss the factors that slow it. Individuals may be aware of a symptom, but unable to put their finger on the cause until they look at the whole process from end to end.

For example, the default process depicted in Figure 6.1 was originally used to issue invoices for time and material contracts to a government agency. It took approximately three months to generate a single invoice. The primary culprit was endless uncoordinated and partial reviews and data supplied by external organizations. A series of project workshops were conducted to analyze the process from contract set-up, through time recording, procurement, accounting, and billing. This was done to establish the default "baseline" process.

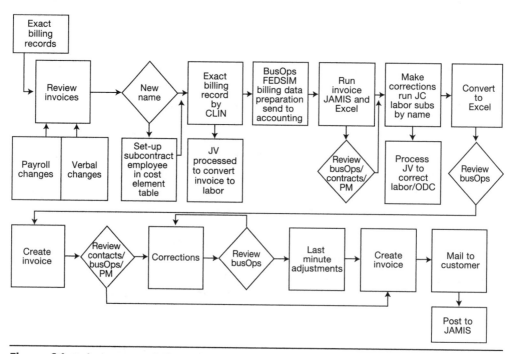

**Figure 6.1** Default process (before Six Sigma workshop).

The cross-functional team that attended the Six Sigma workshop generated a series of ideas to address the endless "bureaucracy." The ideas were evaluated, and those that offered the greatest opportunity for improvement were incorporated into a series of actions that met the original process objectives. Then the team developed a new process that addressed all of the discontinuities and "black holes," resulting in endless loops in the original (default) process. Their new process is seen in Figure 6.2.

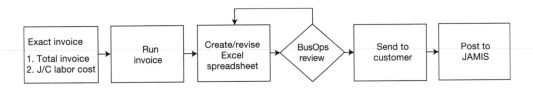

**Figure 6.2** New process (after Six Sigma workshop).

The new process reduced the effort to produce a time and materials invoice from 23 steps and three months to six steps and two weeks. This represents a 74 percent reduction in effort and 83 percent reduction in cycle time. These savings were achieved through workshops that were concluded within a single week, and all actions to implement were completed within 30 days following the workshop.

Because the users of the process devised the solution, the new process is "owned" by the whole team and not imposed on them by outside parties, which are not part of the organization or its culture.

Cross-organizational communication channels were opened, which permitted the process team to continue to make improvements beneficial to the whole organization long after the workshops were concluded. Support for process improvement was created through the success of the workshop-led changes. Individual team members took ownership for the changes, which became a key determinant of the willingness of others to look at what they did and determine further methods of improving upon it.

## SUMMARY

Bureaucracy is everywhere and it is nowhere. Bureaucracy is not people slowing work, it is a process that forces people to work at tasks much longer and harder than they need to. Performance improvement can be accelerated through an objective cross-functional look at how an organization does its work in an intense workshop format. This chapter has provided an overview of where to look and an understanding of how it comes about. A workshop approach is proposed to bust the bureaucracy and drive performance improvement. With this knowledge, leaders are better equipped to eliminate this barrier to improved performance.

# 7

# The Phases of Six Sigma

SIX SIGMA CRYSTALLIZES A CHANGE IN CULTURE, DEVELOPMENT TOOLS, AND A
METHODOLOGY TO CREATE AN INNOVATIVE ENVIRONMENT IN WHICH INTERDISCIPLINARY
TEAMS COLLECTIVELY INVENT BEST VALUE PROCESS/PRODUCT SOLUTIONS.

Six Sigma is a significant paradigm shift from the traditional sequential processes used throughout industry. It is a concurrent process that brings together the customer, the supplier, and company personnel in creative workshops at key intervals throughout a program or product lifecycle.

Each effort is preceded by rigorous planning sessions and concludes at a "management out briefing" with specific actions identified for implementation, as well as schedules, cost and risk reduction evaluations, and concrete objectives and metrics that measure successful achievement.

An example of the effectiveness of this approach is a value-added computer system reseller. Through a series of tactical transformational workshops their production processes were completely redesigned. They validated the business redesign resulting in a 300 percent increase in throughput with increased quality while effecting a 33 percent reduction in personnel and 66 percent reduction in shipping costs.

This chapter introduces the main phases of a typical Six Sigma project, some of which will be addressed in more detail in subsequent chapters.

## BUSINESS ANALYSIS AND PROJECT PHASES

The three main phases of a Six Sigma project are:

• Planning and initial data collection

- Workshops

- Implementation

The *planning phase* typically begins about a month before the workshop with a meeting of the Six Sigma staff, Program Manager, and key personnel. Process discipline is maintained by completing the preparation checklists that identify project and logistical details, such as identifying the specifics to be analyzed. A planning meeting is also where specific and measurable objectives for the workshop are set, and, depending on the task, specific cross-functional team participants are assigned to each aspect to be reviewed.

The planners select approximately 10-14 people, including key process personnel and those who interface with the process, and, in some cases, suppliers, customer personnel, or outside process experts (or all three) to review each major element of the process or product.

## The business analysis (data gathering)

The business analysis team gathers data from multiple sources to understand the current nature of work performed. Those invited to participate in the workshop may be asked to draw an "as-is" version of their processes prior to the workshop so that a baseline process exists to serve as the focal point of the initial analysis. Additional data are collected as determined in the planning phase.

Part of the baseline setting may be an abbreviated QFD or similar Six Sigma tool, which is designed to bring a clear understanding of the customer expectations to the surface. A complete data collection and analysis typically takes two or more weeks to complete for a full baseline. However, if the intent of the workshop is to rapidly resolve a single problem or issue, a mini-baseline or Kaizen blitz can be conducted in a much shorter time frame. In this case, however, the focus is strictly on "low-hanging fruit."

The mini-baseline can be a first step toward providing immediate attention to an area where resources are insufficient to attack larger systemic issues. However, a band-aid can only cover and protect small wounds. For larger issues, it is incumbent upon the organization to address a full business analysis activity in the future to achieve further gains.

## Workshop phase

The *Six Sigma workshop phase*, which typically takes from one day to two weeks, depending on the complexity of the process or product, is the point where transformation occurs. It may begin with the workshop staff teaching Six Sigma methodology and developing a Value Stream for the customer immediately prior to analysis.

Training is just-in-time. It includes a structured nonconfrontational workshop exercise. The training exercise not only familiarizes all participants with the process, but also begins team formation work on a nonthreatening task, building a team that is sensitized to a philosophy of group creativity. It may also provide practice in looking at a process or product that has been examined before, but this time thinking about the process or product in terms of what can be simplified or removed. The participants forget that they represent different functional areas or backgrounds and begin to work toward the common goal of reducing the cost of producing a concept without losing any of the process or product functionality and still exceeding customer requirements and expectations.

Depending upon the size of the project team, all work may be either done as a whole group or broken into subteams. For complex programs or processes, the participants are usually assigned to submodules of the unit in cross-functional teams of seven or eight persons. Each team is provided all the information it needs to perform the analysis, including baseline processes and data, and the objective or target information, which is the expected result of the workshop. With cost, quality, performance, and schedule or cycle time targets and requirements clearly in mind, the team uses a set of tools to understand the issues and concerns regarding the baseline process or product and generates a set of ideas or opportunities by which improvement may result.

At this point the key to the process is the brainstorming of innovative new ideas to satisfy the customer or management's requirements. Creativity is unleashed. One participant's innovative thoughts are built upon by other team members. Alternative concepts for the same issue, concern, or functional point are invented to address effectiveness in terms of:

- Eliminating redundancy
- Combining/consolidating functions or activities
- Relaxing specifications or requirements to optimize performance
- Using standard tools or commercially available alternatives
- Eliminating expense drivers
- Reducing steps or time drivers
- Using collective approaches
- Upstreaming activity or moving it to the fastest or least-cost point in the process
- Reducing supporting functions or requirements
- Simplifying what is to be done or accomplished

Several alternatives are solicited for each issue, concern, or functional point of analysis. In each case, the important criterion is meeting the cost and cycle time or schedule requirements or targets. Essential to this process is the ability to rapidly estimate cost and schedule impacts of the proposed actions. Several different tools may be used to generate this information. However, in most cases members of the project team have the expertise and knowledge necessary to be able to provide these estimates within the workshop. If the project team members do not have this knowledge, then those who do possess it are brought into the workshop to contribute the necessary information or data to successfully complete the analysis.

A major difference between the parallel actions of the project workshop and the classical sequential processes employed to analyze workflow or product development is direct, clear communication among all functions, and immediacy of action. If there is a question concerning the capability of a particular element or function within a process, a representative of that area is present or brought into the room. If the team looks for an upstream opportunity, a representative of that area is either participating or is quickly located and can "reality test" the idea and determine the feasibility and report on other consequences of such proposed actions. If there is a question about management support, a member of management is either in the workshop or available to discuss the issue and give clear guidance. It is not unusual for team members to work well into the evening to validate a concept. Because of this creative atmosphere, innovative approaches or concepts are frequently worked out on a flip chart or process map.

Working through lunch is the norm if food is provided. Thus, participants are protected from interruption, and they have everything they need at hand to make decisions and initiate changes. There is no waiting for several days to pass while someone researches an issue and writes a report to be submitted for consideration.

At the conclusion of the Six Sigma project workshop, the teams prepare a project plan, task statements of work, metric templates. Cost and cycle time or schedule savings and quality or performance improvements are documented including a Net Present Value (NPV) analysis so this investment can be evaluated along with all other corporate investments. Finally, a management report and presentation of their results completes the documentation. The report includes the alternatives considered and the recommendation. Implementation resources, schedule, and required personnel to perform the necessary implementation actions are detailed in a searchable database. This provides management with a tool to track the implementation and monitor progress according to individual, date, or task. The risk analysis details the consensus perception of the various ideas or opportunities to improve the process. Historically, low-risk changes alone will achieve a one-third cost or cycle-time improvement on average while not adversely impacting either quality or functionality.

## Implementation phase

The final phase is the *implementation of results*. Program management defines and implements the final action plan after considering the cost benefits of the changes. Projects conducted early in the development cycle or early in the establishment of operations usually implement all identified improvements because the implementation cost is low and the development time is available. For projects conducted late in the development cycle, or for long established processes, other considerations, not the least of which are development cost and time or overcoming inertia and resistance to change, play important roles in determining which actions are actually implemented. Changes achieved at the front end are much less costly. These changes add profits directly to the bottom line through avoidance of rework or duplicated effort.

A common thread through the entire Six Sigma project process is facilitation. The Six Sigma team drives process improvements that increase the range of application, such as software, program plan and schedule validation, business processes, supplier development, quality systems, and strategy/capability alignment. The programs using Six Sigma to address performance issues are in many locations throughout the United States and abroad, and include those where a multiplicity of companies in many different countries have teamed on common efforts.

# OUTCOMES

All Six Sigma efforts develop several skills among the participants, such as the following.

## Team building

The first benefit is team building across functional disciplines. This team building opens communications through nontraditional channels across the organization. Where functional responsibilities often create an introspection of the workgroup, the project team focus introduces opportunities for representatives from nontraditional work pairings from cross-functional task teams to build relationships and new communications channels.

## Rapid resolution

A second benefit of Six Sigma is rapid resolution. Projects are action oriented and focused on immediacy of results. The knowledge and skills that the workshop participants bring are the primary factors needed to instigate change. A ground rule is that only ideas that can be acted on and accomplished by members of the project team, or those brought in during the development of the project to ensure their complete buy-in, may be adopted. Thus, the resolution may be rapidly reached because the project team members have the capability to implement the changes to which they agree.

## Problem solving

*Increased problem-solving ability is an inevitable outcome of every project.* The entire process teaches each participant how to unlock his or her own creative problem-solving abilities. The sharing of these skills in a group setting energizes and empowers the individual and provides an opportunity to practice and develop these skills and abilities where the results lead to positive reinforcement. Learning theory teaches that positive reinforcement engenders further attempts to use the skills and employ the knowledge gained.

## Implementation skills

*Implementation skills* are a consequence of Six Sigma project participation. Working together, team members determine a comprehensive set of actions that will lead to process or product innovation and change. The team briefs management on the implementation plan. Management then empowers the changes and is provided with a set of tools to track and monitor each team member as she or he completes the actions necessary to effect the changes agreed to by the project team members and management during the "management out briefing" presentation.

## Common culture

*Creation of a common culture* is a consequence of Six Sigma projects. When participants come from different organizations, communication barriers are broken down. Through the process of the project workshop, common understanding of how each group works results. The team building, which is necessary to achieve an analysis and redesign of either a product design or process, results in human understandings. This leads to positive work relationships that will breach the organizational barriers. It opens opportunities for a new culture to emerge and captures elements of the various cultures, but blends and creates something totally new, a common culture, which can be understood and embraced by those familiar only with the constituent cultures existing prior to the project workshop.

# SUMMARY

One Six Sigma team innovated beyond the design environments from which they emerged as a need was identified to improve organizational performance as well as designs. They evolved to embrace all design opportunities for both hardware and software, and on to business systems, program acquisition, program close-out, strategy/capability alignment, and transition/cultural integration of diverse organizations.

The improvements in schedule/quality/functionality have been tracked and have averaged in excess of 40 percent while cost reductions have averaged in excess of 30 percent across more than 700 Six Sigma business analyses and projects. Examples such as a value-added computer system reseller have validated whole business redesign that resulted in a 300 percent increase in throughput with increased quality while effecting a 33 percent reduction in personnel and a 66 percent reduction in shipping costs. Such dramatic results are indicative of the power of Six Sigma projects.

# 8

# The Power of Six Sigma
# Workshops

THE SIX SIGMA WORKSHOP FORMAT GREATLY ACCELERATES RESULTS.

Change that might take years to happen, even with proper management support, is now happening in days or weeks. A typical Six Sigma workshop is somewhere between two days and two weeks in duration, and the resulting changes are normally achieved within two months following the workshop completion.

This short time frame is achievable because the expertise to determine the best course of action is resident within the firm; it is just locked in many different minds and perceptions. The workshop format provides the key to unlock those minds. The quality of the ideas and the synergy of solutions that happen within these workshops is the power that jumpstarts and drives organizational change.

## HOW THE WORKSHOP WORKS

A workshop team comprises people who are experts in what they do. The problem is that they generally do not have time or a forum (or permission) to come together to compare what they know, test their perceptions, and work together to devise a better way of performing their work. But workshop team members know better than any outside firm the terrain of their organization. They do not need time to come up to speed on what their organization does. They do not have to learn about their corporate climate and culture. They are internal experts and they know how to navigate the implementation minefields to ensure that their expected results are achieved.

In the workshops, the root cause of a problem is attacked rather than taking action against symptoms, which does not cause a permanent improvement to the process issues. A comprehensive approach is taken because a systemic answer to a problem allows it to be addressed once, rather than multiple times.

# WORKSHOP PHASES

Clearly, the Six Sigma workshop format has helped large organizations with extremely complex processes that have evolved into something less than optimal by default. However, it has been found equally applicable in medium and small organizations where workers have slipped into the black hole of bureaucracy or find themselves feeling trapped by the "We've always done it that way" syndrome.

Typically these workshops last two and a half days, although with very complex processes they may last up to two weeks. During this time the cross-functional team reviews the baseline (default) process and identifies issues and difficulties that cause problems across the organization. Even processes that appear at the surface to be functioning well are found to be cumbersome and time-consuming to the people involved in performing them.

The process depicted in Figure 8.1 shows the three phases that constitute a typical Six Sigma project workshop. Each phase is as important as the others. Without proper planning and preparation, the results of the workshop are minimized, and without a properly executed implementation plan, the workshop is not able to deliver the promised improvements.

## Preparation phase

At least one week prior to the workshop the Six Sigma team must define who, what, where, and when. (See the Project Planning Checklist in Appendix A.) The Six Sigma team works with the organizational sponsor and any other key players to define the objectives and choose the participants. These two steps are critical, as the team will not know whether the objectives are achieved unless they are specific and measurable. Likewise, they will not be able to achieve those objectives unless the people who know the current process and the problems it engenders are in the room for the discussions.

The team also needs to invite influential leaders who will be able to persuade those unable to attend that the outcomes will benefit everyone so that they can be implemented expeditiously.

Prior to the workshop, a flowchart or procedure that captures the way the process is currently being done needs to be created (baseline). Only when workshop team members understand what is currently being done will they have the ability to see what can be done differently. This baseline process, if shared prior to the workshop, can start participants thinking about what is being done and how it could be done differently, which accelerates the start of the workshop.

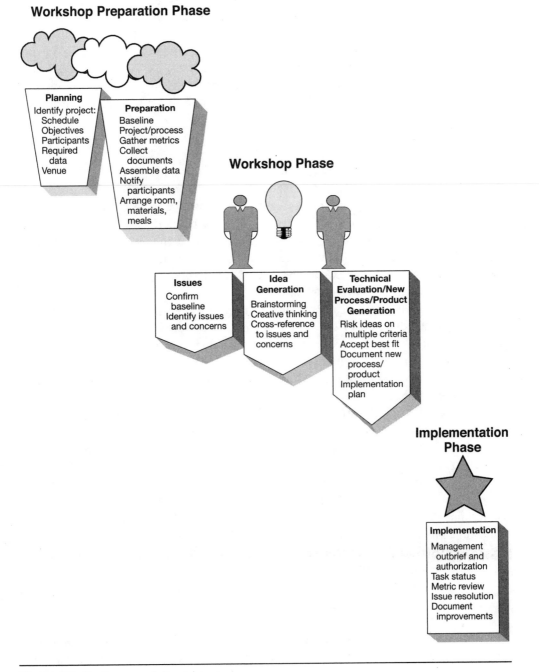

**Figure 8.1** Six Sigma workshop phases.

The final aspect of the preparation phase is to gather as much information about the process or product as possible, arrange for the venue, and notify the participants. Although this may seem like minuscule detail work, it is important. If the room is not reserved, or the room is not conducive to a workshop, the results will be affected. If participants do not understand what is expected to happen, why they are doing it, or what their expected role is to be, then valuable time is diverted in the workshop to bring the team to the same point in preparation.

## Workshop phase

One of the first activities in the actual workshop is a review of the baseline. Even after hundreds of workshops, the author has yet to see a baseline developed outside of the workshop that everyone agreed was what was actually being done in the organization. This is why it is so important to verify the baseline. Once this is done, the workshop team members are more familiar with the process and are better prepared to discuss the issues and concerns with the existing process. These issues and concerns are captured and saved for use later in the workshop.

Once the main issues are captured, the next activity is to generate ideas to improve the process. Once this part of the workshop begins, the ideas are often rapid-fire and synergistic. Often when the ideas are combined together they create a novel and comprehensive solution to the problem. But in some instances, the ideas are mutually exclusive and the team must determine which ones among the competing solutions they will further develop to resolve the issues.

When all ideas/solutions have been captured, a cross-check is performed to make sure that viable ideas/solutions have been generated to address each of the original issues that were recorded. If any issues have not been addressed, more ideas are solicited to address the open items.

Each idea/solution is evaluated across multiple criteria, which address the objectives of the workshop. In this technical evaluation phase, each idea/solution is analyzed to determine the merits and effects across the organization if the idea/solution is implemented in a process change. Once all the ideas/solutions have been evaluated, the team accepts those that will improve the process, thereby addressing all of the issues and concerns reflected in the objectives of the workshop.

## Implementation plan/phase

Once the ideas/solutions are accepted, a new process is drafted, including an estimated time required to perform, cost to perform, and cost to implement. Each accepted idea/solution is either documented within the process or assigned to an individual to put into effect. The individual writes a Task Statement of Work (see Appendix G for a sample) to ensure that the workshop team as a whole agrees with the way in which the individual expects to incorporate the idea/solution into the process. When all are in agreement, the Task Statement of Work and a schedule as to when the work is to be complete are included as part of the overall implementation plan.

Training is an output of every workshop. If a process is changed, then those who perform it and those who use it must be trained in the changes. If a product is redesigned, those who are going to do the final design must be trained in how the product design has been changed, along with any new processes or methods incorporated by the workshop team. The final task of the team is to develop a "management out briefing," to explain the plan, expected improvements, and the actions necessary to implement.

The "management out briefing," documents the changes to be made, the implementation plan, the training requirements and plan, and the new process or design. Management issues or concerns about the proposed actions are reviewed and addressed. Specific management actions necessary to implement are discussed.

Once management has approved the plans, an on-going task status reporting is necessary, along with metrics capture and review. If issues develop that affect the implementation, the team is responsible for resolving those issues and keeping the implementation on track. Finally, the implementation team documents the improvements and reports them to management.

## ENTERPRISEWIDE PERFORMANCE IMPROVEMENT

Six Sigma workshops are capable of addressing a wide range of organizational needs leading to performance improvement. As shown in Figure 8.2, these workshops are able to address processes across the entire enterprise lifecycle.

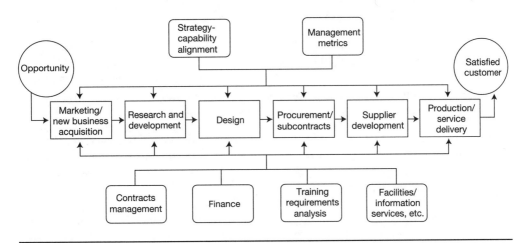

**Figure 8.2** Typical enterprise lifecycle processes.

# TYPES OF WORKSHOPS

The following list summarizes the types of workshops that have been used to accomplish various organizational requirements.

- Strategy/Capability alignment—To determine what is needed for the organizational capabilities to support the corporate strategy, and then create a roadmap that defines the transition to alignment.

- Training requirements analysis—To accelerate the process of defining the organizational requirements for training and maintaining a highly skilled workforce.

- Process documentation—To capture and validate the processes that exist in an organization and determine how the work is actually being done. Essential for knowledge capture and sustained organizational improvement results.

- Process improvement or innovation—To determine how a process can be improved or replaced by inventing a totally different approach to doing the work.

- Process optimization—To work through the issues within the process to determine the optimal method of doing the work required.

- Schedule/Plan validation/verification—To bring together cross-functional teams to determine whether a schedule or plan can be met and determine what actions can be taken to improve upon the current plan/schedule.

- Organizational integration—To define the best methods of transitioning from the current state to one that is built upon the strengths of the new players. This is used after acquisitions or divestitures occur, or significant reorganizations change the responsibilities in the organization.

- Performance improvement—To look for root causes and opportunities for improvement in a facilitated cross-functional team where open and direct feedback on observations, concerns, and ideas lead to a new depth of understanding of cross-organizational discontinuities and opportunities. Used when organizations perform suboptimally or behind plan/schedule.

- Design for manufacturing, design for assembly—To use a designated set of tools within a facilitated workshop to create a best value product design that minimizes cost and cycle-time to produce while ensuring that performance and quality targets are reached.

- Synchronous workflow analysis—To bring together cross-functional teams to maximize concurrence in the processes used to produce or deliver services to customers.

- Supplier development—To bring together cross-organizational teams to clearly express expectations to vendors and determine methods and means that will permit the vendor to meet those expectations. May apply tools such as those used in DFM depending upon the product or service to be acquired.

- Software development—To harness the power of cross-functional teams that include customers and vendors to optimize the development process. This process creates a consistent approach by the development team and minimizes steps and tasks, thereby reducing cycle-time and cost while reaching quality and consistency targets of the final products.

## BENEFITS OF SIX SIGMA WORKSHOPS

Six Sigma project workshops have substantial beneficial effects, such as:

- Reduction in cycle-time. This is the amount of time that it takes to execute a process or build a specific product. It is accomplished by placing a task where it is performed with highest efficiency. Elimination of duplicate or unnecessary tasks also reduces the time that is necessary to execute a process. Improving hand-offs, which tend to be points of substantial discontinuity, also eliminates rework or duplicate efforts.

- Reduction in cost. Time is money. The leaner the process, the faster it may be performed. However, a reduction in cost is not automatically a reduction in headcount. Often, in growth organizations, the result of a Six Sigma project workshop is for existing staff to be able to process increasing volumes of work, which eliminates the need to add to staff. Thus, the efficiency does not result in the elimination of existing personnel, but rather the ability to contain cost increases while managing substantial increases in business activity.

- Reduction in space requirements. Most organizations do not engineer their workflow. Functional organizations may not be co-located with other organizations with which they conduct the most business. Workshops are often able to identify opportunities to rearrange the workflow to make it more efficient. In so doing they often identify opportunities to reduce space requirements.

- Align organizational strategy and capability. Strategy is derived from perceived opportunity. In small organizations it is clearly evident whether the organization has what it takes to execute a strategy. In larger organizations, especially those that experience high turnover, the ability to execute a strategy is not as apparent. In any size organization, a forward look toward expected opportunities and the requirements necessary to execute them can position the firm for growth. Organizations that must acquire skills, knowledge, and experience in particular labor markets will always be playing catch-up to those organizations that have internally developed the capabilities necessary to execute a variety of related strategies. Strategy/capability workshops focus on creating the roadmaps necessary to ensure the ability of the organization to survive and prosper in turbulent markets.

- Capture intellectual capital. Workshops capture the ideas and processes that the cross-functional teams generate. This knowledge capture permits the organization to create repeatable processes for areas that otherwise may be single-point failure candidates. Knowledge captured in the workshops may permit cross training, allowing some individuals who are single-point failures in their current positions to move to growth opportunities. By documenting their processes, others are now able to perform the functions that previously only they understood.

- Integrate cultures. When companies acquire other businesses or merge activities with other organizations, the cultures of the combined companies are usually very different. In addition, roles and responsibilities change as the companies combine. Workshops are able to bridge the cultural differences by bringing elements of each former organization together to focus on how best to get the work done. Ownership is not the issue. The process is the issue, and the participants are forced to move beyond ownership of "turfs" to design the best way for the new combined organization to perform its work.

- Build ownership and analysis capability for processes. After an intensive effort to look at how a process is conducted and create a new process that improves upon the old, those involved develop a sense of ownership for what results. With team members putting their name on the process, they want to make sure it works. The workshop teaches the basic process for process improvement, and as members of the on-going process team, they have a responsibility to make continuing changes that enhance the process.

- Build cross-functional communication and teamwork. Workshops are two to three days of intensive communication and relationship building. The teams are cross-functional and thus the relationships developed in the workshop open new communications channels that may not have been available previously. The fact that the team members share an understanding of the process permits them to understand the issues other team members raise relevant to the process and permits them to understand opportunities to improve that process.

- Improve performance across the organization. As areas of former "under-performers" become more efficient, the organization as a whole begins to take on a winning team attitude. When a baseball team loses a few games and gets into a slump, everyone wonders, "When will they win again?" Some teams write off the season. Other teams address their weaknesses and prepare for the playoffs. Organizations develop similar attitudes toward themselves. When they see their weakest links working hard at fixing themselves, they begin to believe that the whole "team" can reach the playoffs. Individuals are willing to take more chances because the rest of the team is working together and playing to win.

# SUMMARY

Six Sigma has been used to address issues with abstract processes such as aligning organizational strategy with capabilities and with concrete processes such as billing and collections. It has been effective in small businesses and on complex multinational multibillion dollar system integration programs. Thus, it truly is an enterprisewide set of tools that can be used to address a wide variety of performance issues.

Six Sigma is a concurrent process that brings the customer, supplier, and company personnel together to change and/or integrate cultures, using development tools and a methodology to collectively invent best-value process/product solutions. A major benefit is that it is an intense, disciplined activity that quickly and decisively improves processes or designs while reducing cycle time and/or cost, and increasing performance and/or quality.

Six Sigma may be used as a rapid integrator of diverse cultures and a method of resolving transition-related issues. The author has confirmed the methodology applicability, identifying average cycle-time reductions in excess of 40 percent, as well as dramatic cost savings in more than 700 business analyses and projects over the past 10 years. Six Sigma principles have been adapted to diverse applications, and these same principles have demonstrated effectiveness in small businesses such as simulation-based flight training organizations as well as on single multinational complex system integration programs with total improvements value in excess of $1 billion.

One of the chief lessons the author has learned in conducting Six Sigma business analyses and projects is that no process or design change can successfully operate in isolation from the rest of the organization. The Six Sigma tool set, when properly adapted to the needs of the organizational "sponsor," addresses all key development and manufacturing processes including design, development, and production, as well as business processes such as business development and acquisition, program management, supply chain, supplier development, finance, and training needs analysis.

# 9

# Accelerated Needs Analysis

SIX SIGMA WORKSHOPS PROVIDE A FORMAT FOR ACCELERATING THE
DEVELOPMENT OF NEEDS ANALYSIS BY TRAINING ORGANIZATIONS.

The key to effective training is a careful analysis of the needs. Once the needs are identified, the training requirements can be defined and the training itself developed.

One Six Sigma team developed a methodology to accelerate the definition of training requirements while simultaneously creating demand for the training in the organization. Their analytical work was accomplished through Six Sigma workshops.

In the Six Sigma workshop, the team reviews how work is currently being accomplished and the problems and difficulties engendered by this work method. Then they create a new, highly efficient process. In designing the new work process, specific training requirements are defined, targeted to making new seamless work processes operational. The project workshops are conducted in less than a week, with targeted implementation scheduled within 30 to 60 days. The organization fully endorses the resultant training in support of efficiency implementation.

There are two basic approaches to conducting an accelerated needs analysis. One approach is a *strategy alignment* workshop and the second is a *process improvement project* workshop, as described in the previous chapter.

## STRATEGY ALIGNMENT WORKSHOP

This activity identifies where an organization has capability shortfalls in executing the strategy. When applied to a corporate university or organization with large training or educational systems, it reveals where the curriculum is not addressing strategic needs.

For example, a strategy alignment workshop resulted in a training curriculum for country and regional managers.

The goals of this effort were to:

- Define the overall job requirements for a country and regional manager.

- Define the level of knowledge required for a country and regional manager.

- Identify the customer interface requirements for the internal and external customers.

- Recommend curriculum and courses for the development of country and regional managers.

The overall goal was to achieve a broadening of the skills and knowledge of the country and regional managers so they would be able to manage their country operations as though they were an independent business. This required a broadening of the skills, knowledge, attitudes, and experience of this group of employees.

The expected outputs of the workshop were:

- Job task analysis

- Profile of skills/knowledge required for success

- Curriculum

- Instructional delivery methodology

- Recommended learning materials and references

- Evaluation methodology

- Certification criteria

The phases of the strategy alignment workshop are:

- Planning

- Current job content analysis

- Current organizational strengths, weaknesses, opportunities, and threats (SWOT) analysis

- Futuring (SWOT analysis projected 18, 36, and 60 months into the future)

- Job content analysis across knowledge, skills, attitudes, and experience

- The creation of a job description that meets the new future-oriented organizational needs

- A training curriculum that addresses the needs of existing incumbents as well as any additional training needed for new hires

- An action log assigned to specific individuals with completion dates established

In the model validation workshop the participants represented eight different nations within Europe. Thus, the analysis addressed cultural, national, and legal differences, as well as the commonalities of the corporate expectations. The workshop did not seek to impose a consultant solution upon the team; rather, it utilized the expertise within the organization to come to agreement on the strategy and methodology necessary to achieve the stated goals and the organizational performance expectations.

The participants were able to identify specific training that would provide the skills, knowledge, attitudes, and experience necessary to meet the agreed-upon objectives and methods. For certain types of training, specific instructors were identified. The group identified a certificate as the output, which would be most important to them. Such a certification would provide the professional recognition that they desired as the outcome of the investment they would be making in time and energy to complete the prescribed course of study. (For more details on this particular example, refer to Appendix I: Developing a Curriculum for Country Managers.)

Whether the outcome is a strategic plan or a training curriculum, the essential process is identical for strategy alignment and planning. Such activity is able to identify means and methods of bridging the gaps and making the necessary transitions so that they can be positioned to execute the desired organizational strategy.

## PROCESS IMPROVEMENT WORKSHOP

Most project workshops result in specific training courses that are developed to effectively implement the required changes and maintain their effectiveness over time. Since the leadership has already made the investment to determine how to improve what they are doing, they usually buy into the training to make the improvements successful.

While early intervention provides the greatest gains in performance, few organizations benefit from catching processes or products early in the development cycle. That is because "crisis management" mode dictates that issues only be addressed when the smoke gets thick and someone in the process or product team has already become toast. Consequently, most project workshop interventions occur later rather than earlier.

For those project workshops that are conducted late in the development cycle, or for long established processes, other considerations (such as development cost and time, or overcoming inertia and resistance to change) play important roles in determining which actions are actually implemented. Changes achieved at the front end are much less costly and drop profits directly to the bottom line through avoidance of rework or duplicate effort.

A common thread through the entire workshop process is facilitation. The project workshop team drives process improvements, which increase the range of application, such as software, program plan and schedule validation, business processes, supplier development, and strategy/capability alignment discussed earlier.

# SUMMARY

Accelerated needs analysis is a result of workshops for either strategy alignment or process improvement. Such project workshops have applicability across all enterprise processes from business acquisition through product design, development, and production through delivery and post delivery support, as well as all organizational support functions such as finance, human resources, and general administration.

Project workshops, regardless of their type, generate training requirements and create management support for the investment. New processes detail cost and cycle-time savings. The investment in training to make the new processes successful generally has a very short return-on-investment cycle. While this chapter looked at two specific workshop models, each type provides the organization with tremendous leverage in enhancing performance with small and rapid investments in manpower development.

In the course of his work, the author has validated the cross-cultural applicability of project workshop effectiveness. For multinational organizations, this cross-cultural applicability is a key element.

# 10

# Six Sigma-Led Deployment of Sarbanes-Oxley Section 404 Internal Controls

Six Sigma provides a structure for accountability.

The Sarbanes Oxley Act of 2002 and the American Institute of Certified Public Accountants (AICPA) report of the Treadway Commission on Internal Controls are summarized in Section A. This AICPA report is known as the COSO framework, which stands for Committee of Signatory Organizations that supported the efforts of this commission.

## SECTION A—SARBANES-OXLEY REQUIREMENTS

The Sarbanes-Oxley Act of 2002 is intended to bring about a new level of attention to corporate governance and to strengthen the public reporting requirements of firms that publicly trade their stock in the United States. There are multiple sections to the act encompassing many facets of corporate governance. Among them are two that directly prescribe a series of actions that must be taken to ensure the adequacy of the internal controls of all subject firms.

Section 302 requires quarterly certification by the CEO or CFO of all companies filing periodic reports under section 13 (a) or 15 (d) of the Securities Exchange Act of 1934 regarding the completeness and accuracy of such reports and the nature and effectiveness of disclosure controls and procedures supporting the quality of information included in such reports.

Section 404 requires an annual report (an assertion) by management regarding the effectiveness of the internal controls and procedures for financial reporting, and an attestation by the company's independent auditors as to the accuracy of management's assertion.

## Deploying world-class controls

This simply-stated requirement of Federal law, applying to all publicly traded companies regulated by the Securities and Exchange Commission, is the tip of a very large iceberg. The undertaking can be quite large for companies that have not previously had formal assessments of financial internal controls.

The example that follows describes the approach taken by one major company to leverage its companywide investment in a Six Sigma infrastructure to employ the skills, tools, experience, and abilities of highly trained Black Belts and Green Belts to deploy a set of world-class internal controls that assures compliance with the requirements of the law and at the same time improves operational efficiency, productivity, and reporting accuracy.

## Document the processes and controls

The essence of the task is to document all major financial processes in each major business and identify and characterize the controls in each process. This activity was seen as providing the objective evidence of controls for each process. This is used to substantiate the control effectiveness in three rounds of assessments in the first year.

The first assessment round is conducted in a blitz format by the deployment team and is led by internal Six Sigma Black Belts. Internal auditors conduct the second round. This audit team is removed from the deployment process, and looks at the data with fresh eyes. The third round is by the independent auditors, who attest to management's assertion regarding the effectiveness of the internal controls.

## Identify insufficient controls

A component of each of the first two rounds to identify controls that are insufficient. This identification results in the assignment of a Green Belt project to analyze the control issues and put into effect improved controls through a team project. The result is that before the next round of assessments identified deficiencies will be strengthened through improved or redesigned controls.

There are two levels of controls that must be assessed: the entity control environment, also known as the tone at the top, and the activity-level or transaction-level controls.

## Entity control environment

The nature of communication with the organization and the demonstrated leadership of management in conducting business determines the entity control environment. This assessment relies mostly on personal interviews with business leaders and obtaining objective evidence of their honoring of the systems put into place to regulate individual behavior, whether ethical or otherwise, which can be summarized as:

- Integrity and ethical values

- Commitment to competence

- Management's philosophy and operating style

- Organizational structure

- Assignment of authority and responsibility

- Human resource policies and practices

- Entitywide objectives

## Activity- or transaction-level controls

The activity- or transaction-level assessments are oriented toward whether those responsible for financial process management have established a system of highly effective controls and whether those controls are adequately monitored and adjusted with the needs of the business, which can be summarized as:

- Risks

- Managing change

- Information and communication

- Manage the enterprise

- Monitoring

- Separate evaluations

- Reporting deficiencies

## Evaluate the controls

The assessments seek to understand the nature of the control activity, and to make one of the following five assertions regarding each control evaluated:

- Existence or occurrence—Assets, liabilities, and ownership interests exist at a specific date, and recorded transactions represent events that actually occurred during a certain period.

- Completeness—All transactions and other events and circumstances that occurred during a specific period, and should have been recognized in that period, have, in fact, been recorded.

- Rights and obligations—Assets are the rights, and liabilities are the obligations, of the entity at a given date.

- Valuation or allocation—Asset, liability, revenue, and expense components are recorded at appropriate amounts to conform with relevant and appropriate accounting principles. Transactions are mathematically correct and appropriately summarized and recorded in the entity's books and records.

- Presentation and disclosure—Items in the statements are properly described, sorted, and classified.

## Define the internal controls

COSO defined internal control as a process, effected by an entity's board of directors, management, and other personnel, designed to provide reasonable assurance regarding the achievement of objectives in the following categories:

- Reliability of financial reporting

- Operational effectiveness and efficiency

- Compliance with applicable laws and regulations

The internal control objectives are achieved through five components, which are:

- Control environment—Sets the tone of the organization toward control consciousness.

- Information system and communication—Establishment of an information system to manage and communicate the organization's activities and prepare financial statements.

- Risk assessment—Identification, analysis, and management of risks affecting the organization.

- Control activities—Policies and control procedures to address risks and accomplish management objectives.

- Monitoring—Mechanisms to provide feedback on whether internal control is operating effectively.

## Validate the control environment

The control environment reflects the overall attitude, awareness, and actions of the board of directors, management, owners, and others concerning the importance of control and its emphasis in the entity. Seven factors collectively affect the control environment:

- Integrity and ethical values—Code of conduct; use of appropriate incentive schemes.

- Audit committee and board of directors—Oversee accounting policies and practices.

- Philosophy of management and operating style—Attitude toward financial reporting, approach to risk.

- Assignment of authority and responsibility.

- Commitment to competence—Ensuring competence, requisite skills, knowledge for particular jobs.

- Human resource policies and procedures—Sufficient, competent personnel with adequate resources.

- Organizational structure—Assigns authority and responsibility.

## Align the information system and communication

Communication involves providing a clear understanding of individuals' responsibilities for internal control over financial reporting, including reporting exceptions to an appropriate higher level within the entity. Communication takes such forms as policy manuals, accounting and financial reporting manuals, and memoranda. Communication can also be made orally and through the actions of management.

The information and communication component includes the accounting system. The accounting system consists of the methods and records established to record, process, summarize, and report an entity's transactions and to maintain accountability for the related assets and liabilities.

- *Identify and record all valid transactions.* This objective concerns the financial statement assertions of existence or occurrence and completeness.

- *Describe on a timely basis the transactions in sufficient detail to permit proper classification of transactions for financial reporting.* This objective concerns the financial statement assertion of presentation and disclosure.

- *Measure the value of transactions in a manner that permits recording their proper monetary value in the financial statements.* This objective concerns the financial statement assertion of valuation or allocation.

- *Determine the time period in which transactions occurred to permit recording of transactions in the proper accounting period.* This objective concerns the financial statement assertions of existence or occurrence and completeness.

- *Present properly the transactions and related disclosures in the financial statements.* This objective concerns the financial statement assertions of rights and obligations and presentation and disclosure.

## Conduct risk assessments

The purpose of an entity's risk assessment is to identify, assess, and manage risks that affect the entity's ability to accomplish its major objectives. Once risks are identified, management considers their significance, the likelihood of their occurrence, and how they should be managed. Management may initiate plans, programs, or actions to address specific risks or it may decide to accept a risk because of cost or other considerations. Risks can arise or change due to change in regulatory or operating environment, personnel, or information systems; rapid growth; and new technology, lines of business, products, or activities. Change can also include:

- Rapid growth

- Corporate restructuring

- Accounting pronouncements

- New lines, products, or activities

- New technology

- New information systems

- New personnel

- Changes in the operating environment (for example, increased competition)

- Foreign operations

## Document control activities (same as control procedures)

Control activities are the policies and procedures that help ensure that necessary actions are taken to address risks and achieve management's objectives.

Control activities can be thought of as:

- Segregation of duties—the assignment of duties such that no one person is in a position to both perpetrate and conceal errors or irregularities in the normal course of processing information or data. Separate custody, authorization, and record keeping.

- Information processing—this includes:

  1. General controls

  2. Application controls to check accuracy and completeness

  3. Authorization controls over transactions

  4. Document controls, which may include record specifications such as:

     – prenumbered

     – multiple copies

– proper records for detail and control

– exceptions investigated

- Performance reviews, such as comparing actual with expected performance.

- Physical controls, including those designed to:

  1. Restrict access to computerized systems.

  2. Complete an independent reconciliation of accounting records and the underlying physical assets.

  3. Safeguard assets.

## Monitor internal controls

The design and operation of internal control should be monitored by management to consider whether it is operating as intended and that it is modified on a timely basis for changes in conditions. Monitoring is a process that assesses the quality of the internal control system's performance over time. Monitoring can be done through ongoing activities or separate evaluations, such as:

- Internal auditors

- Continual management review of exception and operation reports

- Periodic independent audit

- Regulator's suggestions for improvement

- Review/response to customer complaints

Documentation may include questionnaires, flowcharts or narrative. The advantages and disadvantages are summarized in Table 10.1.

**Table 10.1** Documentation methods.

| Method | Advantages | Disadvantages |
|---|---|---|
| Questionnaire | Easy to complete<br>Comprehensive<br>Weaknesses obvious | May be completed without thought<br>Standardized questionnaires |
| Flowchart | Good for systems<br>Easy to follow<br>Fairly comprehensive | Time consuming<br>Weaknesses not always obvious |
| Narrative | Detailed analysis<br>Tailor-made | Same as flowchart |

# SECTION B—SIX SIGMA LEADERSHIP FOR SARBANES OXLEY DEPLOYMENT

Six Sigma has several natural alignments with the Sarbanes-Oxley activity outlined. One major corporation subject to the requirements of this law recognized early the opportunity to reduce the cycle time required to map financial processes and characterize the controls that are in place, and conduct assessment blitzes, which leverage the investment in a Six Sigma capability across a new opportunity.

A second opportunity was identified, which was to use the performance improvement tools and methodologies of Six Sigma to identify the controls' insufficiencies or weaknesses.

The continuous improvement philosophy and structure of Six Sigma also provides a means and method to rapidly evaluate the identified controls' weaknesses and insufficiencies and launch evaluations and projects that will materially strengthen the overall system of financial controls. This approach is summarized as follows.

## Five-phase Six Sigma evaluation of internal controls

The Six Sigma approach to internal controls evaluation is a five-phase effort (see Figure 10.1):

- Process mapping/controls identification and characterization

- Controls assessment through Six Sigma blitz

- Controls audit by internal auditors

- Assertion by management (business units and company)

- Audits by independent auditors and attestation of the leader assertions

## Corporate organization

The success of any effort is largely dependent upon how well it is organized. What follows is one example for establishing projects and teams in a large company. Establishing similar committees and teams will need to be scaled to the size and needs of one's own organization.

### Establish the corporate project office

The corporate project office needs to be a group of people who are carefully selected to have the right blend of controls expertise, audit and compliance focus, along with Six Sigma and project management experience.

### Establish a corporate disclosure committee

The corporate disclosure committee and subcommittee on Sarbanes-Oxley 302 and 404 assessments and management assertions is a group of people who will review the

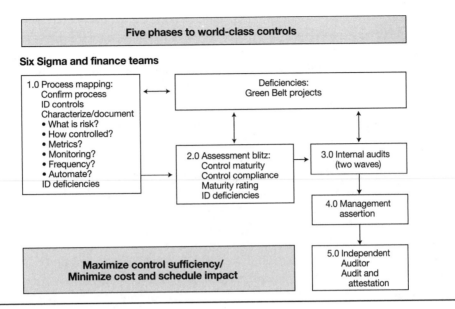

**Figure 10.1** The business-unit level deployment flow.

work plans and schedules, and monitor progress made against the schedules and budgets. They should report back to the corporate board audit committee.

### Review the framework

The COSO framework from the Treadway Commission is a document that provides the overview on the theory of internal controls and the logic behind the compliance and audit structures that will be employed in preparation for the independent auditor's attestation of management's assertion.

### Select deployment and Six Sigma project leads

The deployment leads and Six Sigma project leads are the basis for forging operational teams at the business and corporate levels. The finance organization needs to own the deployment of an internal controls system and the auditing of those controls. Therefore, the deployment lead for each business should be a respected leader from within that finance organization. The Six Sigma lead is an enabler who brings the tools and process experience/training to assist the finance organization. The goal is to not only meet the requirements of the audits, but also to ensure that controls sufficiency exists. While the law requires that the internal controls systems exist and be sufficient to ensure accurate reporting of the firm's financial condition, the management of the firm is required to make this assertion and can be held personally liable for deficiencies leading to fraudulent behavior and disclosure. For this reason management has a very large stake in ensuring the adequacy of these controls and will want the best expertise applied to making sure this is the case.

## Review proposals for assessment and control tools

Obtain and review proposals from audit consultants for assessment management tools and control design activity. Home-grown tools to manage internal controls can do the job; however, the big four accounting firms and other consultants have also developed tools that effectively manage the data required to ensure compliance with the act. Many of these tools are specific to the requirements of Sarbanes-Oxley. If the management of the firm is focused only on compliance with the act as currently constituted, these tools are, for the most part, adequate. However, some firms have looked out and are concerned that the requirements as currently constituted may not resist further elaboration over time. Therefore, the tool flexibility becomes an important consideration in the long run. Companies do not want to find themselves forced to acquire a new tool in three to five years and go through the process of loading data and history into the new tools. Therefore, some tool sets that are designed more for risk management may provide flexibility down the road that is worth investing in today.

The accounting firms also offer technical assistance with the deployment of the internal controls evaluation process. These technical services encompass the gamut from complete outsourcing of the documentation and internal assessments to assistance with redesign of specific controls identified as being insufficient. Each firm will need to decide to what extent it needs the assistance of outside firms.

To many executives the idea of outsourcing the entire responsibility is counter intuitive to the reason firms have been now required to perform these tasks. For that reason these executives and boards are requiring that the firm "own" this process and be responsible to ensure that the law is properly complied with. Independence of the attesting audit firm must be ensured to avoid further scrutiny of the internal controls of the firm.

## Select management tools and consultant firms

A set of criteria should be established to assess the capabilities of the candidate firms to provide these services. The criteria must be developed in concert with the finance organization leadership and with consultation and advice of the audit committee where needed. This action will shape to a great extent the nature of the internal activity required. Firms with specific experience in the industry of the firm and independent audit engagements for firms in the same industry bring a level of credibility and access to knowledge and experience that can expedite the process of deploying a proper internal controls evaluation set of tools and procedures. Their expertise may also be instrumental in designing controls systems that address weaknesses or insufficiencies identified.

## Brief the disclosure subcommittee on tools and recommendations

Once the program office selects the tools and consultant, the disclosure subcommittee should be briefed on the recommendation and be afforded documentation on the selection criteria and results of their evaluations to provide a set of outside eyes on the logic and consequences that can be expected from the recommendation. This group should have an instrumental role in challenging the logic of the recommendation and provide insights of how the recommended consultants can be expected to perform in the environment of the firm.

### Obtain board audit committee approval on consultant recommendation

Once feedback from the disclosure subcommittee is factored, the recommendation should go to the CFO for presentation and approval at the board audit committee. This group may also be an important source of feedback about both the recommended tool and consultant role in the deployment of the assessment system and methodology.

### Map financial statement accounts to processes

In order to ensure that the material balances of the financial statement at the corporate level are accurately represented, the various accounts must be mapped to the processes that control the development of the numbers represented on the financial statements. Since companies have many accounts and processes, the auditors who attest to the management assertion want to know that they are in fact auditing the controls structure that affects material balances on the financial statement.

### Map control objectives for each process

Once the processes have been identified it is essential to understand the control objectives for each process, what is it that must be controlled to ensure that the financial statement balances are accurate. Map control objectives for each process, key assertion for each process, risk for each process, and develop model controls for each anticipated control point. Once the control objectives are known, the answers to several key questions should be explored.

- What is the assertion that the management of the firm intends to make about the controls in that process?

- Is the assertion that the balances represent the complete set of transactions during the affected period?

- Are the balances for valid transactions where there will be no future period adjustments because all sales were valid and all relevant costs were properly matched with the revenues for the period?

- Has controlled access been maintained during the period to ensure that only authorized individuals have initiated and approved each transaction?

- Is the assertion that the transactions represented are accurate as to the amounts and that there have been no calculation errors incurred as a result of manual calculations as opposed to system generated calculations?

To ensure that the controls address the actual risks that are inherent in the process, the risks should be captured and recorded for each. Finally, model controls should be identified from the best-practice literature to have a basis for comparison. If all controls represent best practices then world-class controls exist. However, few firms have best-practice controls deployed across all processes, and, thus, identifying the best practices apart from the actual assessment activity provides a standard against which the current control structure can be measured. This activity also provides guidance where control weaknesses or insufficiency are identified.

### Disseminate information to deployment teams

Once the data are captured, they should be disseminated to the deployment team leads. The more information that is provided to the teams at this stage, the greater the acceleration in project completion that can be realized. This information can provide a framework for key financial process mapping and control characterization. In addition, this effort also increases the probability that there will be uniformity in how the businesses conduct their data gathering and assessments, as they are provided with not only a common structure but are capturing data about their processes against a uniform standard and with the same starting point.

### Hold kickoff meetings

A key to getting uniform results is to get everyone on the same page at the beginning. This entails a kickoff meeting where the deployment leads and Six Sigma leads are able to see the same demonstrations, ask questions in such a manner that everyone hears the answers at the same time, and the deployment leads and Six Sigma leads are obtaining the same guidance. If a pilot activity has been conducted this is a good opportunity for everyone to see what has been done at the pilot site and ask questions about what worked well and what problems were identified.

### Train users in assessment tools and management systems

The kickoff meeting is also a good opportunity to train the deployment leads and Six Sigma leads in the use of the assessment tools and management systems. This should be scheduled close to the time when the actual process mapping and controls characterization takes place in the businesses. A refresher may be required at the time the actual assessments begin; however, such a refresher may be done using e-training tools such as SAMETIME or eROOM.

# PROCESS SUMMARY

## Phase One

- Review process maps according to tier priority.
- Identify controls per control objectives and types (data provided from corporate team).
- Characterize the controls:
  - Record control objective and location of control on process map.

- Record and describe the control itself (how it works).
- Record the types and source of metrics about control performance.
- Record who monitors/reviews the control metrics.
- Record frequency of monitor/review activity.
- Identify opportunities to automate the controls.
- Six Sigma Green Belt projects result from identified control deficiency.
- Consultants available to assist with control design issues.

## Phase Two

- Conduct a Six Sigma blitz to obtain evaluation of control performance.
- Use automated Web-enabled tools to record information and evaluations.
- Conduct assessments by Six Sigma team and review by Sarbanes-Oxley deployment lead or designee.
- Assessments roll up to business unit and then to companywide levels.
- Green Belt projects result from controls deficiencies identified.

## Phase Three

- Internal audit conducts internal audits of the control systems across the company.
- Identified control insufficiency will result in Six Sigma Green Belt projects, which must be completed prior to independent audit.

## Phase Four

- Business unit leaders (CEO and CFO) assert that the system of internal controls is sufficient to ensure that the financial statements released by the company are accurate.
- The CEO and CFO of the parent company also assert that the system of internal controls is sufficient to ensure that the financial statements released by the company are accurate.

## Phase Five

Audits by independent auditor lead to attestation of the corporate CEO and CFO assertions of sufficiency of the system of internal controls.

## Sarbanes Oxley

### Control migration

In Chapter Six: Eliminating Default Processes, the discussion centered around how processes drift over time as a result of many factors. This process drift also is a central element of the assessments conducted as a result of Sarbanes Oxley.

Control migration occurs, not as a result of planned changes, but as a result of the many small changes in personnel, requirements, systems, customers, environments, mergers, acquisitions, and so forth. When assessments are conducted a central element must be to assess the effects of control migration and determine control changes necessary to realign the process with controls to ensure proper process functions.

# SUMMARY

The Sarbanes-Oxley section 404 requirement to provide an annual assertion by management as to the effectiveness of financial internal controls presents an opportunity. These assessments of the internal controls of publicly traded companies when integrated into the Six Sigma capabilities of an organization:

- Leverage investments in Six Sigma.

- Reduce cycle time to analyze and characterize the control system.

- Provide an opportunity and method to quickly resolve controls deficiencies and insufficiencies.

- Reduce disruption to normal activity.

- Result in a superior set of financial processes and controls to monitor those processes.

# 11

# Software Innovation
# Workshops

SIX SIGMA, WHEN APPLIED TO SOFTWARE DEVELOPMENT, HAS SIMILAR LEVERAGE
IN PERFORMANCE IMPROVEMENT AS WHEN IT IS APPLIED IN MANUFACTURING.

The *Software Innovation Workshop* is a shift from the traditional methods of software process improvements. Methods such as tailoring documentation, chartering process improvements teams (PITs), establishing quality circles, using the latest computer-aided software engineering (CASE) tools, and setting up cross-functional integrated product teams (IPTs) have all produced increased efficiencies, but not the degree of change that we refer to as "quantum results."

The Software Innovation Workshop is different from other workshops such as DFM, Synchronous, and Picos, which are typically targeted at hardware products and manufacturing processes. With the focus on software, this workshop is designed to ensure that neither the Software Engineering Institute Capability Maturity Model (SEI-CMM) nor ISO 9000 requirements are compromised.

The workshop process can be applied to any software development methodology, including waterfall, spiral, rapid prototyping, or incremental software development. The process is equally viable to top-down structured programming, functional decomposition, or to object-oriented analysis, design, and programming. In addition, it extends the methodology to not only include existing processes, but also to derive new processes where none exist. Because the fundamental workshop principle, to ensure efficiency, is included in the derivation, the newly derived processes also begin efficiently.

Repeated applications of the workshop process to software preliminary design, software integration, systems engineering of software systems, software configuration management, and software testing have all yielded results that are consistent with the expectations and predictions of the process.

# SOFTWARE INNOVATION WORKSHOP FORMAT

1. Planning
   - Identify project (objective/goals)
   - Prepare schedule
   - Identify participants
   - Determine/capture plan format

2. Work preparation
   - Collect documentation
   - Collect materials
   - Make physical arrangements
   - Notify participants

3. Baseline project
   - Current processes
   - Organizational context
   - Current metrics
   - Current results

4. Root-cause analysis
   - Identify causes of current results
   - Analyze complexity drivers
   - Select and prioritize

5. Innovation ideas
   - Brainstorming
   - Creative thinking
   - Hypothesizing

6. Feasibility/Evaluation
   - Affinitize ideas into actions
   - Prioritize
   - Cost savings/investment
   - Assign actions

7. Develop task plans

- Develop Task Statements of Work: Capture who, what, and when, in detail

- New process map

- Define Metrics and capture process

8. Implementation

- Management presentation

- Management support/approval

- Authorize and empower the task teams

- Tracking closure

# WHERE IT BEGAN

Development of the Software Innovation Workshop began at a contractor for NASA and the Department of Defense (DoD) in the spring of 1995. At that time, the NASA Space Station Training Facility (SSTF) had been in development for about five years. The contract was to develop approximately two million lines of ADA code and deliver it to the NASA Johnson Space Center Mission Operations Directorate in phases over 10 years.

As time progressed, radical changes in the Space Station Program at NASA resulted from changes in the political process in the U.S. Congress. These radical changes resulted in redesigns, reduced budgets, and having to produce more for less. Since the largest portion of SSTF costs were for software development, headquarters and divisional personnel needed to work together to find a way to save money and do more with fewer resources.

In September 1995, the Six Sigma team/facilitators held a week-long workshop to examine the SSTF software integration to subsystem test process. The workshop included software engineers from headquarters and the division, configuration management experts, representatives from SEI, NASA customer representatives, and observers. The most significant outcome of the workshop was an altered culture between NASA, the customer, and the prime contractor. Interactions took on a team approach where everybody became part of the solution. The culture no longer reflected the long-standing "us" vs. "them" mentality of former days.

The monetary value of this innovative process has been enormous. Millions of dollars in savings have been identified on the SSTF project alone. The future value promises to be even more substantial in terms of meeting cost requirements necessary to win major new programs in an increasingly competitive marketplace. In addition to the current program savings, the Six Sigma Software Innovation Workshop is being included whenever there are major modifications to existing NASA contracts to ensure that the contractor can meet the customer's needs in an ever-changing environment that requires every player to do more with/for less.

# FINDING THE "MONEY LEFT ON THE TABLE"

The experience of software development in the United States has been more dynamic than that of other nations. Approaches such as object-oriented code development have simplified the process of developing new software, making it more repeatable. However, even with the full range of new methodologies used to speed new product introductions, there is still a lot of "money left on the table" with every new software product introduction. In other words, there is almost always an opportunity to reduce cost, content, and schedule on software development projects.

Evidence of this was clearly found during an engagement by one Six Sigma team. This group was asked to assist the software development group at the contractor's NASA operations. The development group found that it was continually falling behind schedule in attempting to produce the software needed to provide new functionality as required by the contract. One of the adages in project management is that "time is money." This was true in the SSTF project as well. The more the company fell behind schedule, the more unbudgeted development time was being consumed, thus adding large additional cost to the project. Clearly the whole approach to development for the new functionality needed to be reviewed to find the "points of pain" that were the root causes of the schedule slips.

The Six Sigma team first met with management, then with a variety of people throughout the software group to gain a feel for the nature of the issues. The Six Sigma team met people in their offices to put the working environment into context. The building where the work is performed is a seven-story structure, which isolates the teams from each other and reduces on-going interfunctional communication. The physical context and the mood, demeanor, and appearance of the work teams provide additional indications of the issues that affect performance and yet do not show themselves during management discussions on issues.

Listening carefully to the issue discussion, the root causes that management ascribed to the problem, and the efforts that management had already undertaken to solve issues, permitted the Six Sigma team to flag the holes and build an overall understanding of the most fruitful areas for investigation. The team then established an overall set of objectives that management had for improving the software process and the goals and targets that the customer had established for the product. This process of contextualizing and setting goals and objectives provided the framework for scoping the activity necessary to reach the objectives and customer expectations.

In this particular case, while the customer (NASA) had a schedule objective that was driving the requirement to work differently, the contractor's site management also had a second objective, which was to develop a standard process for software development that would reduce the development effort to achieve results. In essence, the management team was looking for a cheaper and faster model of how to develop the software to meet the NASA customer requirements for upcoming projects.

While the objectives were high level, the need to operationalize them and achieve results was pressing as missions were already scheduled that required the availability of the trainers to prepare the crews for these missions. Schedule delays on the software would require a slip in the launch dates on a one-for-one basis. This was clearly unacceptable for NASA and the various governmental agencies and corporations sponsoring research efforts aboard the shuttles. The visibility of such delays made any schedule slips totally unacceptable to the contractor's management.

# SIX SIGMA SOFTWARE INNOVATION PROCESS

The Six Sigma team selected a four-step approach to rapidly change the software development processes and thereby achieve tactical transformation. These steps were:

- *Document (baseline) the existing processes* used to develop software.

- *Identify the problems and issues around the current processes*, the time required to perform steps at each point along the way, and the metrics that are captured regarding the performance of the existing processes.

- *Innovate and develop new processes* to meet the specific performance objectives of management and the customer. Determine estimated cycle-times, select management metrics to control and improve the new processes, and compare to benchmarks.

- *Develop specific implementation plans*, driven by individual task statements of work, integrated into a master schedule with implementation tools, training, culture and change leadership, rewards, and reports.

While not a specific element of the process, the Six Sigma team assisted the company teams to present the results of their work to management and obtain the commitments to proceed and resources necessary to achieve the transformation specified in the original planning session. The Six Sigma team periodically checked back with the implementation leaders to ensure that the resources that were identified – human, technical, and financial – were provided and adequate to complete the tasks assigned.

## Results

The result of the NASA effort was a reduction in the necessary lines of code needed to meet the system functionality requirements of the customer by 28 percent from the previous standard solution. This reduction in code requirements was equivalent to a total cost savings on the project of more than $34 million.

## Lesson Learned: Skip the "low-hanging fruit"

One of the biggest hurdles to achieving the management objectives for process efficiency was the need to "partition the tasks" that made up the components of the total development process. Since the original objectives set by management were very high level, this left a great deal of room to seek opportunities anywhere in the processes.

It was imperative that the teams assigned to review the processes and innovate them focused on only a very small step in the overall development process. The tendency is to go broad, looking for "low-hanging fruit" and declare victory with very little effort really expended. This is the mistake that results from teams under duress to make a schedule, wanting to minimize the time away from their task. However, one of the first lessons learned is that low-hanging fruit rarely gets one to the goal. It provides a measure of immediate results, but only fixes symptoms and not root causes.

Partitioning the work adequately in the beginning provides structure for the work effort. It sets a scope early and keeps the team working as they see how much fundamental change means to overall cost savings and efficiency.

## Lesson Learned: Strive for simplicity

The simplest design is the best design. This holds for software as well as hardware. Software has an incredible amount of interconnectedness. When complexity is the approach to a functionality solution, it will almost always lead to further complexity needed to resolve functionality dependencies impacted in the original solution. When a patch is applied to fix one functionality issue, a dysfunction inevitably happens elsewhere. As programs become larger and more complex with added functionality, the need for simplicity escalates geometrically.

## Lesson Learned: Dig deep for the root cause

It became evident during the process of analyzing the various elements of the process that the team did not want to go too deep in analyzing the process issues. The tendency was to keep discussions at a relatively high level to race through the process quickly. The Six Sigma team/facilitators continually forced the discussions deeper until they were able to find the root causes of dysfunctionality or inefficiency.

## Lesson Learned: Get other expert perspectives

To innovate processes requires the ability to step back from the familiar context and challenge every assumption. One means of forcing such an analysis was to bring in experts from other areas (or other organizations) who were selected because they were highly effective within their organizations. These outsiders also had a different contextual understanding (and often a different set of credentials), which led the teams into fruitful discussions and explorations that the team members would otherwise have overlooked because of their own assumptions and experiences.

## Lesson Learned: Resistance is not everywhere

Resistance, which is assumed to be a universal reaction to change, stems from fear of the unknown and unfamiliarity with how management intended to use the information developed in the work effort. During the course of the project, the Six Sigma team found that as individual process efforts were completed and the team members were able to attain visibility on their issues, much of the resistance melted away. Individual resistance prevailed throughout when individuals were asked to make radical departures from how they were currently operating. However, knowledge reduced the resistance almost immediately and the team as a whole, when supporting the changes, also had a big impact on reducing the resistance. Individuals would overcome their own fears when those they knew and trusted assured them that the entire group would take responsibility to ensure that the new method of doing work would improve the overall effort for everyone, or change it so that it would. When such assurances and operating rules were confirmed, individuals were much more openly supportive of the overall effort.

## Lesson Learned: Implement as you go

One of the tendencies of change efforts is to wait until the end to make changes. In the NASA workshops implementation was continuous and ongoing even while other change efforts were underway. The progress made and results realized actually had the impact of increasing the motivation of team members to pursue more and more innovative approaches. They were able to see that management would support differences in the way that software is written and the processes and procedures to accomplish the work.

Everyone knew that they were inefficient in the approaches taken. However, the NASA ethic of over-engineering for safety permeated the process of all vendors including the contractor's team. The over-engineering approach led to added complexity even when it was not warranted. Simplifying the process actually made the software applications safer by removing interactability unknowns and reducing dependency-driven performance errors.

Each Six Sigma Software Innovation Workshop creates a dedicated team of contractor personnel, customers, in-house subcontractors and suppliers that enable and catalyze the collective invention best value design solutions.

# GLOBAL CONSIDERATIONS

The United States has long been considered to be the global leader in software development capability. It was first to establish the standards of software development capability maturity through the Software Engineering Institute (SEI) at Carnegie Mellon University. There has been a strong focus among software intensive development organizations to establish a repeatability capability. However, comparatively little emphasis has been placed on design efficiency or cost/schedule issues as is prevalent on the hardware side. This lack of emphasis has probably resulted from the incredible advances on the hardware side that provide quantum leaps in speed and storage capacity.

Until recently, the software development industry as a whole has not had to seek out efficiency because a better product would provide adequate rewards even if the solution design was not elegant or efficient.

Meanwhile, other nations have watched the American experience with software development and have slowly begun to mount a challenge to the U.S. dominance. An international body has begun to agree on a common standard that would be linked to the International Organization for Standardization (ISO). This standard, known as SPICE (for Software Process Improvement Capability dEtermination) has a different focus than the SEI-CMM. The SPICE standard is intended to provide a singular standard that is focused on continuous improvement for the specific applications of the development organization. This is in contrast to the level achievement focused on repeatable processes as found in the CMM. Of interest is that the ISO body is departing from its traditional documented and repeatable process approach to certification (which is in line with the CMM) to a continuous improvement model for certifying software development organizations.

While the SPICE standard will in time migrate to the United States as part of ISO certification, it is already being used (as a test standard) in Europe. One of the objectives of the European testing is to determine if companies and organizations that use this standard can achieve rapid progress in making their software designs competitive with American software products.

If the intent is only to "catch up" with American product quality and have all boats come up with a rising tide, that is one thing. However, continuous improvement, by its very nature, provides competitive advantage to those who are most skilled at continuously and methodically making little changes that sum up to systemic improvement and change over time.

## SUMMARY

Innovation is a key to achieving world-class process excellence in order to build a product or provide a service "better, faster, cheaper" in today's fast-paced, ever-changing environment.

The Six Sigma team used this innovation to find the "money left on the table" by most of the software development groups that participated in the workshops. There is almost always an opportunity to reduce cost, content, and schedule on software development projects when cross-functional teams are brought together with set objectives, empowered, and rewarded for their success.

In the case of the Six Sigma team highlighted in this chapter, their innovative efforts resulted in a 28 percent reduction in lines of code for the NASA Space Station Training Facility (SSTF), which led to a total project savings of more than $34 million from software alone.

---

**Note**: Each year, NASA presents the John W. Young Quality and Process Innovation Award in recognition of individuals or groups that promote quality and create innovative methods to achieve quality process or product improvements at an exceptionally high level of excellence. For its repeated application in the contractor division, the Six Sigma Software Process Innovation Workshop received this prestigious award.

# 12

# Design for Six Sigma

DESIGN FOR SIX SIGMA (DFSS) MAXIMIZES RESULTS OBTAINED, BUT IT IS A
LONG PROCESS TO DEPLOY AND EMBED IN THE CULTURE OF THE ORGANIZATION.

What is Design for Six Sigma (DFSS)? According to one firm, it is a change from a deterministic to a probabilistic culture. One sign that this culture change has happened is that product designs incorporate a statistical analysis of failure modes, not just in the product but also in the process. Another sign is the modification or elimination of any design feature that has an unacceptable statistical probability of failure. Essentially, the culture change reflects the shift from a "factor-of-safety" mentality to a quantitative assessment of design risk.

DFSS is considered to be a logical evolution and the complement to the traditional manufacturing and production statistical focus of Six Sigma, which itself is rooted in the overarching concept of concurrent engineering (CE) that encompasses tools, technologies, and methodologies such as team design, simultaneous engineering, robust engineering, producibility engineering, concurrent design, transition to manufacturing, and integrated product development.

According to the Institute for Defense Analyses (IDA) Report R-338, "Concurrent engineering is a systematic approach to the integrated, concurrent design of products and their related processes, including manufacture and support. This approach is intended to cause the developers, from the outset, to consider all elements of the product lifecycle from concept through disposal, including quality, cost, schedule, and user requirements."

The critical elements of the DFSS approach include:

- Design for producibility (design for manufacturing and assembly)

- Design for reliability

- Design for performance (technical requirements)

- Design for maintainability

# TOUGH YOGURT

Changing the culture of a design organization is a long-term effort. Engineers tend to be concrete thinkers who do not invite changes to the way they work. Quick-fix processes do not impress them, nor do the rapid realization of results, regardless of how remarkable they may be. Changing the culture of any organization is a deliberate, long-range, visionary, top-management committed, evolutionary, and revolutionary journey. Depending on the starting point, it may be necessary to amplify all of those efforts an order of magnitude to win over the engineering/design community.

The plethora of tools, technologies, and methodologies that have been used on the continuum to perfection provide evidence that the journey is underway but incomplete in most organizations. Most everyone is at least somewhat familiar with quality circles, continuous measurable improvement, ISO standards, total quality management, reengineering, concurrent engineering, and even Six Sigma. The success of any of these approaches relies – in great measure – on the culture of the organization.

One firm in the aerospace industry reported that it has been nearly a 20-year journey. Elements of the probabilistic approach have been in use for many years (for example, probabilistic fracture mechanics), but only in the last few years has the firm wholeheartedly embraced the integration and incorporation of broadly applied statistical design methodologies.

Most of the firms that were contacted indicated that DFSS is not yet firmly rooted in their cultures. For the most part, it is only in use in selected design groups, and only when certain requirements are to be analyzed. Notable exceptions are the firms that reported substantial success from their organizationwide adoption and use of DFSS on every project. Data from these firms indicate that there is a critical level of utilization/application at which time the additive effects become multiplicative.

# THE JOURNEY TO DFSS

The remainder of this chapter consists of 15 lessons learned about DFSS deployment that resulted from a series of interviews with top Six Sigma consultants or Six Sigma leaders from major companies in different industries.

Their collective stories have been condensed and consolidated under four main categories of experience:

- DFSS as a growth strategy

- DFSS as a way to serve customers

- DFSS as a product-process fusion

- DFSS in the engineering organization

# DFSS AS A GROWTH STRATEGY

## DFSS is the result of an evolution, not a singular event

General Electric, one of the most outstanding models of Six Sigma success, progressed through the following six distinct phases:

- The journey began in the late 1980s with a program of town meetings focused on empowerment and bureaucracy-busting known as WORKOUT.

- They looked outside the company for productivity models and best practices.

- They initiated process improvement through continuous improvement and reengineering.

- They developed a change acceleration process that focused on increased success and the rapid adoption of change.

- They incorporated key strategy initiatives with a focus on globalization and productivity.

- They adopted a culture change effort to integrate Six Sigma as the way the firm works. This was only upon the successful completion of all five of the previous phases, which spanned a period of 10 to 12 years.

## Key learning

*Achieving world-class performance is more than a good set of tools. It takes preparation and foundational change efforts leading to capability.*

### Paper and electrons are a better investment than tooling and retooling.

It is a "catch-22" when firms do not have the money to properly plan and validate a design, but they do have the money to fix problems with the product that result from the comparatively small investment that would have been required in the beginning. Most who were interviewed agreed that DFSS is capable of standing the traditional spending profile on its head...and also capable of moving defect detection and elimination up front, where it can be most beneficial, during the design planning cycle.

*Rule of thumb*: 75 percent to 80 percent of cost is locked in at design. One firm reported it was necessary to conduct a return on investment analysis to determine the effect of *not* making the investment up front in DFSS before investors "got it."

When DFSS efforts are linked to public and frequent rewards for the individuals and teams involved, significant progress is made. In one firm 30 percent of the engineering workforce have stock options in the firm. "The individuals who drive DFSS here are rewarded very, very, well," said the spokesperson for this firm.

## Key learning

*DFSS is an investment that grows into program profits in direct proportion to the size of the initial investment. The more the initial investment to eliminate design issues the greater the lifecycle profits that will be realized later.*

## Leadership commitment and the alignment of rewards are essential

One example of improved results obtained by adopting DFSS occurred at a firm where DFSS involvement was linked directly to management rewards. This firm established a requirement for senior management to spend 30 percent of their time on DFSS activity. Linking this to the reward structure, a significant portion of the executive bonus compensation was tied to achieving predefined improvement targets. This particular firm limits the number of initiatives that can be undertaken simultaneously to permit intense focus on achieving aggressive improvement goals, which permits the senior executives the opportunity to commit large blocks of time to mentoring and reviewing projects undertaken by Black Belts and to be involved in setting the priorities for action and targets for improvement. It also husbands the resources necessary to get the work done by planning for them in advance.

## Key learning

*A structured compensation system that substantially rewards leadership cooperation and co-ownership for successfully implementing cross-functional DFSS projects significantly improves the bottom-line.*

## Leadership involvement establishes and maintains momentum

One aerospace firm that has come a long way toward achieving true DFSS integration and adoption across the entire organization offers the following glimpse into their journey:

- Master Black Belts and Black Belts were selected from only the very best people within the organization.

- During the first year all leadership teams met weekly to discuss, review, and adjust the strategy and implementation of DFSS.

- The senior leadership conducted off-site quarterly reviews, to discuss and adjust the strategy to accelerate results.

- Senior leadership reviewed all Black Belt projects at all phases and publicly rewarded the results of these projects.

- Vice Presidents of engineering personally reviewed each DFSS Black Belt project during the first year.

- All Master Black Belts and Black Belts were established as full-time in their Six Sigma positions; funding and resources necessary to support annual Six Sigma activity were planned, budgeted, and scheduled at the beginning of the year.

- Training was owned and provided locally. This permitted site personnel to conduct the training and use local examples in the training exercises and projects conducted.

- Everyone who contributed to the success of the efforts received significant rewards both as members of teams and individually.

- Six Sigma was viewed and openly discussed as a leadership development program, thus becoming a desired career development path.

- Business practices and results were measured and compared to find opportunities for immediate impact.

Core concepts were driven and reinforced across the entire company:

- Critical to quality (CTQ) – what is a defect and what is variation

- Processes used to make products

- Process capability

- DFSS (a process not a chart to report)

## Key learning

*Leaders, especially middle managers, need to be selected, prepared, and trained much earlier in the process to achieve desired levels of commitment.*

# DFSS AS A WAY TO SERVE CUSTOMERS

The best customer involvement is early and often.

The customer is essential to the DFSS process. World-class organizations establish unbreakable bonds and long-linked partnerships with their customers. The wise supplier knows that every customer is also a supplier to another customer in an almost endless supply chain, which resembles a beautifully constructed web of interconnections. The most proactive organizations are working together with their customers to build and strengthen that web.

What Sun Tzu said regarding knowing the competition equally applies to knowing your customers and suppliers. One could as easily substitute the word "customer" or "supplier" for "enemy/competition" and the insight would be just as significant and meaningful. The wisdom is ageless:

> *If you know the enemy and know yourself,*
> *You need not fear the results of a hundred battles.*
> *If you know yourself but not the enemy,*
> *For every victory gained, you will also suffer a defeat.*
> *If you know neither the enemy nor yourself,*
> *You will succumb in every battle.*

## Key learning

*Continual customer feedback and ideas are essential to achieve a partnership with the customer. In an age where competition for customers is a relentless pursuit, those companies that make the customer a partner in the Design for Six Sigma activity and maintain that partnering throughout the product lifecycle have a customer for the product lifecycle.*

## DFSS needs funding and support like any other project or program

Several of the firms reported that the introduction of Six Sigma was imposed upon the organization without proper planning, budgeting, or scheduling of the activity that was to follow. This created many instances where Six Sigma activity was in constant competition for funding and personnel resources to undertake the required efforts. When the Black Belts are scrambling to find charge numbers to ensure the week's salary there is a distinct lack of focus and dedication to getting results. It is also a clear sign from management that they do not value the work or the expertise/contribution to be made by Black Belts and their teams, nor is management fully committed.

Several of the organizations adopted a model of functional Black Belts. These individuals had dual responsibility to manage their normal jobs *and* lead Six Sigma efforts. Seldom is the individual given relief from the prior intense schedules they maintained. This conflict of priorities results in the Six Sigma activity suffering for lack of time. It becomes just one more thing to squeeze into an aggressive schedule. Since the Black Belts tend to be among the most capable individuals in the organization, they are usually the ones with the "go to" mentality, which makes the dual responsibility approach possible, but suboptimal. Sometimes this causes a no-win situation for both the individual and the firm.

At one government contractor, individuals who are selected for a Six Sigma Black Belt assignment will rotate back into a line or support position upon completion of their temporary, but full-time Six Sigma role. The expectation is that they will then lead their organizations using Six Sigma methodologies and tools. In this instance the full-time assignments provide the experience and knowledge to apply the right Six Sigma approach and tools to derive the data and information that will lead to the decisions that improve overall organizational performance.

Several firms discussed Six Sigma and DFSS as leadership development activities. Those who master Six Sigma and DFSS and achieve results applying them are rewarded with more responsible assignments and a fast track to significant leadership opportunities.

The up-front investment is significant. One company reserves 5 percent of the design engineering budget for DFSS staffing and projects. This organization dedicates the best design resources to DFSS on a full-time basis encompassing Master Black Belts, Black Belts, and a number of tools and training specialists. It is a significant investment in customer satisfaction through unparalleled product quality, but the project and savings metrics, along with customer satisfaction ratings, justify the investment.

## Key learning

*If DFSS is to be the driving force, the heart and soul of a business, then adequate dollars, time, and resources must be incorporated into the annual budget, just as with any other project or program, to ensure the company's success. Success is rarely the result of an unplanned, fortuitous accident.*

## Product development is an enterprise activity

One spokesperson said, "Traditional product development is just an engineering activity. But to be successful it really needs to be a principal focus for the entire enterprise, not just engineering. It makes a difference to involve manufacturing, pricing, marketing, and others early in the planning process."

Everyone needs to be involved in making it the way the company does its work. One particular aerospace firm trains everyone, all the way down through the lab technicians, in DFSS. This way everyone knows the tools and how to use them as a team to conduct the DFSS activity.

But not everyone is a willing participant at the beginning. One of the strategies that design engineers have used to avoid DFSS is to put "red-line drawings" from manufacturing engineers into a drawer until it is too late to take action on the recommended revisions. To address the accountability issue, one firm has made its design engineers accountable for producibility and reliability and its systems engineers accountable for the system performance. The objective is to bring 90 percent of every measurable characteristic above Six Sigma. The designers create the scorecard. The impact has been to break the material review board (MRB) cycle on new part introductions and to greatly reduce the number of MRBs and changes required to achieve low-cost, mature production.

## Key learning

*DFSS must be inclusive and everyone must make a conscious effort to weave it into the fabric of the entire organization. Everyone must understand how it works and why it benefits the customer, the business, and themselves.*

# DFSS IS THE PRODUCT—PROCESS FUSION

## Design and process need to be driven together, not separately

Design engineers often become enamored with a technical solution without understanding the implications to the process. The most successful designs result from a fusion of design and the processes required to make the product. Process and product technology must be compatible.

The American automotive industry, for example, expends roughly 95 percent of its research and development budgets on product technology and only 5 percent on process technology. In the Asian automotive industry, however, roughly 75 percent of their research and development expenditures are on process technology and only 25 percent on product.

Process technology is the key to product innovation because it is what enables the design capability. Where the process technology permits greater flexibility and range of capability, the design engineering staff has greater freedom in establishing the design parameters. The range of solutions is extended and permits the manufacturability of a different and, from a Six Sigma point of view, error-free product. Reworking a product to eliminate manufacturing defects at the design stage saves significant costs, increases product lifecycles, and reduces warranty and other post-delivery costs while dramatically increasing customer satisfaction.

Many firms have developed comprehensive product development processes and methodologies. While such global design processes introduce a standard and rigorous process for product development, they often are so complex that they drive surreptitious behavior. Rather than following the processes, some engineers and program managers decide they can make up for cost and schedule challenges by noncompliance with the processes, or by simply tailoring out the discipline-inducing elements of the process along with those that truly are unnecessary to a given product.

## Key learning

*Drive product and process compatibility across the entire value chain and the product life cycle.*

## Major suppliers need to become partners in the design process

Design improvement cannot stop at the door of the design center. It incorporates the customer as discussed earlier, and also major suppliers, whose components and sub-assemblies have enormous impact on the quality and functionality of the product.

At one firm, a decision was made to have a subcontractor provide advanced part prototypes because they could react faster than in-house production teams. However, supplier prototypes were not successfully transitioned in because the supplier used different processes.

The solution first adopted was to do all advance technology prototypes in-house. This permitted the firm to put the production processes in place one time, knowing that yields would be representative. This solution eliminated the discontinuity issues for parts that the firm intended to make in-house, but did not address the discontinuity that continued to exist between parts that were to be supplied by subcontractors for production. Process differences continued to make successful product integration difficult for reasons that were not intuitively obvious. The solution was to select sole source suppliers and involve them at the beginning allowing the firms to design together and build compatible processes.

Worldwide supply chain management is generally focused on pushing for material and subcontracted savings even from the low-cost supplier. However, the lesson learned by this particular firm is that it is not always the best approach and generally adds to lifecycle costing.

Many suppliers "walk the walk" but don't "talk the talk." They may do the right things in designing components to achieve lifecycle gains; however, they don't use Six Sigma terminology to describe what they are doing or why. Obviously, this doesn't make them less successful, but it does lead them to the possibility of not providing their prime contractors with responsive communication, which could lead to misjudgments by the prime and lost contracts.

Lock in long-term risk-revenue agreements with suppliers. Share the risks and the rewards. Balance requirements and share opportunities with the suppliers. This approach eliminates sandbagging on the part of the supplier where they low-ball to win business and then come back and negotiate a recovery or refuse to deliver product.

### Key learning

*The value chain of your customer includes everything that is incorporated in the final product. Substantial elements often come from suppliers and subcontractors. If they are not integrated into the DFSS activity then the final product is suboptimized.*    .

## DFSS reduces the introduction of new variability to the factory floor

Most Six Sigma efforts focus on getting the variability out of the factory rather than on attacking the design. But this is absolutely the wrong philosophy. While the Six

Sigma teams are working hard on taking variability out on the floor, the design community is continuing to introduce more variability to the front end with new designs. This is a losing battle.

American firms have generally "decimated the manufacturing engineering knowledge base. This skill set was often eliminated because they were overhead costs," according to one American automotive firm. "We generally don't do a lot with the data we collect. Teams understand every process step and understand what are good and bad operations."

To focus the teams on the data, this manufacturer has instituted pre-production Kaizen (also known in this company as Manufacturing Systems Design) events to solve problems before they happen. Kaizen events are very short-term focused analyses followed by rapid implementation of changes to achieve desired results. The director of innovation at this company wants his people to become visionaries. His focus is to develop data before they traditionally become available from prototypes and pre-production lots. Conceptual data are developed and driven throughout the design process to validate the models used to create the design. The Kaizen events force the Six Sigma teams to reduce the complexity of discussions, making them understandable to every production person.

Efforts are focused wherever measurements are necessary. For example, what is measurement capability? Do we have good data? What does it mean? In some instances, the data collected resulted in throwing away "good" parts and keeping "bad" ones.

The Kaizen events help the teams look at current products today and help build the bridge to new technologies. The need is to "think common."

When the process of bridging to new technologies is well done, the new products eliminate recurring problems. However, often the old products end up still being made the old way. When this happens, it introduces two standards and two processes on the factory floor, creating the opportunity for confusion and suboptimization. Six Sigma requires firms to drive to common processes on old and new technology. In order to reduce variability and have an effect on commonality, the Six Sigma teams are finding they must give engineers more guidance.

## Key learning

*Factory Six Sigma activity to reduce variability is a losing proposition if the new designs that are being introduced cause new variability. DFSS is intended to reduce the introduction of new variability and achieve process stability and uniform quality faster.*

## Metrics tell the story and should be displayed publicly in every area

Metrics are metrics. However, metrics that don't tell a story are simply busy work. The metrics must capture, track, and help to explain performance at every level of the organization. In the specific case of DFSS, the Design Quality Scorecards must incorporate, at a minimum, the three key design areas of producibility, reliability, and performance. The focus must incorporate not only product quality, but also cycle-times and systems engineering elements. Both direct and indirect savings need to be recorded. The result is that the engineering organization comes to understand the financial workings of the business, which was seen as incredibly valuable in aligning work with the business needs.

For credibility, the savings need to get tied to the bottom line through auditable results. Yet those at several organizations discussed how their accounting systems were not integrated with the Six Sigma savings. One admitted, " I never did like to use 'Six Sigma savings' because the savings are never shown in the Six Sigma budget. Usually we find that it never had a budget before so it must be a cost. On the other hand, the ROI from Six Sigma in terms of the target process and organization providing savings is usually significant."

Since cost avoidance was the focus in many instances, it was difficult to establish systems that would capture auditable savings, particularly when the design savings would not really be seen for three years or more into the future. One approach to this problem that was discussed is the ability to take cost profiles from previous product designs and compare the new product to the old product throughout the lifecycle and track the savings in this manner. The problem identified with this approach is that the savings are recorded over an extended period of time and management usually wants to see the savings immediately.

One aerospace firm discussed how improved reliability on the part level drove multi-million dollar savings in businesses that were tied into long-term service agreements and fixed price contracts.

## Key learning

*Metrics must tell the story of the organization's performance and they must be discussed regularly among the staff in each area.*

## Design and production need to be integrated and balanced

In most of the companies surveyed, the design community still throws its designs over the wall to manufacturing with some low level of follow-on. Even though this traditional approach has hindered performance improvement efforts, many organizations are slow to embrace the DFSS approach. At one American automotive firm, the rule of thumb is that initially 10 percent to 25 percent of all projects are done through DFSS. However, they anticipate that the percentage will increase as they move from a problem-solving to a problem-prevention culture. The plan is to eradicate variability from the factory floor while simultaneously eliminating it from new designs that are entering the factory floor.

In production, an example is the opportunity to eliminate change-over. (Consider fixture transfers from machine to machine rather than part transfer to new fixture. This is an example of a fact-based decision).

DFSS has application across many products and industries. A pre-release Kaizen revealed the position of a car radio was such that it was hard for the driver to see. After a few minor adjustments in the CAD system, the driver had no difficulty seeing the radio. Making the adjustment in the "electron stage" rather than the prototype stage saved the firm a great deal of design cost and rework.

In the pharmaceutical industry, on the other hand, DFSS could be used to accelerate testing by using Design of Experiments to generate statistical predictions of efficacy and speed new product introduction. However, as one survey respondent lamented, regulatory bodies are not advocates of statistical analysis and in fact create substantial impediments to product improvements and increase overall cost by requiring unnecessary analysis by means other than statistical.

## Key learning

*DFSS is applicable in diverse industries, including non-traditional ones like pharmaceuticals, if the design and the production application is integrated and balanced.*

# THE DFSS ENGINEERING ORGANIZATION

## Design team demographics slow the pace of change and evolution

The demographics of product development teams find no one in the middle. Old designers are leaving and young ones with appropriate skills and product domain knowledge are getting harder and harder to find. With mentors leaving the organizations and newer engineers short on domain knowledge it is difficult to introduce rapid change. The design groups are struggling to staff projects and deal with increased design rework resulting from lack of experience.

Recent time studies on teams revealed that at an American automotive firm, the design engineers are spending more time out on the production line floor to understand product problems now in effect and understand field data on how the product operates in the field. Many of the engineers brought into the DFSS teams are those who started out on the manufacturing floor and worked their way into the design community. They understand the importance of process and the impact that DFSS can have. The focus is on product quality. In the automotive industry, however, they find they often can't link field results with product quality. This identifies a need to calibrate quality measurements with field results.

## Key learning

*Design organizations are struggling with the loss of domain knowledge and lack of experience and skills among the teams themselves. This slows the movement to probabilistic design approaches, as there seems to be little time to meet schedules and conduct thorough analysis using statistical tools.*

## Managing a Six Sigma Enterprise requires a change of philosophy

The greatest opportunity to reduce product lifecycle cost is in the design stage. However, even Six Sigma teams find it difficult to overcome "conventional" wisdom that dictates minimizing program start-up costs. It is nearly impossible in many firms to change spending patterns, even though these spending patterns are linked to outdated measurements and reward structures for program management.

No new designs enter production flawlessly. However, it takes a very strong program manager to overspend the budget this year in order to save more next year. Conventional wisdom and the current system of rewards drives teams to spend the money later, even though the amounts are much greater and the firm has already lost the confidence of the customer by being late and dealing with last-minute quality fixes.

Short-term results are the driver for "conventional" wisdom. Most managers find it unreasonable to invest in cost avoidance that won't be realized for three years when today's emphasis is on next-quarter results.

One respondent observed that to change this short-term focus, several firms have design engineers actually building the product themselves to better understand the impact their designs have upon production. They also have placed program management and even site management into the career path of the design engineers, who are most successful realizing significant lifecycle performance, reliability, and producibility gains by adopting DFSS.

In the automotive industry, the respondent made six key observations:

- Many engineers are working their way up from the factory floor, and these engineers tend to have a good feel for the DFSS philosophy and methodologies.

- Engineers going out on the shop floor don't follow a product all the way through to delivery to understand the full range of production issues and opportunities.

- When design engineers have the opportunity to progress through program management and plant management, their interest and dedication to DFSS is elevated.

- Several of the automotive companies have developed pilot plants where engineers replicate the processes to be used and build the designs in a pilot atmosphere using engineers as the production staff. Integrated product teams encompass manufacturing, design, and process engineering to identify the design-production transfer issues on a small scale and find solutions before implementing a full-scale production facility.

- Design engineering has in some places become responsible for parts, parts failure mode analysis, and parts logistics. They are charged with integrating just-in-time suppliers into the manufacturing processes to increase the number of inventory turns. Some automotive companies conduct a design failure modes and effects analysis (DFMEA) of the parts and subassemblies they acquire and this information is utilized in the analysis and evaluation of suppliers.

- Some firms are doing pre-production Kaizen on the CAD system to save proto-type costs. The ability to examine a part in 3-D reveals improvement opportunities much earlier. However, it is often difficult to obtain production-related measurements at this point in the design cycle. Some do the pre-production Kaizen as an activity for the suppliers to prove that they can run at rate before production commences. Others conduct a pre-production Kaizen, but only make changes that can be completed immediately. The idea is to celebrate and walk away, attacking the next problem area. However, this approach requires unusual levels of discipline to gather the data first and limit action to the next 30 days.

## Key lessons

*Enlarging the responsibility of design engineering to follow the product from start to finish creates ownership that changes the approach to product design. It accelerates the incorporation of lessons learned outside the design community.*

## Culture change requires a change in the engineering hierarchy

The culture of engineering must change to make DFSS successful. In some companies the design engineers consider themselves supreme beings. This limits the communications among design, manufacturing engineering, and production. The cultural hierarchy perpetuates suboptimal results, introduces variability, and ensures production difficulties at start-up and during the early phases.

At the same time, more and more firms have begun to regard engineers as a commodity. This approach introduces even greater variability into designs and products because product domain knowledge is required to design and build increasingly defect-free products. To reach increasingly defect-free design requires data-intense analysis. Traditionally, operators collect the data and engineers evaluate them. However, if the operators do not participate in the resulting design activity, the data collection does not have meaning to them. The validity of the data cannot be ensured, as it is a required rather than a vital task.

Reliability engineers need to be part of the design team. Monte Carlo Analysis results in the probability of various scenarios essential to the identification of failure points. The essential element is to describe statistically the best lifecycle design. This permits the design team to understand the cost and maintenance implications of requirements provided by the customer. In many instances when faced with the costs associated with their requirements, the customers will change their requirements to lower-cost solutions that have similar functionality, reliability, producibility, and performance.

Innovation and continuous product and process improvements are inextricably linked. It is important to work to integrate initiatives and get everyone going in the same direction. Problem prevention is key to the success of any variation reduction effort. Everyone needs to be trained in product and process elements. To validate this, the career paths in some firms require both product and process knowledge.

Career paths for probabilistic design engineers will be a necessity as we continue the movement from reactive firefighting to one of prevention, one where problems are solved at the "risk" stage, before they happen. The adult learning process must be designed and enhanced around career interests. Further, redundant training that exists across functional silos needs to be eliminated so that the time can be devoted to developing the competencies required by our organizations when they are needed (just-in-time philosophy).

One of the respondents has observed many instances where business managers, not trained in statistics, remove statistical analysis and introduce significantly increased variability because they are not able to base design decisions on lifecycle models.

## Key learning

*The trend toward engineering efficiency (assigning engineers from pools to cover short-term assignments) has made engineers a commodity at just the point in time when the loss of domain knowledge has made the need for longevity in an organization essential.*

# CHALLENGES TO SUCCESSFUL IMPLEMENTATION

## Probabilistic design is not well understood

Probabilistic design analysis is not generally part of the engineering curriculum. It is only taught at a few universities. Thus, firms seeking to establish DFSS as the approach to product development must train their engineering teams in basic probabilistic design methodologies. The training encompasses tools and methodologies, but the firm must simultaneously manage the culture change required to make DFSS the way that business is conducted.

Several respondents also commented that regulatory agencies and bodies continue to require testing that adds no value to the analysis of product failures or quality. The issue is that the key personnel in the agencies have not been trained in probabilistic design, do not understand it, and therefore are skeptical of those who advocate its use.

## Implementation continues to be uneven

Some leaders understand and embrace probabilistic design while others continue to resist. Much like the point in "Indiana Jones and the Last Crusade" where Indiana Jones must decide whether to step off into what seems to be thin air to reach the other side, these leaders hesitate. It is the fear of the unknown. Few have received formal education in probabilistic design. Even though they may understand the concept and even the methodology, it is not what they have been educated to use. It is not the approach that led them to their present positions. They erroneously think they must abandon what they already know to reach results through an approach that contradicts the logic and experience they possess.

Too often DFSS is imposed from above rather than resulting from the pull of middle management and individual design engineers. When this happens, it is regarded as extra work and extra cost rather than the way that designs are created.

## Everything has to be Six Sigma

Many firms in the midst of deployment of DFSS have found themselves in the trap that "every analysis and every improvement effort must be considered a Six Sigma project." Several respondents agreed that the answer to this question is no. DFSS should only be used where it makes sense. At one aerospace firm approximately 20 percent to 25 percent of the projects conducted are DFSS and many efforts are not Six Sigma because the tools are not appropriate to the results or the effort can be completed more economically without a formal effort. The return on investment analysis indicates whether a full DFSS effort is warranted.

## Lack of discipline

When meeting with Six Sigma Black Belts, nearly all will bring up the lack of discipline as one of the root causes for designs that are difficult to manufacture or assemble easily. In nearly every engineering organization the need is to respect data-driven decisions and to suspend opinions in the face of facts. This drives to more discipline in setting and flowing down requirements.

## The phased implementation approach

The deployment of the methodology and the training to establish it is a concurrent effort that takes three-to-four years to complete. One firm specifically discussed how licensing the tool they had developed accelerated their deployment by two years. They have since refined the tool, tailoring it to their specific applications and integrating it directly into their computer aided design (CAD) systems to accelerate deployment even more. The lesson is that organizations that believe they must reinvent the wheel will spend much more time achieving the same levels of capability.

## Reliability

One firm discussed the difficulty they had in obtaining valid data from the field. Their solution was to solicit customer feedback through Web-based scorecards that the customer is able to customize and report data on. Allowing the customer to customize the metrics captures the most important measures, according to the customer, and also creates the incentive for the customer to maintain them. Examples of customer-defined metrics are: performance, reliability, cycle-time to problem resolution, and cycle-time to delivery on spare parts. However, one of the hurdles to deploying a customer maintained scorecard is it sometimes makes data available to customers who are competitors in other products.

# SUMMARY

This chapter is based on interviews with Six Sigma leaders at market leaders such as Raytheon, GE, Delphi Automotive, Pratt and Whitney, Allied Signal, and consulting firms such as The Pendleton Group that shared stories about implementing DFSS in their respective organizations. When Six Sigma is introduced at the "electron stage" rather than the "prototype stage" substantial savings are possible.

Fifteen lessons learned were identified about DFSS deployment that resulted from a series of interviews with top Six Sigma consultants or Six Sigma leaders from major companies in different industries.

Their collective stories have been condensed and consolidated under four main categories of experience:

- DFSS as a growth strategy

- DFSS as a way to serve customers

- DFSS as a product-process fusion

- DFSS in the engineering organization

Also identified were six challenges to successful DFSS deployments. These are:

- Probabilistic design is not well understood.

- Implementation continues to be uneven.

- Everything has to be Six Sigma.

- Lack of discipline.

- The phased implementation approach.

- Reliability.

# 13

# Black Belt and Green Belt Preparation

LEARNING BY DOING AND APPLYING THE TOOLS AND METHODS UNDER THE WATCHFUL EYE OF A MENTOR WHO MODELS BEHAVIORS IS THE PREFERRED MODEL FOR DEVELOPING SKILLS AND KNOWLEDGE OF THEIR USE.

In World War II, officers were recruited and put through an accelerated officers candidate school, generally in three months time. They were derisively known as 90-day wonders because few of the soldiers they were leading into battle believed these individuals had the skills, knowledge, experience, or intuition necessary to keep them alive in the thick of battle.

Now, at the turn of the millennium, Six Sigma often trains 90-day wonders to become Black Belts, particularly in companies that are just beginning the journey. On-the-job training may last a few months longer than 90 days, if the company allows the Black Belt an opportunity to get a few work projects under his or her belt. This permits the Black Belt candidate to actually practice using the tools that were only briefly displayed during the formal training classes.

The author had the luxury to work one-on-one for two years with Ron Carmichael, a vastly more experienced Black Belt, before taking a lead role in day-to-day performance improvement activities.

During this intensive mentorship, tools were applied many times with an experienced eye looking over the shoulder. Methods were explained and modeled so that they became nearly as automatic as breathing. The intangibles of dealing with people in intensive group settings where participants' sacred cows were gored on a daily (and sometimes hourly) basis were dealt with professionally and then discussed in detail over many evening beers. Insight was gained over an extended period of trial, error, analysis, correction, and discussion.

# LEADERSHIP UNDER FIRE

Six Sigma 90-day wonders generally do not have an opportunity to grow before they are called on to lead. In World War II, the casualty rate among the 90-day wonders was extremely high, and there are numerous stories about "fragging," where the leader was inadvertently (but deliberately) a casualty of the people he was leading. When the soldiers did not have confidence that their leader was going to keep them safe, the 90-day wonder was eliminated in the hope that someone with more experience and better judgment would replace him.

After being mentored for an extended period by one of the best Black Belts in the business, it is hard for the author to imagine trying to conduct complex Six Sigma activities after simply sitting through classes on the subject. Those who have just completed classroom training (and perhaps a cooperative project with other Black Belt trainees) have virtually no experience to be able to apply to the problem-solving situation they are facing. In most cases, they gain a real (yet unnecessary) appreciation for the situation faced by their WWII counterparts.

The author has witnessed numerous Black Belts who start a project and apply the tools, but never complete the data acquisition phase. Instead, they take the partial data and apply them to "solve" the problem. In other instances, the data are fully captured, but the application of analytical tools is wrong. In still others a number of tools are applied, but the Black Belt cannot figure out how to integrate the data into a meaningful analysis, let alone a valid predictive tool.

The situation for training Green Belts is even more troublesome. In several organizations Green Belt training consists entirely of classroom instruction by a single instructor, who comes in and flips through slides for the prescribed number of hours. Upon completion of the class trainees are sent forth with a mandate to conduct a project of their choice, *if they can get funding from their manager to do so.* Completion of a project is supposed to be mentored by a Black Belt who may know nothing about the area he or she is mentoring and even less about the validity of the data or analysis conducted.

While these examples are extreme, the fact that they occur at all should be troublesome to anyone who cares about leaders in training or the credibility of Six Sigma in their own organization.

# TAKING INEXPERIENCE OUT OF THE TRAINING EXPERIENCE

The lack of practical experience is the shortfall of most training programs. However, there are numerous ways of making the training more relevant to the needs of the Green Belt and Black Belt candidates. The following sections describe the author's practical experience in taking the inexperience out of the training.

## Planting seeds and growing fresh Green Belts

To address Green Belt concerns, the author prepared Green Belt training at his organization that armed the individual candidates with relevant experience before they were requested to go forth and complete a project. The method was to break the time out across several weeks rather than the two-day model that was then prevalent. By doing so, he was able to conduct a live business assessment as the class.

## Planning for practical experience

Prior to the training sessions, the Black Belt instructor signs up candidates and talks with them individually. The instructor chooses a valid project that one of the candidates would like to conduct and basic data are gathered using the Project Planning Checklist found in Appendix A. From the planning data, a more detailed data capture tool is designed by the Black Belt and validated in conjunction with the Green Belt candidate prior to the training session. (See the Sample Questionnaire in Appendix D.) A list of data sources and contact information is compiled.

Just before the first training session, the list of candidates is used to make assignments for the data sources that will be used during the collection phase.

## On-the-job classroom

On the first day of class, the Black Belt instructor provides a three-hour overview, emphasizing the objectives and anticipated outcomes. The last hour is used to introduce the business assessment that the class will conduct as a Six Sigma project team, review the data collection tool, and make assignments. Class members are given a notebook of reference materials and a deadline of the end of the week to gather the assigned data and send them back to the Black Belt instructor, who compiles and analyzes the data.

The second class consists of four practice hours with relevant Six Sigma tools. The tools for this session are selected by the Black Belt instructor, and based on the specific work assignments, to familiarize the class with the tools they are most likely to use in their projects.

A week later the data are presented to the class and the data analysis techniques discussed. This is followed by a session to capture the undesirable effects of the situation. The project sponsor, who is a member of the class, validates the undesirable effects.

The final half-day consists entirely of applying analytical tools to the undesirable effects, generating the ideas that lead to improvements, evaluating the ideas and selecting the solutions that will become the subsequent projects to improve performance.

Project and mentor assignments for the next step in training are made before awarding the certificates. The certificates simply celebrate the completion of the initial training. A duplicate certificate is provided to each individual's supervisor, along with specific information on the project and mentor assignments.

The Black Belt mentor meets with the supervisor and Green Belt candidate to discuss the project and to ensure that adequate time and resources are available to complete the project. A timetable for project completion is agreed upon, and the Black Belt mentor advises the supervisor that she or he will be getting progress reports from the mentor through project completion.

The principle behind this approach to training Green Belts is that the individuals need more than a classroom presentation about tools. They need to participate in the process of using them, in a real situation, to experience a business analysis from end-to-end. In doing this they gain an understanding of why the project is important, how it was developed, and that the sponsoring supervisor fully supports the time and resource commitment to getting the project done.

### Just-in-time celebration and recognition as a reward

Celebrations are as important during the training as they are during the real project teams. In this class they were built into the process along the way. There happened to be a Krispy Kreme Donut shop on the Black Belt instructor's way to work. He would buy two dozen of these melt-away donut treats for the team as a means of rewarding those who got to the sessions early (they got their choice) and to keep everyone's blood sugar soaring through the work that day. Subsequent training sessions quickly became known as the next Krispy Kreme team.

Monthly, when the projects are complete, the Green Belt candidates are awarded their certificates by the divisional general manager, who takes the opportunity to talk about the individual projects completed by each candidate. Much emphasis is placed on the importance of each project to the division in making its goals for the year and sustaining competitive advantage into the future. He also individually thanks each candidate for caring enough about the company to become part of the company's future leadership through their knowledge of Six Sigma and skills in applying it to their everyday work.

## PREPARATION FOR AN APPRENTICESHIP

Training Black Belts is a more complex issue. The theory behind the 90-day wonder approach to training Black Belts is that the people being recruited to Six Sigma are already experts in various elements of Six Sigma methodology. Candidates who have years of experience in specializations such as design for manufacturing, lean production, software process, product development process tailoring, supplier development, and organizational development, for example, should be able to pick up the other concepts around Six Sigma relatively quickly.

What happens more times than not is that these specialists attend the classes, learn the proper terminology, and then return to their previous position. In some instances they apply a few more, or different, tools to accomplish the same results that they got before. In other cases these experienced individuals are recruited to become instructors to the waves of new recruits that are coming through as the company gears up for Six Sigma deployment.

The net result is that the most knowledgeable people are minimized in their direct contributions coming out of the training they receive. Rather than applying their broadened knowledge to making quantum improvements in company performance, their contribution opportunities are marginalized.

The author's contention is that the most effective model to train and deploy Black Belts is not classroom instruction but rather an apprenticeship program. Machinists who produce high-value products within tight tolerances are trained on the job by more experienced machinists. Likewise, it only makes sense for Black Belts who need to be able to wield the right Six Sigma tools in the right way to solve complex problems of high value to the organization to be trained on the job as an apprentice to other highly experienced Black Belts.

The apprentice concept works because the novice not only learns how to use the tools, but also when to use them to obtain the desired final product to meet the specifications and quality requirements.

A Black Belt apprentice has a more complex role to master than a machinist does because the Black Belt works with people, which introduces infinite variations of unpredictable factors and behaviors to deal with in attempting to achieve results. The "job" is to lead project teams of "volunteers" to obtain dramatic performance improvement while training the team members and mentoring their results and personal growth.

This is clearly not a skill set that can be taught in a classroom. It can only be developed through application and repetition, solving the varying problems inherent therein and gaining insight over time.

Where a Six Sigma program is established and functioning well within a company, the apprentice program becomes a viable option to consider. But what of the situation of a company putting Six Sigma into place where nothing currently exists? How can the company apprentice Black Belts where there are no masters to work with?

The simple solution is to hire Master Black Belts and create the core from external sources. The limiting factors in this approach are that the Master Black Belts may not be readily available in the marketplace. If they are available, they may not have industry-specific product knowledge and will not have company-specific process knowledge. This results in a learning curve for the Master Black Belts before they can become effective in instructing the Black Belt candidates.

The most common approach is for consultants to be hired to provide the Master Black Belt core for a period of time until the Black Belts can be mentored to the point of mentoring other Black Belt candidates. This is generally a multiyear process. The use of consultants broadens the experience basis, which could accelerate the learning curve and address the industry-specific knowledge issues. The use of consultants, however, is also a temporary solution in that the consultants will leave at some point and the domain knowledge leaves with them. While the apprenticed Black Belts should have the company-specific knowledge and newly learned skills to continue the work, the depth of Six Sigma knowledge remains a concern.

A hybrid solution appears to make the most sense to an apprentice approach to rapid Six Sigma deployment. Hiring a small cadre of experienced Master Black Belts who are teamed with a small group of external consultants and an internal leadership steering team creates the nucleus that resolves the domain knowledge issues of retention and lack of knowledge among the Masters who lead the deployment and development of the apprentices.

The involvement of the leadership team as a steering group permits the mentoring process to start early. Pairing new hires with external consultants leverages knowledge and experience, and allows for the rapid development of Black Belts who, with the internal core of Master Black Belts, may be able to assume the roles played by the consultants at the end of their assignments. This built-in early promotion opportunity for Black Belts provides an incentive for high-quality people to get involved with the effort early on.

During the initial deployment phase it is important that the Green Belts obtain their training and certification as a matter of working with the Black Belt teams on actual business analysis and projects. Green Belt certification is awarded upon successfully leading a project to achievement of expected results or better during this phase. The rationale for this is that the Black Belts are not sufficiently knowledgeable and experienced to mentor the Green Belts apart from a business analysis or project they are working on under the direction of a Master Black Belt.

## SUMMARY

An apprenticeship model for Black Belt training and certification is preferred to the 90-day wonder approach that is common throughout industry. The apprenticeship allows the Black Belt to master use of tools and methodology, and establish a core of competencies relating to leading project teams to the successful realization of performance improvement. The "learning by doing" approach is better suited to the human dynamics skills and abilities that a Black Belt must master to be effective in deploying an effective culture of Six Sigma improvement and performance.

For Green Belts, a training approach that also permits modeled behavior and participation in an actual business analysis to show how to lead projects and achieve results is preferred to one that simply provides an overview of the tools, methods, and philosophy of Six Sigma and instruction given to "go forth and do good."

Six Sigma is much too complex to be able to read about it and make it happen. The primary reason is that it blends the statistical data capture and analysis of engineering disciplines and couches it within the complexity of human dynamics. Generally, individuals who are very good at statistical analysis do not find rewards in leading project teams to achieve performance improvement analysis and projects.

The reason an apprenticeship is the best approach is that it blends the objective with the subjective to achieve a fact-basis for rational decision-making to assist people in bridging the chasm between their own strengths and weaknesses.

# 14

# Beyond the Black Belt

The Master Black Belt and Champion have an obligation to develop the personnel applying Six Sigma and to be proactive in returning Six Sigma Business Leaders into roles where they can leverage business results from their training and experience.

In some Six Sigma organizations the site leader for Six Sigma activity is a Master Black Belt. In other organizations they are called Champions. The primary difference between the two designations is that the Champion is usually an administrator and not a practicing Black Belt, although this is not always the case.

The site leader generally plays two different roles: first as a mentor, and second as a leader and representative to the site Leadership Team for the Six Sigma Black Belts and Green Belts.

The site or divisional leader for Six Sigma generally does not have line responsibility and thus acts as a consultant to management. In this consultant role the Six Sigma leader may or may not have a direct staff of Black Belts. The leader may or may not control the budget, selection of Black Belts, or projects to be undertaken. The nature of the role varies greatly from location to location and from one type of business leader to another.

Some business leaders want someone who will ensure that the organization meets the expectations of higher management but leaves the *how* up to the site Six Sigma leader. Others truly want to embrace Six Sigma and look to the Six Sigma leader to be a mentor, confidant, and strategist. Business leaders may put the Six Sigma leader on a short leash if they are only using Six Sigma to comply with requirements, or they may give them broad latitude if they not only "get it" but also practice it.

Six Sigma leaders must have the ability to achieve results through persuasion, and the ability to sell others on the opportunities that are available to the organization to achieve improved results and higher levels of performance. Achieving results without the authority to direct work performed requires a different skill set than the typical manager uses in the daily performance of management.

Interestingly, the skill sets align with three different groups of people: executives of voluntary and membership organizations, where the leader must appeal to something other than monetary rewards to obtain cooperation and results; outside consultants who are brought in to provide specific knowledge or skills for a short and defined project; and Six Sigma Black Belts, where results are obtained through teams that do not report to the Black Belt, have only a temporary relationship with her or him, and yet look to the Black Belt for leadership, knowledge, and guidance.

So, an effective Master Black Belt uses the skill sets needed to manage Six Sigma organizations on the larger scale; the issue, however, is senior management support and willingness to appoint an individual Black Belt to the position. Reluctance often comes from not having seen that individual in a management role where sustained performance and results are the measure of success, rather than project performance.

## MAKING THE TRANSITION

Making the transition from Black Belt to the next level is clouded with nonobjective factors, as is any personnel decision. Underlying this issue is the concept of Six Sigma Black Belt as a leader. Earlier chapters described the skills and traits that make Quantum Leaders, which are the best of the best. Quantum Leaders, however, are what every investor wants running the firm in which they invest their hard-earned savings. Quantum Leaders are what every board of directors wants at the helm of the firm for which they set policy.

The essential task for the Six Sigma Black Belt seeking to make the move to Six Sigma leadership in an organization is to spend time with the Leadership Team to become known to them, learn what their concerns are, and look for opportunities to address (or whenever possible teach them how to address) their concerns.

At the end of the day, what determines who is selected for a role within an organization is the ability to impress those who are going to decide that the candidate has the knowledge, skills, ability, and desire to do what is necessary to achieve the results expected by management.

At the same time, one must not lose sight of the need to build personal relationships, perform consistently at very high levels, and demonstrate knowledge of business issues facing the management team by offering recommendations on how situations can be resolved to the best advantage of the firm.

It is also imperative that this not all take place in the last few days before a decision about a new Six Sigma Leader is to be made, but rather be a part of the daily approach to doing the job one has now. Being openly ambitious works in some situations. Being involved, knowledgeable, and a consistent performer builds a level of trust and expectation that is a better basis for obtaining such a position. As most managers know, the last thing they want is a surprise, and when someone is unknown to them, the probability of a surprise is greatly increased.

# THE SUCCESSION PROBLEM

One of the major issues that Master/Champions must deal with is the career path open to Black Belts. Some firms have discussed dual-track approaches where Black Belts have the opportunity to move either into a general management track or a "scientist" accredited technical track. In either track the Black Belt has the opportunity to move to the Master level upon achieving defined levels of experience and training. What happens beyond that is the focus of the career track.

Some individuals are more comfortable as "tool masters" who become the company resident experts on the application of a particular tool, such as Design of Experiments. This individual is content to work on the most challenging problems the company faces in applying a particular tool to obtain the data required. The "tool master" generally has little interest in management roles within the firm and for this reason a "scientist" track becomes appealing. There is and will continue to be a requirement for such "tool masters." However, in relation to the total population of Black Belts within most organizations, those who intend to follow such a track should be small in number as there seldom is a substantial need for a large cadre of such experts. In most cases, for even a large organization, two or three masters of a single tool will be sufficient.

Movement into the general management track thus becomes the focus for the majority. In the initial selection of Black Belt candidates the expectation is that those applying for such positions are those whom the company hopes to see move into general management positions in engineering, production, and the various support function areas. Six Sigma Black Belts become the company experts in knowledge-based management, fact-based decision-making, and the merciless pursuit and elimination of waste and variation.

The company needs to establish a rotation policy in relation to Black Belts. How long does the firm want to keep Black Belts focused on Six Sigma assignments before redeploying them into line roles?

One firm decided that the goal is to move Black Belts back into the line as soon as possible and established a 24-month assignment period as the norm. Subsequently, the firm elected to lengthen the assignment periods to try to increase domain knowledge of Six Sigma and leverage results from higher skill levels resulting from the number of projects completed. But for the remainder of this discussion, the 24-month period will be used as an illustration.

# THE SUCCESSION TIMELINE

The rotation time line for a 24-month assignment would look something like this:

| Month | Six Sigma assignment |
|---|---|
| Month 0 | Selection for Six Sigma assignment |
| Month 1-5 | Training and OJT teaming with an experienced Black Belt |
| Month 6-12 | Leadership of increasingly complex projects |

*continued*

*continued*

| Month 13 | Certification |
|---|---|
| Month 13-18 | Leadership of increasingly complex projects<br>Green Belt mentoring<br>Leveraging results |
| Month 19 | Assessment and negotiation of development plan<br>Assessment of areas of greatest potential contribution by leadership<br>Selection of career track/next assignment |
| Month 20-22 | Leadership of most complex projects<br>Select and conduct capstone project<br>Green Belt mentoring<br>Leveraging results |
| Month 23-24 | Mentor replacement<br>Transition responsibilities<br>Complete capstone project |
| Month 25 | "Management out briefing" experience to leadership<br>Capture lessons learned and recommendations<br>Transition to new responsibilities |

One issue to address is preparing the methods and procedures to identify and transition replacements into these roles as Black Belts vacate them. It is far superior to have a defined methodology and clear expectations about the process than to operate in an ad hoc fashion. "Ad hoc-racies" tend to deliver inferior results. In this case, it would tend to bring individuals who may not be the highest potential individuals into Six Sigma. This situation would clearly limit the effectiveness of the entire Six Sigma effort if the quality of replacements were not as high as those they replace.

The other side of the coin is the methods and policies that surround the move and transition of Black Belts into "leadership" positions (see Figure 14.1). One firm used as a recruiting tool a commitment at the commencement of the Six Sigma effort that Black Belts would serve 24 months and then transition to leadership positions. When increasingly large numbers of Black Belts completed training, it became evident that 24 months was not going to permit the firm to obtain a high return on the training investment from the savings achieved. As a result of this understanding, they increased the average assignment period to three to five years.

It next became evident that there were not enough "leadership" positions opening up in the company to accommodate all of the Black Belts coming off assignments even with extending the assignment period. Many of the Black Belts who were expecting leadership roles upon completion of their assignments became frustrated. As a result some agreed to take positions that were essentially at the same level they left when they accepted the Six Sigma role; some sought out nonleadership positions, but in other organizations; others simply accepted opportunities outside of the company.

The clear lesson learned is that companies deploying Six Sigma efforts must have a clearly thought-out strategy for career paths, handling length of assignment, and end-of-assignment transition if they are to leverage the full benefits of the investment being made in human capital.

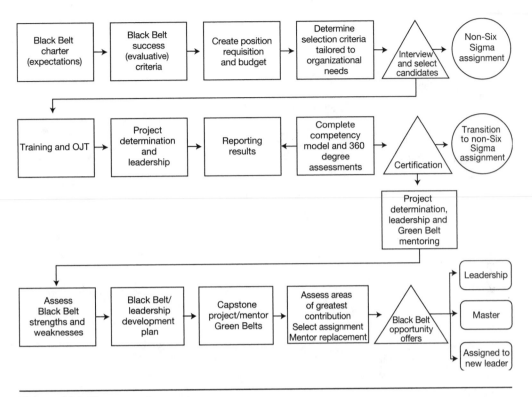

**Figure 14.1** The succession process.

## ESSENTIAL SUCCESSION SELECTION CRITERIA

Selection of replacement Black Belts should be based on the same criteria as the original selection, and this will vary from organization to organization. There are many considerations that go into this subjective evaluation of potential. These considerations are not only in what it takes to do the Six Sigma work and obtain results, but also in the contribution that the individual is expected to make to the firm when the assignment is complete. While no list is exhaustive or tailored to the specific needs of any organization, what follows is a list that was prepared for a market leader to define what those criteria should be.

- High potential employee
- Demonstrated leadership
- Strong customer interaction capabilities
- Ability to negotiate with and mentor Leaders
- Broad background
- Willingness to learn

- High energy

- Results orientation

- Good presentation/facilitation skills/ability

- Demonstrated organization skills

- Delegation and supervision effectiveness

- Motivational

## SUMMARY

Master Black Belts and Champions have a very diverse role. However, it is often removed from the daily realm of business analysis and projects. The role is one of leadership and contributing indirectly to the performance gains that the company makes. It is a role focused on the development and deployment of effective leadership assets across the business to ensure that the annual objectives are met, as well as creating and ensuring that the leadership capability of the company rapidly develops ahead of the requirements for specific leadership skills.

Succession of Six Sigma leaders is a critical issue. Not only is the timetable for such transitions of concern, but the very selection process raises other issues. This chapter provides both a model succession timetable and set of selection criteria for your consideration.

# 15

# Six Sigma as an Integrating Force

SIX SIGMA PROVIDES A COMMON VOCABULARY AND SET OF TOOLS THAT PERMIT
PEOPLE FROM DIFFERENT ORGANIZATIONS AND CULTURES TO WORK TOGETHER.

Six Sigma is a powerful force for bringing together people of different cultures because it reintroduces common values, beliefs, expectations, experiences, norms, focus, and language.

The Six Sigma culture focuses on performance and results. Six Sigma people mercilessly hunt down and eliminate all sources of variation and defects. Zero tolerance for waste and inefficiency becomes a way of life.

This becomes increasingly important as more and more companies, driven by the quest for ever-increasing results, buy and sell business units. The rearrangement of deck chairs moves whole groups of people from one corporate culture to another.

Some Leadership Teams, in a deliberate attempt to shake organizations loose from their prior cultures, have adopted the approach of "shuffling the deck" or routinely reorganizing entire reporting structures and relationships. They break their organizations down and send the pieces back up to completely different reporting structures.

The assumption behind shuffling the deck is that it breaks down complacency and increases competency by forcing people to work with and within other organizations. Working relationships are no longer based on tradition, but rather on current need. Conceptually this idea has merit, but in reality it has produced less than optimal results. Change for the sake of change is disruptive.

It is clear that when an organization changes hands, people will be forced to make changes to accommodate systems, processes, procedures, cultures, and norms that will be new. Adding further change into the mix overwhelms individuals and results in higher-than-necessary turnover. This leads to loss of domain knowledge, customer relationships, and processes and systems that actually may be superior to the ones that were bought or brought in to replace them.

Individuals need established relationships as an anchor to help them weather the storm of organizational change. When the coherence of the work group begins to break down as a result of a loss of identity within a new entity, it is not only the poorer performers who seek the haven of a new shore. The best people always have other options. When change loosens the ties that bind them, moving on becomes a more viable option to most people.

If organizations can leave the companies they acquire intact and operating as a separate division, they can achieve minimum turnover. In addition, keeping as much of the former leadership intact as possible minimizes the impact of the change from independence to that of integration into a much larger organization.

## SIX SIGMA AS A UNIFYING FORCE

Leadership Teams, and Quantum Leaders in particular, have found that Six Sigma provides a means of bridging the divide between the new culture and the old. The Six Sigma culture centers on the elimination of defects and variability, and on continuously improving product designs, processes, and organizational performance. It is this common ground that forms the cultural bridge.

The common value of Six Sigma organizations centers on the contributions of all members leading to desired results. Further, Six Sigma organizations are customer focused and driven to deliver products and services that exceed the specifications and expectations of the customers and any regulatory bodies.

The Six Sigma belief is that empirical data are the best source for decision-making. Everyone in the organization has the ability to acquire, validate, and analyze the data. Every decision made will benefit the customer, employees, stockholders, and society at large equally in the long run.

The Six Sigma expectation is that all contributions will be fact-based decisions resulting from the use of Six Sigma tools, methodologies, skill sets, experience, and resources in the acquisition, validation, and analysis of all relevant data. Everyone's contributions are valuable, from the leadership all the way to the lowest paid employee, and all contributions are expected to improve performance and the overall results of the organization.

The integrative force of Six Sigma is not isolated to merging organizations. It can powerfully accelerate the process of bringing work groups into the fold and individuals into their teams.

Learning new job responsibilities is accelerated as a result of the training and experience in process design and analysis. Individuals are able to rapidly assess the requirements of the position and optimize the workflow and requirements to best suit their own abilities and interests.

This ability to optimize the workflow still must be managed by the larger work group and the management of the area. The optimal situation for one individual may be to only perform one step repeatedly. If the previous position holder performed 10 steps in the process, then to optimize the new individual either requires hiring additional employees to perform the other nine steps or throws the responsibility onto the shoulders of the other members of the work group. For this reason, specific data must be gathered, validated, and analyzed so that changes can be negotiated and incorporated within the total scope of the work team or group.

Processes may be redesigned annually or whenever new members join the process team. At that time, processes may be adjusted significantly if new skill sets differ from the optimal design previously adopted.

## SUMMARY

The shared values, beliefs, expectations, norms, focus, and language of Six Sigma bridge the gaps between people regardless of former work situations and employers who may be competitors, or of a different national origin, race, religious belief, gender, or other social or cultural differences.

For this reason, Leadership Teams, and Quantum Leaders in particular, use Six Sigma as an integrating force to take advantage of the common ground, common language, common experience, common methodologies, and common focus on a set of tools that permit people from different organizations and cultures to work together.

# Section C

# Tales of Transformation

SIX SIGMA TOOLS AND METHODS, WHEN ADAPTED TO A PARTICULAR
ORGANIZATIONAL NEED, CAN RAPIDLY ACHIEVE RESULTS EVEN IN STRATEGIC
AND KNOWLEDGE-BASED APPLICATIONS.

Six Sigma is an enterprisewide effort that can bring about the transformation of an entire organization regardless of the nature of the business that is conducted. The last set of chapters present success stories and lessons learned from a variety of real-world applications of Six Sigma, ranging from improving a relatively simple single-component design all the way up to addressing complex strategic analysis and governance issues.

*Chapter 16: Tactical Transformation* discusses how the key to leveraging internal assets for growth and market leadership has become rapid process innovation. One approach to stimulating this kind of innovation is through tactical transformations or single, highly visible, opportunities for achieving rapid results. This chapter distills some of the author's varied experiences in creating tactical transformation within companies, government agencies, and municipal governments around the globe.

*Chapter 17: Product Development Transformation* describes the transformation that occurred in a workshop environment in Italy resulting in the construction and adoption of a totally new product development process in less than a week. This chapter illustrates how the tactical transformation process can be applied to bring together groups that are at odds with each other for the common good enabling quantum levels of improvement and results, even in complex environments.

*Chapter 18: Creating Customer Partnerships* provides a glimpse at the opportunities typically overlooked in early engagement of Six Sigma on program initiation and execution. The conventional wisdom in Six Sigma and the various performance improvement initiatives/approaches is that early engagement leads to geometric improvement in savings and/or schedule. Yet the author's career and that of many other Six Sigma Black Belts has been centered on repairing the damage done because companies are not engaging Six Sigma early. This chapter documents the process one major defense contractor went through to engage early and the estimated results that were achieved as a result.

*Chapter 19: Supply Chain Applications* investigates another target-rich environment, suppliers, in which only a few firms are effective and consistent in realizing Six Sigma improvements. The chapter, offered by Dr. Antone Kusmanoff, illustrates a different perspective on how to enlist supplier support. This approach is a supplier day conference in which supply chain applications, tools, and methods are explained and discussed, and a favorable business proposal is made to the candidate suppliers.

*Chapter 20: Global Transformation—Lessons Learned in Europe* disproves the often-espoused theory that knowledge businesses are often considered difficult environments in which to achieve Six Sigma results. This chapter recounts the considerable successes achieved by one Six Sigma team working primarily in Europe for business units, suppliers, and customers of one multinational firm.

*Chapter 21: Globalizing Knowledge-Flows Management* raises some interesting issues about capturing and using knowledge in multinational environments. Six Sigma Black Belts and Leaders are most effective when they are able to look at global and systemic issues and offer suggestions that will improve performance. This chapter demonstrates such an analysis, which extends results through application of knowledge gained in Six Sigma efforts.

*Chapter 22: Mapping Migration Paths for Corporate Education* discusses the strategic involvement of Six Sigma in determining the best path to create or acquire the skills knowledge and leadership required to successfully launch new businesses, products, or services and reposition the company in existing markets to extend product lifecycles. This illustrates how Six Sigma can be applied to strategic level activity to accelerate the process and broaden the base of input and resulting support.

*Chapter 23: Governance and Governance Transition* introduces a Six Sigma deployment model from a governance point of view and offers an evolutionary concept of how the governing council migrates missions over time. Once the initial Six Sigma initiative is deployed, multiple questions must be addressed, such as:

- "What happens to the governing structure over time?"

- "What becomes the focus of the deployed teams?"

- "How do the teams organize for results?"

*Chapter 24: The Myth of Measuring Cost Avoidance* describes the difficult issue of trying to measure Six Sigma success on the basis of cost avoidance, rather than hard dollar savings.

*Chapter 25: The Six Sigma Journey Continues* summarizes the book with the premise that Six Sigma is fertile ground for leadership development – growing the Quantum Leaders of the future.

The issues throughout this section relate to the fact that Six Sigma is not static; it evolves, grows, and transforms the way the leadership leads and the entire workforce conducts business.

# 16

# Tactical Transformation

STRATEGIC CHANGE CAN BE REALIZED THROUGH SIX SIGMA TACTICAL
(TARGETED) TRANSFORMATION WORKSHOPS.

In a global community, staying focused on growth is difficult when everything that is familiar can change with a morning announcement in a far-off city or nation. The out-of-control pace of technological change can literally kill a company, even if it has always been the undisputed leader in the particular markets it serves. Still, change *within* a company remains as slow and difficult as "threading a needle" in a dark room.

Management teams have used a variety of process and performance improvement techniques to meet the challenge of threading the needle. The resulting changes have, in most cases, made their companies more responsive from a customer service perspective and more competitive in price, schedule, and quality.

Performance improvement efforts have a quick payback. They can transform the groups within the company that are actively involved in the efforts and offer tangible evidence that the company is trying to get better at what they do. The culture shifts to one where complacency is no longer acceptable because everyone knows that doing business as it has always been done will cause the firm to drown in its own inefficiency.

## BEYOND PROCESS IMPROVEMENT

While significant for most organizations, the changes that result from performance improvement efforts may be inadequate to ensure growth, or even survival, in the current world at the current velocity of global and technological change. The key to leveraging internal assets for growth and market leadership has become rapid process innovation.

A preferred approach to stimulating this kind of innovation is to gain successes through tactical transformations or single, highly visible, opportunities for achieving rapid results. They require a Six Sigma team to think small, act fast, and move on.

Any Six Sigma team with a portfolio of successful tactical transformations builds respect, trust, and a core of support for more ambitious activities within an organization.

Black Belt Ron Carmichael and the author built an impressive tactical transformation portfolio over the past 10 years, by completing more than 700 engagements aimed toward achieving process and performance improvements in comparatively short time frames. This chapter distills some of their varied experiences in creating tactical transformation within companies, government agencies, and municipal governments around the globe in a variety of areas, including:

- Business acquisition and marketing

- Program planning and start-up

- Product or service design

- Software development

- Procurement, supply chain management, and supplier development

- Production of simple and complex systems including hardware/software integration, factory floor layout, and service delivery processes

- Distribution

- Finance

- Human resources

- Contracts administration

- Customer service center operations

- Information systems migration for commercial firms

- Senior management metrics, communications, and strategic planning

- Services organizations such as translation services and simulation-based pilot training.

For governments:

- Reduced permitting cycle times

- Procurement

- Legal document processing, storage and retrieval systems

When asked about his experiences on Six Sigma Innovation projects, Ron says, "Every month I go into another company that can't understand why someone else is 'eating their lunch.' I walk the floor, talk to the people, and I see the fear in their eyes.

The average worker in these companies knows that they have lost the edge. They are waiting for management to show them the path back. Unfortunately, neither they nor their management have realized that the path is right before their eyes."

The Six Sigma Tactical Transformation and Innovation methodology incorporates elements of:

- Design for manufacturing
- Synchronous and lean engineering principles
- Process improvement
- Strategy development engagements
- Training and education
- Process and culture change implementation

The Six Sigma Innovation methodology has four essential elements:

- Strategy development and planning
- The innovation workshop
- Implementation
- Training

# STRATEGY DEVELOPMENT AND PLANNING

## The initial planning session

The planning session for a Six Sigma Innovation project starts with a face-to-face meeting with the top executives in the organization. First, the team leader captures their general observations and concerns about the process or performance issue. Next, they "walk the floor," paying close attention to working conditions and workflow and meet the people, asking them questions to get a sense of the culture and their perceptions about the "way it is now." In some cases, they will also seek opportunities for independent discussions with a cross section of customer or supplier representatives, or employees. They are most interested in anyone who may either have a significant impact on or be significantly impacted by the proposed innovation activities.

## Setting the workshop and project objectives

After gaining a firsthand look at the situation, the team coaches management in how to set specific and measurable objectives for the innovation activity. For a Master Black Belt, being a teacher and mentor becomes as natural as breathing. He or she uses every step in the process as an opportunity to teach people how to "fish" (do the steps in the process) for themselves so that they can perform subsequent innovation activities on their own.

Objectives are based on priorities that have emerged during various discussions. The emphasis is on immediate improvement. Longer-term objectives inevitably emerge, which they help management capture for future innovation efforts. At this point in the planning, however, the leaders may remind them how vital it is to keep the scope of the innovation project bite-sized to ensure success.

Sometimes, however, a problem that jeopardizes the organization is so compelling that the leaders instead teach management how to decompose it into a series of small, realistic objectives. In this way a few of the objectives may be incorporated into the current innovation effort. They then assure them, from experience, that accomplishing just one objective toward solving a tough problem can start the dominoes tumbling down. Inevitably when one part of the problem improves, other parts will be helped as well.

## Picking the team

Once the objectives are agreed upon, the leaders work with management to pick the participants for the workshop. They need to be a cross-section at various levels in the organization with the skills and experience that enable them to identify and fix problems. For some issues, outside experts and customers may be invited to participate. Management will need to work with the supervisors of these people to ensure that they are completely free to focus on the workshop without other work distractions.

The leaders also help management to identify "guests" to be brought in only for specific portions of the workshop, either to present information or to assist in a specific analysis or critical decision. Management picks people who would serve in these roles as well.

## Identifying the current state

Depending on the complexity of the process or performance issue, the leaders may work with one or two key players prior to the workshop to create a "picture" of the current state. This may be a flowchart or a step-by-step procedure. It may be formally documented, duplicated, and distributed prior to the workshop or it may be done on the back of a napkin and transferred to a flipchart on the day of the workshop. Either way, doing this step ahead of time saves time that would otherwise be spent during the workshop.

## Details, details

After that, the leaders connect with the workshop coordinator. This person is also someone picked by management in the planning session. The leaders explain the things that need to be done prior to the workshop.

The leaders offer strategies for contacting people, including ways to inform those picked to participate in the workshops, and their supervisors. To preserve the integrity of the Six Sigma activity as a top-down directive, this communication needs to come from top management, but the coordinator can follow up to ensure that it has happened. Management needs to provide the authority and support to ensure that the chosen participants are released from work obligations (and related distractions) on the days of the workshop.

Next, the leaders offer tips to help start the diffusion of the innovation throughout the organization with suggestions on identifying and working with the early adopters and the resisters in the organization. The coordinator may take on this task or just keep the tips handy for the innovation team once they have completed the workshop. The leaders also discuss asking management to offer "special assignments" that will receive special recognition to those who may have bruised egos when they are not asked to directly participate in the workshop. This is done to keep them on board with the innovation efforts, or at least to prevent them from becoming active resisters.

The leaders ask the coordinator to schedule the workshop dates when all (or the best possible majority) of the participants can attend and to make sure that the management team is available for a briefing at the end of the last day of the workshop. They also explain, if there are expert guests coming, how to schedule them into the flow of the workshop.

Other essential items that the leaders ask the coordinator to handle are the "official" participation certificates, the arrangements for a celebration gathering, and the management rewards and recognitions ceremony at the end of the workshop. The coordinator can also work with management on "rewards" for achieving major milestones on the project after the workshop is complete.

The leaders delegate the details for making things happen to the coordinator, because she or he typically knows far more than the leader does about the company's culture and expectations and who to contact to get things done.

---

**Transformation Testimonial**

The former president of a U.S.-owned Rome-based training company is a believer. Commenting from firsthand experience he states, "Performance innovation based on processes is the key to survival. The global communications revolution is changing every expectation. Incremental change is no longer good enough. My clients in Italy have found that the results of these efforts have always exceeded their expectations. It is simply amazing how much can be accomplished in a very short time when cross-functional teams are led through a break-through methodology like this. The impact this has on an organization is just amazing."

---

# THE INNOVATION WORKSHOP

## The ticket to transformation

On the first day of the workshop, the leaders introduce themselves, welcome the participants to introduce themselves, and then provide the participants with a brief overview of the innovation process upon which they are about to embark. They may even ask them to be on a "transformation watch" throughout the workshop (making it a friendly competition) and then point out that they have already been "transformed" from individual workshop participants into an innovation team.

## Telling it "like it is"

Their first activity is to validate the existing process (or create it if not already done prior to the workshop). Someone draws the process "as it is" on a large sheet of paper so the entire team can see it. Innovation team members point out errors or inconsistencies and make adjustments to the drawing, based on their own experience. If disagreements arise, the leaders assist the quarreling team members to rapidly reach a resolution.

Once a baseline is agreed to, the team members walk through each step or hand-off in the process to ensure that it is completely understood by everyone. They discuss not only what is done, but also any significant problems or limitations they have encountered. At the end of this stage, depending on the resources available at the workshop location, they may use a software tool to electronically capture the process as a flowchart or procedural document and distribute what has been discussed so far.

## Ideas from the "out" side

Next, the leaders lead the innovation team in an out-of-the-box experience to generate ideas for the improvement "opportunities" they have identified in the process. Additional facilitators and flipcharts may be brought in, if necessary, to ensure that every idea is captured on a flipchart and to encourage team members to generate more and more ideas. This brainstorming stage continues until they have exhausted the typical solutions and escaped their comfort zones to venture into the realm of radical thoughts, original ideas, and innovative solutions. As Ron might say, "Truly creative problem solving can only happen once you're outside of the box labeled, 'the way it's always been done.' "

## Seeking superior solutions

After enough ideas have been generated, the facilitators refocus the innovation team to select a few of the ideas for inclusion in the action items to improve the process. Part of this process entails assessing each action item for unacceptable risk (according to a variety of factors). After the ideas that were generated become action items to work on to improve the process, the team draws a picture of the improved process (the way it will be), and then they validate the process drawing again and check it to ensure it meets the majority of the objectives set by management. If not, more ideas are generated and the process continues until the objectives are met or can be renegotiated so that management is in agreement with the workshop solution.

## Measuring process progress

Next the innovation team identifies ways to measure improvement to the process. Data capture points are inserted into the process drawing so that they will automatically be built into the implementation plan. These collection points and the recommended methods for analysis will be used over the duration of the project to create incremental indications of improvement that will be visible to management and users throughout the organization.

## Planning for performance

Next the innovation team drafts an implementation plan with very specific tasks to accomplish. After that, the team drafts a training plan to provide adequate instruction on the process or performance improvement. Both the implementation plan and the training plan are included in the final report of the workshop.

## The starting line

Finally, the workshop concludes with a management briefing to ensure that management fully understands the tasks to be undertaken and the resources (including training) required to support the innovation project. At the conclusion of the briefing, the management team recognizes each innovation team member, and presents him or her with a certificate (which serves only as a "starting line" in the race to achieve tactical transformation), and then joins the team in a celebration of the hard work they have completed so far.

---

**Transformation Testimonial**

The manager of engineering for a $125 million value-added reseller of computer systems was required to set up a manufacturing facility and deliver product to the customer within 30 days of contract award. "I brought in the performance innovation team after the first year. I knew that there had to be a better way for us. We ran a series of workshops, which showed us the inefficiencies and a different way to lay out the facility. The result was that we tripled production with only 60 percent of the employees the next year. We also found a means of reducing our shipping costs by 66 percent as a result of the outside expertise we brought in to the workshops.

We had the information we needed locked in our individual heads. The Six Sigma Innovation project workshops were the forum that brought it all out on the table for us to see. Once we knew where we were going and how to get there, the implementation flowed. The results speak for themselves."

---

# IMPLEMENTATION

The innovation team is responsible for ensuring that those directly involved in the process are properly trained on the changes. (Training is discussed separately in the next section.) The team is also responsible for follow-up with management and key influencers throughout the company to ensure that the implementation plan is being successfully executed and completed on schedule. The team has designed all implementation tasks to be completed within 60 days. Any project that takes longer than 60 days risks not being completed once normal business activity resumes and intervenes.

At the end of the implementation phase, the innovation team is recalled to evaluate success and determine any additional action required to enhance the process effectiveness and results. At this time longer-term ideas are reviewed and new ideas are captured and evaluated. A new implementation plan is created. Task descriptions are written, assigned, and followed-up on. A training plan is developed. And the cycle continues...

---

**Transformation Testimonial**

Six Sigma Innovation has been applied to software development. The director of software development for a major NASA subcontractor who worked closely with the Six Sigma team commented, "Software development is often as much art as science. But it is a structured process. The Six Sigma Innovation team methodology lends itself to making dramatic improvement.

Through a series of workshops we were able to innovate in such a way that we reduced our lines of code required by 28 percent. On the SSTL simulator we have documented improvements that saved us $34 million. We didn't stop there, however, we continue to use performance innovation on the International Space Station simulators and are making impressive gains in each area where we apply this methodology."

These efforts led to the company receiving the John H. Young Innovation Award for Process Improvement from NASA.

---

## TRAINING FOR TACTICAL TRANSFORMATIONS

One of the primary reasons that change fails in organizations is that training is not part of the change management process. Without proper training, employees are unable to adopt the changes (or adapt to them). Once time and money have been invested in the innovation effort, the success of the project largely depends on making sure that each individual involved knows what to do and how to do it.

An innovation project is like having actors and actresses in a long-running theatrical production suddenly needing to learn new lines or a new scene, which is why innovation projects are kept small in the beginning. (Imagine how difficult it would be having a whole cast needing to learn a whole new show! Worse, imagine having two or three whole casts having to learn a whole new show that has a limited number of parts. That's what happens in reorganizations, mergers, and divestitures every day.)

Hands-on training sessions (rehearsals) provide relevant practice before the process innovation (show) is performed live for the customers (audience).

## Becoming a world-class learning organization

Training on specific process requirements is just the beginning. The kind of sustainable performance improvement that leads to organizationwide transformation and quantum results involves extensive training and apprenticeship in teamwork, leadership, and macro-process knowledge. One of the issues facing most companies is how to provide just the right knowledge and skills to just the right people at just the right time to enable change.

One company has developed an effective set of tools that may be applied to manage this just-in-time approach. The Raytheon RPS Predictor™ helps managers evaluate skill gaps against validated job families from a variety of world-class companies. Once training gaps are identified, individual training plans for each employee are created to map the employee against the skills and knowledge capabilities of similar individuals at world-class companies. A training management system is used to track the instruction that has been provided and the progress the firm is making in transforming the knowledge and skill capability of its human resources to match world-class standards.

## Creating a collective culture

The role of training is commonly overlooked when the organization is undergoing a reorganization, merger, or divestiture. However, a training activity that promotes the collective culture can bring people together no matter how far apart they were at the start.

Training provides the forum for creating a bridge between the component cultures of the new organization. Working together on something brand new is an important first step in bringing the people in the organizations together. At that point, the activity is not "ours" or "theirs." Instead, it belongs to the new collective group, and every member has a stake in it. While participating in the common activity, participants are reinforced for collaborating and given strategies for working with others in their day-to-day work.

The Six Sigma team can assist in culture change efforts when organizations merge by creating and assisting mixed innovation teams to work through their internal barriers to change, and then by obtaining management commitment to support and provide appropriate incentives to those innovation teams that are able to actually demonstrate the culture changes necessary to ensure the success of the collective company. (See Roles and Responsibility Matrix in Appendix E on the CD ROM.)

**Transformation Testimonial**

The managing director of an international Translation Service in England invited the Six Sigma Innovation team to review a process that his organization had worked diligently to optimize. "When they arrived, we thought that they could not possibly find a way to make the process more efficient. What we discovered was that our process was based on some unrealistic assumptions.

With customer representatives and our vendors in the workshops, we were able to understand the basis of our assumptions and the reality of our customers' and vendors' situations. Together we looked at the barriers, attacked them individually, and developed a team working relationship that ensured that each barrier was removed or a work-around found. We were able to meet our customer's schedule, which saved millions of dollars."

## VERSATILE TOOL FOR TRANSFORMATION

Six Sigma Innovation has a wide array of applications. One example is a small Italian manufacturer of mechanical components for helicopter systems. In 1995, the manufacturing operations were purchased from a larger firm and the new management added the capabilities that were missing to be a stand-alone firm. Since then they have designed new products with significant market advantages. They engaged the Six Sigma Innovation team to validate their next moves into new market segments and to innovate processes to reduce costs to world-class levels.

**Transformation Testimonial**

Bill Freeman, the former general manager of a flight training company in London, remarked, "We were constantly striving to increase the value of our services to our customers. I called the Six Sigma Innovation team to help us look at two dramatically different areas, customer billing and simulator maintenance.

Organizational dynamics as well as inefficient work practices affected each area and the team worked hard to correctly identify the workshop objectives, agenda and participants.

The results were brilliant! In both areas we not only reduced costs but significantly increased the value of our services to our airline customers."

The Six Sigma Innovation methodology is a powerful tool for companies that are reorganizing, merging, or divesting operations. The same process is a powerful tool to compress the planning time, build the teams given the responsibility to execute the restructuring, and meet the goals. After that, the innovation workshop format can be used to define new common processes that jump-start the creation of a new integrated culture. The Six Sigma team also helps to incorporate tools such as culture-change training to speed the process of recovery.

Six Sigma Innovation makes the leap to quantum improvement in cost, cycle-time, and performance. As an example, for a city government in Spain, the permitting process was cut from an average of seven working days to one. A billing process for a government contractor was reduced from three months to two weeks. The purchase order documentation cycle for the German subsidiary of an American company was reduced by 85 percent.

---

**Transformation Testimonial**

The chief engineer for Simulator Modifications for the a major manufacturer of flight simulation systems observed, "We are often asked to do the impossible. So we wade in and get started without fully assessing how we are doing.

Six Sigma Innovation workshops force us to take the time to fully understand the tasks we must perform, get everything down on paper so we can see what we have to do, and let everyone brainstorm risk mitigation. When we do this we make up substantial ground. In fact, we often do what would have been impossible without it. At the same time we forge effective work teams, even when they are from different organizations, who communicate better and continually adjust as we go."

---

What makes Six Sigma Innovation efforts different from traditional TQM and team problem-solving techniques is the compressed time to reach results. The process is a short-term, highly focused effort leading to immediate results otherwise known as tactical transformations.

In one engagement 10 major process areas were addressed in a time frame of five months, with nearly 80 percent of the implementation completed. This resulted in a targeted performance reengineering of the entire operation, but was completed in a much shorter time frame than traditional reengineering projects.

Companies that wish to run with the leaders have no choice but to innovate their processes and quickly implement the gains in productivity and profitability.

According to Ron Carmichael, "It's like when I played hockey. The other team makes some moves on you and puts a few in the net. The impulse is to speed up the ice after them. But resist that impulse and slow yourself down, just for a minute. Suddenly you see what is really happening out there. In that one minute you set your imagination free. The opportunity becomes visible. Now just communicate it to the rest of your team through demonstrated leadership. This allows you to take the puck right to the net. Then the rally is on and the game is yours."

# SUMMARY

Quantum gains in organization performance improvement result from tactical transformation through Six Sigma performance and process innovation. What is meant by this is that bites of the elephant are more effective than wholesale attempts to swallow the beast. If planned in conjunction with each other, then a focus on tactical improvements lead to strategic results. In the course of more than 700 business analyses and projects, one team achieved amazing results from a compressed workshop approach. The core elements of this approach are:

- Slow down to critically assess the situation.

- Free the collective imagination to solve the problem.

- Take the leadership to put the plan into action.

# 17

# Transforming the Product Design

SEEMINGLY SMALL INDIVIDUAL SIX SIGMA PROJECTS CAN LEAD TO IMMENSE IMPROVEMENTS WHEN INTEGRATED INTO A LARGER TRANSFORMATION PROCESS.

When looking for ways to improve a design, most engineers would look to change the functionality, manufacturability, or ease of assembly. They might focus on how to remove complexity, components, or assembly labor in the design. Few would ever take the single most important step back and look at how to improve the design *process* itself.

## A COMPANY IN TRANSITION

A Six Sigma team was invited to conduct a Targeted Transformation performance re-engineering project with an Italian components manufacturer in the aerospace industry. The company was making a transition from strictly mechanical components, used primarily for flight controls, to hydraulic systems. A hydraulic design group had been added as a new entity in the organization.

The new hydraulic team launched into a series of new designs, making adjustments to meet the customer requirements while also attempting to create an elegant solution that would greatly appeal to the customer.

At the same time, the management of the firm determined a need to improve overall competitiveness. In the midst of making the transition into new products and markets it was determined the investment in performance reengineering at that point in time would pay off when the new markets were engaged.

## Identifying the points of greatest pain

When the Six Sigma team first arrived in Italy, they met with management to plan the activity, and then they visited with a cross section of employees and walked the factory. Over the course of two days of interviews and observations, the Six Sigma team determined the "points of greatest pain."

Putting these into a logical order, it became apparent that there was poor integration of the design process with the rest of the firm. The greatest need they identified was definition in how the various functions of the firm could and would work together to form a unified process.

The current product coming toward critical design review had been in development for more than 31 months, and management had set an objective of developing the next new product in only 18 months. Thus, the process and cost associated with the design and development phase would be cut nearly in half.

## Eliminating the elegant solution

Most companies say that they are advocates of design reuse, but in reality (or at least in the experience of this Six Sigma team), few companies currently practice what they say. Finding the elegant solution, not just an efficient one, had become an obsession in the Design Engineering group at this firm. However, elegant solutions – as the name implies – are more expensive to achieve and build.

In an examination of the prototype for the first new product for this firm, the elegant design required a flange in a certain location to eliminate torque. It was placed in this location to allow the user to view the hydraulic fluid level through a window on the side of the device. The problem was that the location of the flange required additional machining, adding cost and time.

The company either needed to change the placement of the flange or the window to reduce the machining and set-up requirements. Neither was accomplished in that the final design had already passed the critical design review with the customer.

The position of the flange and fluid window were inconsequential to the customer. The chief designer was enamored with the elegant solution and the customer was happy to have unspecified functionality, even though it substantially reduced the profitability of the device for the manufacturer.

In the product design workshop, this example was used to show why the first cycle for product development was taking 31 months rather than 18. The Design Engineering group was more concerned with wowing the customer by exceeding the demands and requirements for the product than in maximizing profits. This situation arose because the head of design engineering could dictate what he wanted to do since the firm lacked the expertise to design the product without him.

## Outside expert advice

In the design workshop, an outside expert supplied by the Six Sigma team discussed how the firm would be unable to stay in the marketplace for these products if they were unable to make a profit, since his former firm was already quite profitable in that market space. This concept, while unquestioned by the design staff did not seem to affect the design team. The company was generally profitable. From their perspective, it was not their problem whether the product made money or not. That was an issue for finance and manufacturing. However, since the relationships between these groups were weak, there was little accountability for the business side of the design.

# CREATING A NEW DESIGN PROCESS

In discussing ways to bring the various functions together, the Six Sigma team and management decided that the best approach might be to create a whole new product design and development process that showed the integration of all of the functions and dependencies involved to produce a new design.

For practical considerations, the lead designer was only involved in the initial discussions. The new product process definition was assigned to his operations deputy. That this individual actually had the best working relationship with other staff members from the design department turned out to be fortunate.

Following a typical DFM approach, the management of the firm and the Six Sigma team worked together to select a cross-functional workshop team to address the subject of a unified process.

## The "way it is"

Starting with a baseline for the existing process, and linking in the other functional areas, the workshop team created an integrated "as is" diagram of the process. This diagram was thoroughly analyzed for cycle-time, discontinuities, and metrics to measure effectiveness. It was no surprise that there were rampant discontinuities and no metrics.

The workshop team analyzed the process for issues, problems, and root causes of inefficiency. The discussions, at this point, were very lively, with finger-pointing and blame enough to share across the organization.

Once the Six Sigma team was able to move the project team past the recriminations and focus on the opportunity and the needs of the company and customer to improve the process and turn-around time, the team began to pull together. However, suspicion of the lead designer kept the cooperation at a lower level than was desirable.

## Meeting, not exceeding, the customer needs

The team discussed the customer needs and how the process was affecting the ability of the company to meet those needs, which led many of the participants in the workshop team to new insights. They were, for the most part, unaware of how they were limiting themselves and putting their firm at a competitive disadvantage with their competition.

As these issues surfaced and were examined, the acrimony among the team members also reduced, but still, there were long-term issues that were not going to be resolved in a few days of a workshop. Many of these issues were captured by the Six Sigma team and set aside to be worked on at a later time.

## Drafting the new process

To move the team beyond these limiting factors, the operations director for design engineering met with the lead for manufacturing engineering and one member of the Six Sigma team. The three worked as a subteam on the draft process and the ideas that had been generated in the full team workshop to find an economical means of implementing the changes necessary.

After three intense days, a "straw man" surfaced. The Six Sigma team then brought in the functional heads to review the proposed process and add steps that were missing, elements that were needed, or discuss concerns with the three-man team and any other functional heads that stopped by.

## Collaborating toward consensus

Over the next two days all of the functional heads were able to add their comments and integrate when and how they would need to perform their work in order to meet the 18-month schedule target. When new steps were added to the process, the Six Sigma team was quick to bring in the affected functional lead(s) to discuss the impact and make adjustments.

As a final process evolved from the discussions and drawings, the whole process was transferred to the CAD system. Copies circulated among the leads in both English and Italian. The Six Sigma team was surprised to learn how much of the design terminology used in Italy is actually English.

At this point the lead design engineer and the president were brought in for a briefing by the whole team. Each had minor comments that led to changes in the process that strengthened certain areas, but not dramatically. Everyone agreed that the new process was manageable in the 18-month time frame.

## Complete with roles, responsibilities, dependencies, and metrics

One of the results of this workshop-based process definition was an entirely new product development process for the firm with clearly identified roles and responsibilities, and with dependencies clearly spelled out. The process was tailored specifically to the types of products the firm now designs. It breaks down the old blaming structure in that it is clear who is to do what and when. The new process came complete with new metrics to measure effectiveness and to provide information valuable to improve the process over time.

The final process flow was signed by all members of the workshop team to signify their acceptance and accord with this method of doing business. A direct result was an internal critical design review of the next product in the pipeline with all affected functions present. Up until this time only the design team had carried out internal critical design reviews. A great deal of feedback was given, particularly on manufacturability issues by the manufacturing engineering team and the manufacturing machine operators, whose opinions to this point had never been solicited.

The president was clearly pleased with the results of the effort and the other departments felt for the first time they were being listened to by design engineering. A list of issues and recommendations was published and a schedule of when the issues would be addressed was published so that those with continuing interest in the issue resolution could follow the progress.

## TACTICAL TRANSFORMATION SCORES AGAIN!

The outcome of this effort is a new way of doing business that focused the functional groups to work as a team to meet a cycle-time goal for new product development. The fact that the new process was defined and agreed to in less than a week is phenomenal. It shows that the Six Sigma Targeted Transformation methodology with focused effort can achieve results well beyond expectations when the approach is facilitated, specific, focused, and flexible.

## SUMMARY

Ensuring that design for affordability is achieved may mean taking a step back from the product itself to look at the design *process* and determining whether unnecessary costs are built in by the way in which the process flows.

The fact that the process can, in essence, be redesigned in a very short time frame makes it feasible to periodically reexamine the design process itself, to remove assumptions and dependencies that add cost with no true functionality benefit.

Such a reexamination of the design process is also an opportunity to bring all of the various functional groups together to remove discontinuities and strengthen understanding of the process and the interrelationships the process demands in order to maximize the process utility. This chapter recounts one specific example of doing this with the added complexity of an international location imposing language and cultural barriers into the mix. Despite this the lead team achieved a product development process in little more than one week that reduced the product develop cycle from 31 to 18 months.

# 18

# Early Engagement Part I—
# Creating Customer
# Partnerships

FIXING DEFAULT PROCESSES USING SIX SIGMA ACCELERATION WORKSHOPS AT
THE BEGINNING OF A NEW PROGRAM IN CONCERT WITH THE CUSTOMER, LEADS TO
HUGE GAINS ACROSS THE BOARD.

S ix Sigma has a reputation. For many it is synonymous with, "crisis intervention." When faced with a performance crisis, a Program Manager just dials 1-800-06-Sigma for help (or so it seems to many Six Sigma experts sometimes). Perhaps processes aren't working or subsets of the culture are refusing to work together. In these and many other cases, Six Sigma is an effective tool to uncover and work toward resolving issues thereby putting the program performance back "on the mend."

Because Six Sigma has been synonymous with crisis intervention, few Program Managers have ever considered the effect it might have if applied prior to the "crisis." For example, what if it were applied at the beginning of a program – or better yet, *before* the beginning of a program?

Three vice presidents at Raytheon, a major U.S. defense contractor, pondered that very question one day and decided to put their hypothesis to the test by approving an early Six Sigma engagement for the next major program. Their intent was to establish the validity and value of early Six Sigma activity beyond a shadow of a doubt. This is their story.

## Breaking the default process syndrome

Three months *before* an international, multibillion dollar systems contract was finalized, three Raytheon vice presidents brought on board Ron Carmichael, a Black Belt, as the Six Sigma manager.

In the initial meetings, the Six Sigma manager, the three Raytheon vice presidents, the chief engineer, and the material program manager discussed opportunities to *intentionally* and rationally design and implement process and decision-making protocols.

They knew that "default processes" were encroaching upon and had conquered many parts of the organization. (Default processes are those processes that evolve from the way work has been done on previous programs, regardless of whether there is a new application or differences required by the contract terms.)

They also knew that the effects of default processes and inadequate decision-making protocols were rarely identified (or simply ignored) in the early stages of most programs, where the impacts on cost and schedule were minimal. Instead, the effects showed up in the latter stages of a program, just where the impacts on cost, schedule, and delivery were most severe and the ability to recover most restricted.

## FOLLOWING THE SIX SIGMA MODEL

Multiple variations on the Six Sigma model exist, and they differ from one company to the next. The six-step model used at Raytheon is included here, along with a running narration of the activities performed and products (and by-products) produced at each step. The Raytheon Six Sigma six-step model:

- The Vision
- Commitment
- Prioritize
- Characterize
- Improve
- Achieve

## THE VISION (STEP 1)

Together, the integrated baseline manager and one of the three Raytheon vice presidents established a Vision for the program that integrated: Six Sigma, a partnering protocol with the program customer, the Ministry of Defence (MoD) for the United Kingdom, integrated baseline program management (IBPM), and the product development process (PDP).

For example, imagine each program element as a leg to a four-legged stool upon which program management, cost, schedule, and performance achievement are measured. When the integration of the various program elements is solid and complete, the stool (program) is sturdy and stands on its own.

The program had many elements that added complexity. The first assembly and integrations with aircraft happened at U.S. facilities. Subsequent assembly and integrations with aircraft took place in the United Kingdom. Thus, the processes, procedures, approaches, and decision-making protocols required for all follow-on aircraft needed to be defined and proven on the first aircraft in the United States, and then transferred in their entirety to the United Kingdom. This involved culture translation and process knowledge transfer prior to the beginning of the production stream.

In addition, 31 major suppliers, most in the United Kingdom, would be involved in producing elements of the final system. These suppliers needed to be integrated into the Six Sigma efforts, the IBPM, and the partnering arrangement with the MoD. They also needed to be able to follow Raytheon's PDP methodology.

The Vision was of a flexible collaboration, capable of anticipating, analyzing, and acting upon information. This Vision required well-understood processes and decision-making protocols to build trust and open information flows across the multiple organizations required to execute this complex program.

The early application of Six Sigma was intended to find and deal with program problems one to two years earlier than typically addressed using traditional program management tools. "With two years of hard work in the beginning, we should experience seven years of a great program," commented one vice president. He knew that early identification of issues would permit the program team to have sufficient time to proactively resolve issues that arose, at the lowest cost in both dollars and productivity, since the necessity for rework is radically reduced when an issue is caught early. He knew that schedule slips would be minimized through this approach. Dependencies would be less likely to drive actions when the risks and issues could be identified and resolved early enough to be worked into the schedule dependency hierarchy.

An important aspect of the Vision was that the culture of the program organization already understood the Six Sigma six-step process and had incorporated it into the basic managerial approach to the program. The iterative nature of this process drives conscious decisions to find alternatives that reduce the impact of cost, schedule, and cycle-time drivers. This Six Sigma-literate culture linked to the structure of the PDP, the discipline of IBPM, and the open communications flows of the partnering agreement with the MoD. With this high level of integration, all parties were aware of the kinds of data that would be necessary. Because of this, they were each able to collect, analyze, and use the appropriate kinds of data to make decisions about actions necessary to meet the program objectives in the most expeditious and rational manner.

# COMMITMENT (STEP 2)

Six Sigma is an iterative process. The steps are revisited throughout the process. It is possible to bypass a step and circle back to more fully realize that earlier Six Sigma step later in the process. This is especially true for the *commitment* step, which goes far beyond simply being open for a revisit. It is literally "alive" during the entire course of action and affects the progress of all of the other steps. The commitment step is the root that continually carries life to the Vision.

## Integrated support and commitment: The first key to culture change

Back at Raytheon, programwide commitment required buy-in from System Program Office (SPO) leadership and the entire consortium of players: Raytheon, U.K. customer and suppliers, right down to the lowest level of participation in each organization. The customer was open to a close working relationship on Six Sigma activities, but Raytheon's program team was reluctant to give its full commitment.

Culture issues can hold up, or even stop, Six Sigma progress until commitment is achieved. In the typical, late Six Sigma involvement, the "processors" were replaced as frequently as the "processes." This influences commitment dramatically.

Late Six Sigma involvement can, and usually does, lead to positive results and improved profits, but it does not always mean the full-term commitment to the Vision was achieved. Weak commitment is one reason the same failure modes show up on the very next project start. They fall back into their old "tried and true" methods. It takes time and effort to overcome years of digging in and making excuses to actualize the commitment step.

Early Six Sigma involvement, on the other hand, caused a unique culture confrontation within Raytheon. The program team was not in the desperate condition of a near-term failure, the recognized domain of Six Sigma at that time. Just the opposite! They were coming directly off the success of winning a major multibillion dollar contract. Suggesting that they should now commit to a newer Vision and were in need of support from the Six Sigma team was an extreme test of winning commitment.

## Early customer involvement: The second key to culture change

At reports of program team resistance to Six Sigma involvement, leadership communicated that in spite of a fertile start, there was still significant ground to clear. Doing so now would result in the best crop ever produced. No doubt partial commitment was reached from the extensive training activities provided to every player of the program team. Early training provided a clear and strong view of what was ahead and how Six Sigma would support the project. But the most significant event to convert the program team came from the customer's involvement in the Six Sigma activities.

At that time the customer had been participating only in workshops that were specifically designed to support their activities. But the customer quickly recognized and supported the value of the Six Sigma baseline activities as well as the entire Six Sigma process enhancement capability. After learning more, the customer became committed to the higher project Vision and the Six Sigma path to reach that Vision. They understood exactly how the highest quality and joint success would be reached with the Six Sigma circle surrounding the project.

According to the MoD project IPT (U.S.) team leader, "Before arriving in the United States, the Defence Procurement Agency (DPA) staff, now known as the IPT (U.S.), partook in a structured "breakthrough" process as part of a Smart Procurement initiative transition from functional-based project management to an Integrated Product

Team (IPT) structured organization, similar to that used by Raytheon. The breakthrough process had many similarities with the practices adopted by Raytheon and performed under the banner of Six Sigma. Thus, the culture of change was well underway with the U.K. contingent and [they] embraced new ways of working and interfacing with contractors [,which] was becoming widely accepted."

## Joint customer-program team training

The next step to full team commitment was achieved by holding intensive combined customer-contractor training sessions. This was quite unlike a late-start, crisis-oriented Six Sigma effort, in which there is normally reluctance to open the windows to the customer and even greater reticence to provide for customer involvement. During these early-start Six Sigma sessions it was easy to have open and honest exchange of concepts and ideas flowing both ways.

This was highlighted by the Lead of the MoD Resident Logistics Office (RLO), "A fundamental tenet of DPA's recently adopted Smart Procurement System is the need for authority personnel to work closely with contractor staff in order to satisfy taut contracted cost, performance schedule, and support parameters. Working closely does not mean working in the same building and meeting occasionally to review each other's outputs. Working closely means sitting down in the same room and adopting the Six Sigma approach to discuss, understand, or develop a plan, process, or procedure. Only in so doing will there be a joint understanding, but more importantly, a joint sense of ownership and commitment to the outcome. Additionally, it is far more efficient and effective to have worked the process jointly than to have held separate forums only to then come together at a later date to persuade one another of the relative strengths of each position.

"There may be some concerns about the contractual obligation that exists between contractor and customer and the extent to which the customer should influence and 'own' plans, processes, and procedures. Clearly, responsibility for product delivery to cost, time, and schedule remains firmly with the contractor and the sense of ownership that results from successful Six Sigma efforts implies agreement and commitment by the customer, not assumption of responsibility."

He continues, "I am totally committed to the Six Sigma process. The tangible benefits of Six Sigma are improved processes, for both authority and contractor, a greater understanding of each other's aims and aspirations, and a stronger commitment to those ideas, plans, and processes that have been derived and developed together." He concluded his remarks by noting, "Authority and contractor personnel are truly working together on the project, utilizing Six Sigma and working toward the common goal of delivering a system to cost and schedule that performs to specification and for which support has been optimized."

The customer's early commitment was contagious in this joint environment. In this case, a clear path was forged to a solid, long-term joint commitment. In fact, after completing 36 separate Six Sigma baseline efforts during the characterization step, the indications are that when an early and strong commitment can be established, it has much greater long-term strength. It also appears that a true commitment can be achieved most easily when it is possible to have extensive customer involvement.

Evidence of the strong customer support for Six Sigma on the program was signified by one MoD representative's observation that the early customer involvement was essential, "not only giving an early insight into the methods employed by them (Raytheon) in introducing improved working practices and processes, but (the early customer involvement) also formed a most important strand in building relationships and trust between customer and contractor. These work ethics complement the Partnering Protocol developed and agreed (upon) at the contract award."

# PRIORITIZE (STEP 3)

When a whole program lies before you, and there is so much work to be done to organize and begin, knowing where to begin can be a problem. What is the single most important thing that must be done first? In the case of the Raytheon program, a starting point needed to be invented. There were no examples of early adoption of Six Sigma on other programs to follow that would demonstrate the benefits and results, or even what to do first.

## Attacking the highest priority issues

Raytheon leadership identified material management as the greatest potential risk area. There were 31 major suppliers, mostly in the United Kingdom; major components being produced or integrated by different Raytheon business units (for radar and for final integration); and a total acquisition element that constituted nearly 80 percent of the total program cost.

To kick things off, the Six Sigma manager worked toward establishing a relationship with the materials program manager. The Six Sigma manager met with the materials program manager on a few different occasions and recounted lessons learned over the past 10 years of process and performance improvement efforts he had led.

Once rapport had been established, the materials program manager agreed, provided he received any necessary assistance and support from the Six Sigma manager, to use Six Sigma to define how his team and the integration team would together be able to support the $1.1 billion procurement that the program required.

According to the materials program manager, "The program is one of the largest material content programs ever won by Raytheon. From the onset it was clear that the program 'Vision' would have to be implemented with near perfect execution to achieve the profit/loss objectives mandated for the program. As material is the single largest contributor to the program financial baseline, a major emphasis was put on improving the supply chain processes by the early use of Integrated Product Development Process (IPDS) and Six Sigma tools."

He continued, "It was clear that a total materials roadmap to achieve profit targets was required...at the onset they (the 31 major suppliers) clearly did not result in a combined profit picture that achieved the planned numbers. The goal of the supply chain team was to ensure that 31 precise solutions were developed and implemented that resulted in the overall right answer.

"During the kickoff planning phase of the program, a supply chain gold team Review was conducted to lay the framework for success. This gold team consisted of senior executive management professionals from across varying company entities.

"The program 'Vision' set by the SPO was to ensure that all the best practices and combined knowledge of the company became available to the entire program leadership team at the three primary subsidiaries working the combined project. The supply chain gold team reviews resulted in strategic plans that are currently being implemented on the program."

Parallel procurement organizations were set up in the United States and the United Kingdom which worked the entire project from inception together. The concept was to ensure a smooth and seamless handoff of the project to the U.K. team upon the delivery of the first unit. Each functional position in the United States had a counterpart in the United Kingdom. Each position worked as a team with both individuals sharing responsibility for the entire procurement function, thus ensuring history and knowledge when the U.S. team transitioned everything to the United Kingdom.

The identification of sponsors is a continuous effort. Part of the process is also gathering information about programs where Six Sigma efforts were not initiated early and the eventual costs to the program in schedule slippage and rework. Simply asking someone to sponsor an event is not enough. A case for action essentially is required for every sponsor, for every event.

One of the early priorities was to involve the customer in training for Six Sigma, PDP, and IBPM with the program leadership team. The customer was then invited to be a standing member of all Six Sigma efforts. This is a reflection of the partnering agreement established between the DPA project task leader and the program management.

With customer support for the Six Sigma efforts, resistance was broken down over time, since the customer was able to recognize the value added through these activities and supported the SPO, program manager, and Six Sigma manager in their joint efforts to make it part of the culture expectation for the program.

## Building linkages across all processes

Six Sigma linkages have become an integral part of the product development process. The purpose of these linkages is to ensure the use of Six Sigma is called for throughout the program in the integrated master plan and schedule (IMP/IMS) and is not to be tailored out. It also ensures that the PDP is followed throughout the processes that have been defined and protocols deployed through Six Sigma. Again the emphasis is on early definition of processes and decision-making protocols and the continual re-examination of assumptions and data to be proactive in issue identification, analysis, and action to reduce risk to cost, schedule, and performance.

## Flexible prioritization

While the flexible approach to prioritization is by no means ideal, it reflects the reality of culture change and managerial focus on reducing immediate expense. The program was not bid with the costs associated with Six Sigma implementation built-in.

Performing these activities added unbudgeted costs to the front end. These costs have the immediate effect of reducing program profit, or so it seems to most program managers. It is difficult for them to look to the long-term costs incurred by insufficient process and decision-making definition while still early in the program. They know that final performance directly affects corporate program performance ratings for future competitions, but they do not link Six Sigma activity to improving those ratings and award fees. Those long-term factors are undefined when a program begins, and every manager hopes for the best while identifying risk mitigation plans.

The Six Sigma up-front planning and process definition gets every contributor on the same page early. It identifies risks sooner and therefore reduces the associated costs of mitigating those risks compared to finding them as errors later in the program. And nearly as important, the efficiencies gained in the improved processes are expected to show return on the Six Sigma investment at orders of magnitude greater than the cost of the workshop activities themselves.

The ideal method of prioritization may well be to take all program processes and begin with those that are immediately required for program start-up, prioritized by the impacts from the lessons learned. However, the first lesson learned from the program is that this has a low probability of success except with unusually insightful Program Management. This will remain the case until incorporation of Six Sigma in all program start-ups becomes the norm rather than the exception.

As a company, Raytheon is in a transition from business as usual to business unusual, abandoning old expectations and being open to discovering more effective means of achieving program goals.

# CHARACTERIZE (STEP 4)

After the prioritized list was laid out with the sequences established, the effort to hammer out baseline characterizations began. With the first baseline efforts underway, the program personnel became interested in understanding what benefits could be derived at this early stage. Constant reminders were forthcoming from the SPO that Six Sigma would be employed at every level for all processes and for most decision-making requirements. This drove attention to the results of the efforts. As new members joined the program team, they were trained in the Six Sigma approach and accepted it.

During the first eight months 36 sessions were conducted to define and come to agreement on processes, establish decision-making protocols, and identify barriers and solutions to achieve the program goals for cost, schedule, and performance.

The Six Sigma manager applied the lessons he had learned in performance improvement activities over the last decade to point him to the areas of greatest probable risk to program performance. The priorities shifted according to which managers would sponsor which activities, with some specifically dictated by the program chief engineer. The work-group sizes varied for the various baseline efforts from a handful to a roomful. They were always open to all interested parties. All participants attended at least some of these baseline efforts.

Since the program team was completing only the first aircraft, with the remaining production aircraft being completed in United Kingdom, initial comments from the engineering team included the ever faithful, "How can Six Sigma help me if I am only producing a single item?" When reviewing the prioritized list, the processes that support engineering activities are applied repeatedly. Many processes were iterated monthly, some quarterly, and some were, in fact, only planned to occur once during the program. But one time in the current program didn't necessarily mean the cycle didn't occur repeatedly. The support structure and processes could be applied to other program starts as the business unit aspired to, accepted, and achieved projects.

Even the "one aircraft" statement was a short-term view. One of the larger challenges associated with the program was the transfer of the production of the follow-on aircraft to the United Kingdom. Obviously, efficient and well-documented processes were a key to the successful transfer of the remaining production aircraft. Additionally, the business unit follow-on contract work would benefit from the Six Sigma processes as long as the characterization is true and the improvements are real and achieved.

## Limitation of early program data

The early start limited data collection for the characterization aspects of the program Six Sigma effort. The Six Sigma templates developed for the program could not always be supported by collected data. The program execution was just beginning. When defining the existing process for a project that is not underway, there is some difficulty in being sure that what is currently involved is appropriate in this case. It was possible, however, to characterize the business unit support processes that surround program activity and understand the resource allocation that they demand. A list of baseline processes accomplished at the beginning of the Six Sigma characterization step follows.

Preparation for these baseline efforts began late in 1999, before the contract was signed, and continue throughout the execution of the contract.

- Six Sigma baseline efforts (initial)

- Requirements flow down

- Program plan IPTs

- IPT 10 top risks to program

- Provisioning/requirements

- One database tracking system

- System readiness review (SRR)

- Radar material
- Supply chain
- Subcontract requirements
- Manufacturing, hanger, dock, and line
- Configuration management (CM)
- Quality
- Configuration
- Materials gold team
- Quality (2)
- IPDS/Integrated master plan (IMP)
- Data management (DM)
- Industrial participation
- Integrated logistical support (ILS for MoD)
- CM/DM—IPDS tailoring
- CM/DM budget schedule
- Industrial participation (IP)
- Program schedule
- CM/DM training
- Certification
- MoD certification
- ILS obsolescence
- Business unit procurement
- U.K. procurement
- U.K. subcontracts
- U.K. contracts
- ILS schedule
- Business unit MoD certification signoff
- Commercial processes (U.K.)
- Program materials flow

## Cataloging/planning process

Participating in a number of the Six Sigma efforts and understanding the importance of airworthiness to the MoD, the program system engineering manager took it upon himself to initiate with the customer a series of Six Sigma minibaselines utilizing the talents of his staff.

According to the program system engineering manager, "Airworthiness certification is a key concern of the MoD. Certification involves the coordination of requirements with multiple groups (Raytheon, DAS, local MoD Resident Project Office [RPO], MoD project staff in the United Kingdom and the testing facility also in the United Kingdom) and the accumulation of large amounts of test data. Four airworthiness minibaselines were conducted. As a result of the Six Sigma minibaseline effort, both the MoD and Raytheon have established a coordinated airworthiness certification process." Shown is the first of three sheets that were required to capture the resulting baseline information for the airworthiness certification workshops. This version of the activity flow includes the recommended improvements for the airworthiness certification process. This one sheet is included to demonstrate the efforts and expansiveness of not only this workshop, but also the detail typical in the other 36 baseline efforts.

One staff member of the MoD reflected upon this joint Six Sigma effort. "After the extremely good start to our deployment at (Raytheon) and integration into the (Raytheon) IPT structure, the IPT (U.S.) has found a cross-company willingness to maintain those links developed in the early days and use these to improve corporate knowledge and understanding. This has been no more evident than in the recent development and agreement of a qualification and certification process (see Figure 18.1).

Using the skills of (a Raytheon staff member) as a facilitator, a selected group of IPT (U.S.) and Raytheon engineers, covering aspects ranging from aircraft test, airworthiness, and engineering, was able to identify the key processes and milestones within Raytheon's normal Federal Aviation Administration (FAA) qualification process. A subsequent session was undertaken by the IPT (U.S.) staff, assisted by Raytheon's expert. The purpose was to develop the MoD process, followed by a session to understand where the two processes were common and where they strayed. The whole process was extremely well controlled, allowed good exchange of ideas and views, and as an additional benefit, provided a fast ramp-up learning experience of the necessary disciplines for achieving qualification of the aircraft for most of the participating staff within the program."

## IMPROVE AND ACHIEVE (STEPS 5 AND 6)

Results from the last two steps are projected to be significant, but they are not yet measurable. For this reason this chapter in this Six Sigma story is incomplete. However, the main purpose in initiating this story was to describe some of the details from the early stages of an early involvement effort. At Raytheon, programs such as this are executed over a long-term horizon, in this case, seven years. When the program is completed, the

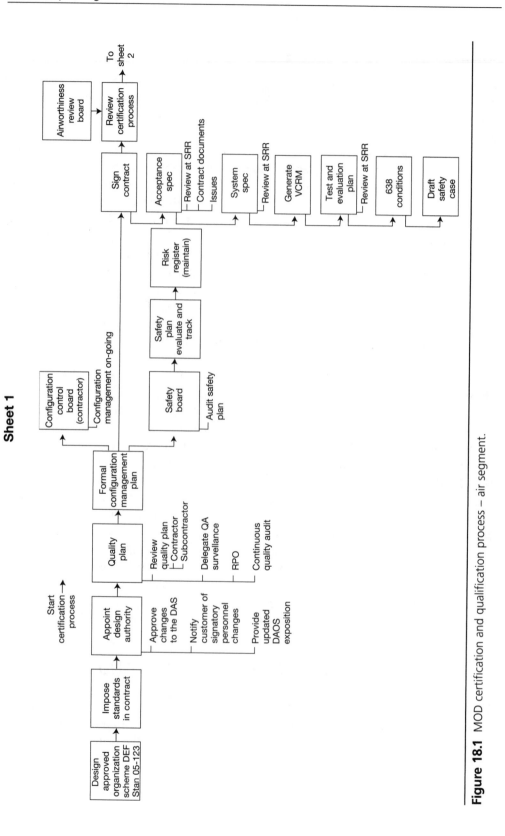

**Figure 18.1** MOD certification and qualification process – air segment.

setup and initiation efforts will have long been just a hazy memory among those who were present at the beginning.

Recording the logic and thinking behind these early efforts leads to understanding the lessons learned that enable us to replicate what is good and avoid the mistakes that lead to suboptimal program execution and final results. Showing how the Vision is translated at this early stage serves as a guide to those who must set up and initiate the next programs. Further, business development is able to glean lessons about building in early customer involvement, which leads to increased customer satisfaction and a strong predisposition to seek Raytheon as a prime contractor for future major systems acquisitions.

## Scalability

What may seem to be a unique set of requirements for the program, namely the large material subcontract content, large number of international subcontractors, midstream program transfer from the United States to the United Kingdom, and the need to work across multiple contractor businesses both in the United States and the United Kingdom, may not prove to be so unique in the future. Raytheon clearly hopes to be able to capture future programs of this magnitude and scale. This program may prove to be a template for future successful program execution. If this is in fact realized, Raytheon can expect to continue to be a major player for such international program acquisitions and executions in the future. Learning how to set up such programs and substantially reduce cost, schedule, and performance risks makes that a profitable future.

According to one staff member of the MoD, "Six Sigma has brought about a change in what was a stayed mindset, giving a means to approach any or all processes or procedures through a method of unhindered lateral group-think tanks using brainstorming. The capture of ideas and identification of issues has made Six Sigma a self-perpetuating process of corporate improvement that the IPT (U.S.) will continue to embrace."

He continued, "The skills shown to us as used in the various (Raytheon) Six Sigma projects have been adopted by the IPT (U.S.) to develop and improve staff roles and responsibilities, communication paths, and other internal processes."

Another member of the MoD RLO, added, "Six Sigma sessions have been used so far in three main areas in the early stages of the project, namely in identifying, establishing, and agreeing on processes, procedures, and best practices for Raytheon, the customer, and jointly owned problems from the start. A little invested up front should pay huge dividends later."

This member of the MoD RLO went on to say, "Benefits to date include clearer identification of complex processes required to effectively and efficiently arrive at an end product; joint understanding and agreement on related procedures; the opportunity to clarify potential misunderstandings; and the building of total project trust and open communication to resolve potential issues before confrontation, if possible. As far as the customer is concerned, the (Raytheon) Six Sigma involvement is the way ahead and full commitment is evident. Watch this space for an increase in the consumption of brown-paper and Post-it notes!"

Personal acceptance of the Six Sigma approach by the customer team members was summarized by this same individual when he stated, "(I am)…a believer in structured whole-team participation to deliver the best possible team-agreed strategy to forge a way ahead…becoming the natural (Raytheon) Six Sigma customer representative. (I have)…since very successfully led internal sessions, participated jointly in facilitating joint contractor/customer sessions, and planned sessions with (Raytheon) Six Sigma management."

## SUMMARY

Six Sigma is generally thought of as a method for recovering from poor program performance and improving overall efficiency. However, the primary benefit of Six Sigma may be realized through engagement at program commencement rather than at program crisis when the impact of error on the program is magnified.

The Six Sigma early engagement described in this chapter reveals that Six Sigma may be *most* effective when employed in establishing the processes and decision-making protocols and a culture of continuous anticipation of program needs through investigation, analysis, and rapid actions to reduce or eliminate risk to cost, schedule, and performance.

Or, in other words, an ounce of prevention is worth a pound of cure. In this example, a highly complex multibillion dollar program undertook to start off on the right foot and use Six Sigma to define how the project would unfold across more than 30 major system suppliers and a transfer of production from the United States to the United Kingdom after the first production delivery. One of the key lessons is that it does not take such complexity for an early program engagement to save the company huge amounts of money and ensure that the project schedule, which also translates into profits and follow-on sales, is met.

# 19

# Early Engagement Part II— Supplier Development

GAINING ACCEPTANCE OF SIX SIGMA BY EXTERNAL MEMBERS OF THE SUPPLY CHAIN IS THE KEY TO LEVERAGING THE RESULTS ON THE MATERIAL SIDE OF THE PRODUCT.

## INTRODUCTION

What follows is an account of a supplier day activity for a large-scale complex program at Raytheon, which Dr. A. L. Kusmanoff recorded at the time. It is reprinted here with permission as both an illustration of strategy and a "Tale of Transformation."

The gathering was unusual. The customer, Raytheon (a defense contractor), and multitudes of subcontractor suppliers were all standing by in the same room at the same time. The event was the Six Sigma Supplier Conference for a major multinational systems contract. The participants were the prime contractor, Raytheon; the customer representatives, United Kingdom Ministry of Defence (MoD); and the program suppliers from 33 separate organizations. The Six Sigma team had developed the agenda for the conference and it was designed to bring this diverse audience with many uncommon goals into alignment with a single common Vision.

The common Vision wasn't that Raytheon is the best in the world at what needed to be done in the program. Yes, that is true enough and was a message that was clearly delivered to the audience by the president of Raytheon's U.S. business unit at the time of the conference in his welcoming remarks. But that was not the common Vision.

The call to unite the diverse group into a partnering community presented by Raytheon's U.S. materials program manager was not the common Vision either. Yes, that was one of the primary objectives of the conference, and a primary result from Six Sigma activities, but no, it was not the common Vision.

And the Vision wasn't a flawless execution of the project by Raytheon's team, again, a true and realistic objective clearly expressed by Raytheon's program manager. The program was built from the starting day with Six Sigma as its superstructure and the way forward. This was more positive evidence of Six Sigma value; however, it was not the common Vision. In fact, each one of Raytheon's leaders presented results that could be expected and results that had been achieved. They were preparing the suppliers to be open and ready to participate in the Vision that was soon to come.

The common Vision was clearly projected to the diligently prepared audience at the Supplier Conference by Raytheon's U.S. supply chain vice president, and his U.K. counterpart. From their dynamic presentations the clear Vision emerged, which could simply be restated as, "There is going to be a superior supply chain developed for this program and for future projects." The details of this common Vision included the real-world key drivers of collaborative planning, continuous product improvement, relationship focus, and E-commerce linkage. The result was a total cost/best value-driven collaboration.

After the Vision statement and supporting elements were loaded and locked into the minds of the suppliers, the conference was ready to move on to the next step in the Six Sigma circle, Step 2: Commitment. Here they were offered an unparalleled opportunity to partner with Raytheon.

The Raytheon U.S. business unit Six Sigma Champion took on the challenge and responsibility of initiating everyone into Six Sigma methods and benefits. He then revealed Raytheon's commitment to deploy Six Sigma into each supplier's "home" at Raytheon's initial expense. This investment in success promised to be "a chicken in every pot" for the willing suppliers.

The Champion continued on to explain that Six Sigma brings the customer, tools, and culture from overlapping circles into alignment, creating concentric circles. This is not through purchase and absorption but rather by open collaboration. He explained how Six Sigma was successfully deployed throughout Raytheon's various business units, and had been applied to this program even before the first subcontract was signed. The results of that effort were what Raytheon's program manager had so proudly shown them during the introductions.

He continued to explain how Six Sigma was being offered to these suppliers to reach the same kinds of results. This idea brought the common Vision into sharp focus for many of the suppliers at that point. More about the kinds of support that were being offered was sampled shortly thereafter in sessions with one of Raytheon's Black Belts and Lead trainers, along with a Lean Thinking consultant. These leaders shared tools that are available, and how Raytheon wants to support its suppliers by selecting and sharing the most appropriate tools from a host of those available in the Six Sigma arsenal.

So sure is Raytheon of the results that it offers the Six Sigma training and workshops for a share of the savings from subsequent Six Sigma efforts. In making this commitment to deploy Six Sigma to every supplier, Raytheon has encouraged and empowered every supplier to climb on board to the benefit of all involved.

While Six Sigma is an important vehicle to help everyone reach the destination, the Vision still represented the destination: a superior supply chain. According to Raytheon's supply base management director, the Vision is realized through an agreement continuum, which is based on long-term relationships with suppliers through mutually beneficial goals, trust, and benefits. The suppliers then got an open view of Raytheon's selection processes and an example of an alliance agreement, which supports the supply chain Vision.

The importance of the message was well understood by the suppliers as it struck chords that they deal with every business day. Improving Raytheon's efficiency through total supply chain productivity would require these first-level suppliers to have second- and third-tier subcontractors stimulated to cost reduction practices. Raytheon's supply base director showed all in attendance that Raytheon has the will, the commitment, and the resources to engage key suppliers in their growth strategies. The Raytheon Supply Chain organization was seeking key stakeholders to participate in the rewards, and the suppliers at this conference were keenly aware that they were the prime candidates.

A sister division of Raytheon was the first supplier to stand up and show how to support the common Vision and the reward possibilities. The program manager for the radar system delivered an unmistakable message: Six Sigma works. Savings of $66 million were directly attributed to Six Sigma activities in his unit. Showing that total cost could be tempered with best product goals, $30 million of that savings was spent as investments reaching for nonmonetary improvements such as performance, schedule, and risk mitigation activities. But with an effort of only 14 months that netted $36 million plus happier customers, this was a target that each supplier in attendance could gladly shoot at in their own arenas.

Joining the program team was clearly not limited to Raytheon and the suppliers. Program suppliers were well aware of the open and strong customer relationship that had been developed by Raytheon and the program team. When the customer representatives in attendance were putting action items on the board of subcontractor's preliminary design review, it was clearly saying that something different is going on in this program. And it happens only through a combination of the unique partnering agreement and Six Sigma, as was so well articulated at the beginning of the conference.

But like all things on earth, somebody has to do the work. The presentation by the MoD resident project officer, a self-proclaimed R6Sigma (Raytheon Six Sigma) doubter at the start of the program, showed that when someone is able to witness the events and actions in place from Six Sigma application, they can be won over for good. Now leading the charge, he explained to the suppliers, his suppliers, that Six Sigma was not just an acceptable route to the destination, but also a required one. It closely parallels the MoD Smart Procurement process, and his office and personnel were not just standing back "being" the customer, but they were working jointly to make the program a success. They are now truly partners. That is the very message Raytheon's U.S. materials program manager was expressing from the start of the conference as an objective for every supplier.

To expand the value of reaching the common Vision, Raytheon's manager of business development expounded on the business that is unfolding in front of Raytheon, not behind it; not specifically more program business, but more program-like activities that will be following the program credentials in Europe and other international locations. The step of building continuous business is as important as the steps to continuous improvement are to manufacturing.

Raytheon's SPO vice president orchestrated the finale. Straight talk, straight from the top of the program. "Six Sigma is a moving train," he said. Every supplier had been selected for the program because they had met the standards in the past, and they were expected to move with Raytheon into the future. Reaching for final commitment, the SPO vice president laid it out clearly, "The train is out of the station. You [the suppliers] have the advantage for now, but you [the suppliers] need to grow to the next level with Raytheon."

Six Sigma is good business. The next budgets won't be smaller because of improved efficiencies and best-buy approaches; they will be bigger because there will be bigger piles to share, which will be driven by the multiple programs inaugurated by the program successes.

Wish you could have been there? It was an exciting one-day event and it was even topped off with a barbeque. Are the suppliers signed up to participate? One of the data link suppliers was already convinced that this was the train they wanted to ride, and they were the "first at the ticket office." They are now working closely with Raytheon's Six Sigma representatives and have developed a working partnership with the Data Link Integrated Product Team and with the customer.

Clearly moving toward collaboration, their representative expressed that Six Sigma processes and tools bring on an open view of the design, manufacturing, and especially the supply chains such that they strengthen the partnerships. It was not clear to him if it is a cause or a result, but either way, a fundamental element of the partnership that he has witnessed is fairness. The result is solving problems and mitigating risks together rather than alone.

Fairness drives long-term professional thinking as opposed to short-term dollar gains for one side at the cost of the other. Making the value grow so that the partners all gain a share of a larger-growing pot as discussed by the SPO vice president requires open fairness. The Data Link company representative attributed many factors to the fairness characteristic, including personalities and processes, but the real mechanisms that unlocked the fairness door were the tools and commitments that came with the Six Sigma business approach.

Six Sigma does not always end up with an idea no one ever dreamed of before; sometimes it is as simple as not doing stupid things. Raytheon's U.S. business unit president, who has led Raytheon's corporatewide Six Sigma efforts from the beginning, finished the conference with a simple but deep thought that helped everyone understand why Six Sigma works. He put it as follows: "Six Sigma is a structured approach which yields uncommon common sense in the way we do business."

Upon leaving the conference, Raytheon's president's powerful message was paraphrased by another supplier's Program Manager saying that he could now see how Six Sigma leads us to do what we should be doing all along, but sometimes we need a "way" to discipline ourselves to do it. The way ahead, the conference common Vision, is to be supported by Six Sigma tools and workshops. With Raytheon as a partner, he was looking forward to reaching the Vision as described, which was precisely why everyone was there in the first place.

# SUMMARY

Probably the most difficult aspect of supplier development is obtaining the cooperation and enthusiastic support of the supplier to undertake an analysis and improvement regime on their internal processes. It requires an "open kimono" that most suppliers shun, fearful that the prime contractor will not want to continue to do business with them if they are aware of just how inefficient and nonlean their operations really are.

For this reason, gaining entry to apply analytical tools and make improvements under normal circumstances is a difficult sell at best and impossible at worst. The purpose of providing this description of a supplier-day activity is to illustrate how one of the most difficult aspects of supplier development, namely obtaining commitment for participation, can be accomplished through an innovative, Six Sigma solution, a solution that can be used to convert reluctant suppliers into enthusiastic partners.

What follows is a list of tools that have proven effective in supplier development activity across hundreds of engagements. The tools are listed according to the impact they have and the stage of program execution at which they are applied.

In the illustration, the commitment was to participate in Six Sigma activities. There are, however, many different tools that can be applied to bring the supplier base into the process of overall performance improvement. These tools offer the greatest leverage when applied at specific points in the life a product or program.

The tools that have the greatest payback beginning with the conceptual design phase through field maintenance and support are:

- *Design to cost/cost as an independent variable:* Set and achieve product cost goals through design trade-off analysis.

- *Performance-based specifications:* Sets a performance specification for a part rather than providing supplier with a part number to supply.

- *Design for manufacturability:* Identify alternative design solutions to reduce design complexity; reduce design cost to build and increase the ease of manufacturing.

- *Design for assembly:* Identify design features that increase the labor time required to assemble a final product and identify lower-cost alternatives.

- *Software innovation:* Standardize cost-efficient software processes tailored to design goals and system requirements.

- *Design of experiments:* Optimize product designs or manufacturing processes through experimentation; changes variables to determine optimal performance outputs.

- *Part selection process:* Standardize on fewer parts and suppliers; reduce part count, and improve part producibility/reliability; strategies to reduce obsolescence risk; and identify and develop strategies to minimize problem suppliers and parts.

- *Design/part failure modes and effects analysis:* Identification of the elements of design or parts used in a design that have the greatest statistical probability of failure and the conditions under which failure is most likely to occur.

- *Continuous flow manufacturing:* Planning for consistent operational performance by improved product and information flow through the manufacturing cycle.

- *Lean manufacturing:* Determining a production flow that eliminates waste and derives maximum value-add to the product.

- *Agile manufacturing:* Determining methods that permit rapid redeployment of assets in response to changing product or process requirements.

- *Kaizen blitz:* A short-term, limited-objective, team effort with the objective of improving the performance of an under-performing process.

- *Process improvement:* A workshop to determine means of improving a process, bringing together process actors and redesigning to speed process flow and efficiency.

- *Acceptance test analysis:* Analyze supplier acceptance test data to identify test reduction opportunities and parameters, which drive yields.

Finally, the Six Sigma Black Belt teams that work in supplier development must understand which tools will achieve the desired results. The supplier development team must help the supplier become comfortable with the tool, the process that the tool uses to achieve desired results, and provide an understanding, prior to project commencement, of the impacts that this method of analysis and improvement will have on his or her organization.

Incentives are essential for the supplier to participate, and these must be structured carefully with knowledge of the program requirements and the supplier's individual situation. The incentives could be anything from splitting the actual savings achieved to a joint venture partnership to develop and manufacture new products. In the end it all starts with the supplier buy-in, and the level of support determines the results.

# 20

# Global Transformation—
# Lessons Learned in Europe

SIX SIGMA IS EFFECTIVE WHEN APPLIED CROSS-CULTURALLY AS LONG AS
THE BLACK BELTS AND BUSINESS LEADERS ARE SENSITIVE TO THE CULTURAL
DIFFERENCES THAT THE TEAMS ENCOUNTER.

The transfer of technology or business process improvement methodology changes radically when done outside of the United States. What works well in one country may produce substandard results in another. When the teams that perform the work are not from the culture, do not speak the language, or lack a firm grasp of cultural norms the stage is set for failure.

One Six Sigma team has, however, been successful in conducting Six Sigma-based Tactical Transformational workshops for business units, their customers, and their suppliers despite of the challenge of a foreign (to them) environment.

## TACTICAL TRANSFORMATION WORKSHOPS

The Six Sigma Tactical Transformation workshops improve business performance by having hand-picked cross-functional teams attack performance problems through structured innovative problem solving. These workshops incorporate elements from:

- DFM

- Synchronous engineering

- Lean and agile manufacturing principles

- Statistical analysis and process control

- Strategic planning
- QFD

## Summary of projects

For more than two years the U.S.-based team conducted Six Sigma Tactical Transformation workshops in several European countries. This experience led to 12 major lessons learned. But first, following are the countries and a synopsis of the results of these efforts:

- *Italy:* Design process, procurement, production planning, machine utilization and scrap, quality systems, management metrics, and strategic planning. The results showed cycle-time improvements ranging to 50 percent and cost improvements in the same range.

- *Germany:* Finance, development, and service delivery processes. Cycle-times ranged up to 85 percent reductions with significant cost improvements.

- *Spain:* Municipal services with reductions in cycle time approaching 85 percent with major improvements in internal controls, systems, and procedures.

- *Pan-European:* Strategic alignment that produced positional job descriptions, future-oriented training, and certification programs for country managers serving a U.S. multinational firm.

- *England:* Reduced cycle time for translation services by 40 percent and up to 60 percent for financial services.

The success rate was uniformly high. The results were similar across very different types of businesses, process areas, predominant languages, and cultures.

## GENERAL ISSUES

### Language/culture

The workshops in Germany were a microcosm of cultures and languages, with participants from 16 different European countries. English was the common language, but it was not the primary language for most of the participants, and it was often difficult to ensure everyone had reached complete understanding.

Cultural issues, however, were not as significant as expected. Individual behaviors typical of a particular culture were observable yet manageable as long as the workshop leader could react in a positive and supportive manner. The workshop leader needed to spend time with the sponsor and some of the participants before the workshops planning and socializing to acclimatize and become sensitized to cultural issues before commencing work.

The sponsor served to clarify meanings, and as a cultural bridge when unfamiliar phrases, similes or metaphors were used. The leader needed to question behavior in side meetings and off-line opportunities. Using gentle persuasion to keep the sessions moving until an opportunity presented itself to learn more about what was being observed seemed to be effective. In the off-line meetings the discussion focused on the impacts on the overall objectives and agenda and the needs of the individual in this setting.

## Planning

During the planning sessions, assessments of the participants knowledge of the subject matter and methodologies were developed through interviews. This shaped a portion of the discussion with the sponsor as to workshop kickoff training and the selection of proper representatives.

Interviews revealed that ISO 9000 was better understood than Lean principles, DFM, and other methodologies. Meetings with the translators were held to establish working relationships and ensure that proper understandings were achieved. Translations of final work products were reviewed for correct technical terminology.

## ISO 9000

In each case, the processes improved were the basis for ISO 9000 revisions or in some cases initial certification. The sponsor tracked implementation effectiveness on Excel spreadsheets that summarized the Task Statements of Work developed in the workshops. This provided the ISO documentation of actions taken and changes to work instructions, procedures, and processes that resulted from the workshops.

## Linkage to ERP solutions

In Germany and Italy, the workshop processes were the basis for new enterprise resource planning (ERP) computer systems implemented by the companies. The type of ERP system did not appear to be an issue, as both Oracle and BAAN systems were involved. The processes were for the most part adopted as defined by the teams.

The ERP systems coded the process steps and data requirements identified into the standard procedure. This ensured compliance. In many ERP solutions the consultants brought in to implement the systems attempted to get the company to revise how they do business to fit the standard system model. However, the model is generic and works for some businesses, but it is not an exact fit for any.

Linking the tactical transformation to the ERP solution allows the company to implement tailored optimized processes that fit the specific business and not a computer systems model.

## Linkage with other performance improvement tools

In Italy, the workshops were the predecessor activity to a job and skills mapping. This is the basis for an employee competence management system. The Predictor ™ system is a product that analyzes the organizational structure and individual positions within that structure. It serves as the basis for development of the individual position holder as well as knowledge, skills, and experience migration needed to meet emerging corporate and market needs.

One U.S. company's Rome-based training office had been successful in packaging the Six Sigma Tactical Transformation workshops, Predictor™, and a training management system as a performance improvement engine. Since many medium- to small-sized firms cannot afford to purchase each element of the package, the president and managing director in Italy offered a shared service for Predictor™ and training management, spreading the costs across multiple users. His company also provides cooperative training programs that meet requirements for member firms of regional industrial associations. Those firms that utilize the Predictor™/training management service determine the primary courses to be offered; however, the members of the industrial associations may request others not specifically meeting the company's client needs if class-size minimums can be reached.

# LESSONS LEARNED

## Transformational efforts are most effective in their native language

Translators for the consultants are effective. However, implementation is driven by the understandings of the participant team. Therefore, it is more important for the team to understand how they arrived at conclusions and the nuances of agreements than it is for the consultants.

This can be very difficult for some consultants to accept as it reduces the primacy of their role. However, in the change management process, the consultant is only a stimulus and guide and not, in most cases, the person responsible for final implementation. In addition, it is essential that the reports be produced in both the native languages of the participant team and the workshop leaders. Only when both groups have an understanding of the results can an effective implementation plan and program be created and executed.

## Decision-making in workshops must reflect the cultural norms

In Spain, the teams had little difficulty voting on alternative proposals for addressing the identified problems and issues. In Italy, the teams were careful to avoid offering divergent opinions, which eliminated the need for voting and possibly "rejecting" the ideas of one of the members. This is not a straight cultural stereotype. Within cultures there are differences that must be addressed. Thus, the workshop consultants must be able to understand the needs of the participants as a group and adjust to the decision-making processes with which they are most comfortable.

The individuals and teams in Italy assigned to plan the implementation were very comfortable taking the ideas offered and combining them into a fewer number of specific actions. These were grouped so that they encompassed the essential ideas that would produce the results desired. In other cultures and companies delegation of such authority would never have been permitted. It is almost impossible to know how different approaches will be accepted in advance. These issues and approaches must be worked out on the spot with the sponsors and participants.

## Consultants must be very flexible in workshop format and structure

In Italy, the workshops were phased with one month between groups of four workshops to provide the teams an opportunity to implement changes. It was discovered that little was accomplished in that month between workshop sessions. To address this issue, the second phase workshops were restructured to eliminate the voting. Time was restructured to spend 50 percent of the workshop time actually working on implementation issues.

This approach permitted the company to achieve 62 percent implementation completion within 120 days of completing the first workshop. The schedule permitted complete implementation closure within nine months. A construction project that needed to be complete to permit moving some functions and consolidating others recommended in the workshops limited the project completion percentages.

## Collaboration creates a stronger package

In Italy and Germany, the workshop outputs were tied directly into ERP systems and formed the basis of new work processes. In Germany, the new processes were also the basis of a successful ISO 9001 certification effort. In Italy the processes were included in a workshop-identified unification of all external certification programs such as Joint Accreditation Review (JAR) Board, FAA, Civil Aviation Administration (CAA), and others with the ISO 9001 certification documentation and procedures. Thus, instead of having to prepare for separate audits using differing documentation, employees only had a single set of requirements and procedures to follow.

## Schedules must fit the work requirements of the teams

In Spain, for example, workshops started at 8:30 a.m., broke from 10:30 a.m. until 11:00 a.m., met until 2:00 p.m., broke for siesta until 4:30 p.m. or 5:00 p.m. and were concluded at 7:00 p.m. or 8:00 p.m.. The teams would then assemble for Tapas at 10:00 p.m., go for a glass of wine or aperitif at 1:00 a.m. and then reassemble at 8:30 a.m. the next morning. One city was an hour drive from the hotel where the team was staying, which made for some short nights between sessions. Normally the workshop team preferred to keep the group together and work through lunch. This was simply not possible with the teams in Spain. Had the consultants not been flexible on these issues, the resistance within the workshops would have made productive work nearly impossible.

## Keep the sponsor involved and informed of progress and issues

In several instances, the project sponsor was able to "troubleshoot" issues that were keeping the workshop teams from making progress. In some instances the teams simply did not believe that the sponsors would actually implement or permit them to implement the recommendations that came out of the workshops. This disbelief caused the team to focus on little things rather than the systemic issues that were limiting their effectiveness.

Bringing the sponsor into the workshop and engaging him or her in the discussion opened up the sessions. It was only when the sponsor was willing to confirm the authority of the group to make such recommendations and that the management was predisposed to implement any reasonable recommendation that dialog finally elevated to systemic levels.

## Workshop teams need help in preparing the plans for action

As part of the Tactical Transformation workshops, the team developed a Task Statement of Work form that each person responsible for a specific action is required to complete prior to the end of the workshop. The task statement identifies the primary planning elements such as who, what, when, where, what will it cost, what will it look like when it is done, and what is the expected benefit. The task statements became the organizing element around the assigned actions.

The assigned individual or subteam was encouraged to combine actions as much as possible to address the essential issues that would lead to transformation. This permitted a reduction in the total actions necessary to implement, reduced the tracking required, and simplified the overall process of change. The task statements are also included in each workshop report and in the implementation manager's schedule book. A master schedule of implementation actions is produced. This is incorporated in a notebook with a copy of each task statement.

Depending on the needs of the implementation manager the tasks could either be sorted by due dates then by individual, or by individual then by due dates. The task statements are then indexed in the notebook in the same fashion.

## Give the workshop sponsor a draft of the report at the conclusion

Too often, the consultant leaves at the completion of the work and takes the information with him or her. The consultants then spend several weeks working on an impressive report to provide to the project sponsor. When the final report is received, all of the workshop participants have been back to their regular work for a month and have forgotten about the workshop activity. Then the tasks become just one more thing that must be worked into the daily routine.

When the draft report is provided immediately after completing the workshop, the individual team members are able to take their action plans with them and begin to work them. When significant actions are actually completed within the workshop, the motivation to continue is higher because the participants are able to see immediate results. Implementation effectiveness is tied directly to the motivation of employees, along with management support and follow-through immediately after the workshop.

## Approach the workshops as a learning experience for the participants

The consultants often have a tendency to see themselves as the outside experts and don't believe the participants have the knowledge or experience to do this kind of work. This attitude limits the effectiveness of the results. In each of the workshops conducted, the Six Sigma team looked for internal leaders who demonstrated leadership in the workshops and could assist the follow-on implementation. These individuals were then given opportunities to provide the leadership in the workshops and to assume increasing responsibility for the workshop results over the course of the work.

This development of the internal capability to self-diagnose and implement change is the primary means of continuing the change effort once the consultants leave. Many consultants fear that this will lead to a loss of follow-on work with this client. What the Six Sigma team has discovered is that the opposite tends to be true. Those clients that actually are committed to continuing the change processes are more likely to bring the consultants back in on new projects to help them set up, kick off and support workshops through to conclusion. Those where the internal support has not been developed tend to dismiss the efforts as only a "one-shot" event imposed from outside rather than something that they own and manage as a way to continuously improve.

## Partition the workshop into smaller packages

Things just take longer in multicultural environments. There are more issues that must be worked through than what one experiences when working in the native culture. There were many instances in the initial workshops where complaints about "that's not how we do things here" and "Americans just don't understand" were voiced in the back of the room. However, in every instance, those who were the loudest complainers were the most ardent supporters of the efforts once they understood that the transformation was really controlled by them. They took time to become comfortable that the Six Sigma team was only providing the methodology for them to look at themselves as others see them and solve their own problems.

The consulting team also became a source for benchmarking data and information on how companies in the United States tended to do things. Once the role of resource person and facilitator was understood, the pace of work accelerated. Once the adjustments to the workshop formats were made to address cultural differences and individual corporate needs, the level of enthusiasm and effectiveness rose dramatically.

## Define the data to be collected

There was clearly a desire on the part of management for the workshops to produce effective metrics and for the workshop teams to define what data are to be collected and how they would be reported to management. In some instances, management also wanted information about just what the metrics meant in terms of probable management response to changes in the metrics.

## Tie improvements to the role of management in strategic planning

When the team conducted workshops and left upon their conclusion without working directly with management as part of the effort, the results reduced over time. One very effective approach is to conclude the workshop series with an experiential learning activity such as those provided at the Raytheon Eurosite near Barcelona, Spain. This team-building experience is a perfect setting to enhance the management team communication and understanding of their roles as a team. Incorporating a workshop focused on communication and strategic planning as a part of that activity had a dramatic effect on the overall transformational activity.

# SUMMARY

This chapter provided 12 specific lessons learned by a Six Sigma team while conducting Tactical Transformation workshops in European settings over a two-year period. The primary issues are adaptation to the cultural and language differences. Many of these issues can be identified in the planning stages, but others are adjustments that must be made on the fly as the work progresses.

Management tends to want to see how everything links together. They want to see how the improvements will affect the bottom line and how they can manage the changes in such a manner that the improvement will continue and not just be a "one-shot" effort that regresses as soon as management gets involved in another issue, problem, or opportunity.

The project team members want to do a good job, but in most instances do not feel empowered. Such bottom-up empowerment is not customary in many of the countries where the workshops were conducted. It was necessary to have the sponsor reinforce the empowerment in the early workshops in order to obtain the focus on systemic issues necessary to leverage the results to the effectiveness levels desired and expected.

Six Sigma-based Tactical Transformation is an effective means of addressing the most significant pain that an organization is experiencing. It allows the firm to put the resources and efforts into the one thing that will boost performance and results immediately. Once a singular success is achieved, the firm builds the confidence that it can address other areas, usually sequentially. They see that they can be as successful in seeing further bottom-line improvements resulting from operational efficiencies, improved products, and customer service.

Six Sigma-based Tactical Transformation is also an accelerated means of inducing change and recovering the investments in making that change occur. In many instances it was seen that the workshop costs were recovered within the implementation periods following them or at least within the first year thereafter. This rapid recovery makes the investment an easy decision for most management teams and has proven to have dramatic effects anywhere it has been used globally.

# 21

# Global Knowledge Network— Forming a Cultural Bridge

SIX SIGMA PROJECTS LEAD TO INCREASING THE KNOWLEDGE OF THE ORGANIZATION, AND IT IS IMPORTANT TO CAPTURE THAT KNOWLEDGE AND SHARE WITH OTHERS.

How does an organization with global operations, customers, and suppliers make it possible for critical knowledge to flow across cultures and languages? Generally, U.S.-based multinational organizations expect their employees to be fluent in English. They also assume that their employees are able to bridge U.S. English meanings, colloquialisms, similes, metaphors, and language conventions. However, depending on the culture and language, building a bridge may be difficult, at best, if a particular point in the discussion has no relevance or comparable translation at the other end.

A second issue, long overlooked by global organizations, is the strategic capability of the knowledge flow. For example, most U.S. multinational corporations do not link employee selection and training with their global knowledge management and resulting strategic capability. An individual may be considered a "knowledge node" within a distributed system. As new "nodes" are added to the system, they bring new information and capabilities. When a "node" attends training, more new information and capabilities enter the system. When a "node" obtains market research, customer information, or conducts product research and development, even more new information and capabilities enter the system.

At some level, all of the information and capabilities of the individual "nodes" reside within the global knowledge network of the corporation. Getting the most out of these resources requires forethought, planning, creative approaches, and strategic decisions about the new capability that will result.

# CREATING CULTURAL COMPREHENSION

## Standard English

Some firms, in an effort to bridge the gaps in understanding, have adopted Standard English as the means of internal communication. Standard English is an abridged and less dynamic version of the common English language spoken in the United States that attempts to eliminate multiple meanings, use of colloquialisms, similes, metaphors, and other regional language conventions and expressions that pose problems when translated.

While spelling and grammar-checking programs exist to assist in applying Standard English to business communications, there are no programs that are sufficiently robust or configured for more complex communications for international use. To address this, linguists, in conjunction with developers, might examine business English applications with respect to commonly understood meanings of English terminology in other languages and cultures.

## Multinational translation software

Several software companies have attempted to build applications that translate text into multiple languages. At a basic level, employees gain a common means of communication. However, technical terminology and other contextual language conventions are rarely built in. Thus, essential meanings may be lost, even though the communication is in the native language of the recipient. This is more problematic than Standard English because a recipient may believe she or he received the communication as intended and the sender may not know how to verify whether the translation is accurate or meaningful, or how to clarify if necessary.

## Language/culture barriers

The most problematic aspect of the language/cultural issue is that most Americans, because of the large scale of their generally unified culture/language, have little appreciation of the vast differences in cultures and language. This leads to a presumption of comprehension that may or may not exist. Confusion is often an output of industries where fast-paced innovation is required, but acronyms abound, particularly since the first letters of the words used in the acronyms don't match their translated counterparts.

When a foreign multinational attempts to do business in the United States the problem is even greater. Most Americans are less prepared to work with cultural or language differences. If the prevailing language were to be German, it would be almost impossible for a foreign multinational to successfully communicate with an American workforce across even the most sophisticated global knowledge network.

Imagine an American firm taken over by a Chinese multinational. If that firm were to assign a managing director who does not speak or comprehend English, the result would be chaos without an interpreter. Even with an interpreter, the cultural barrier would have a severe, negative impact on the receptivity of the workforce to direction from that managing director.

Language and cultural differences will continue to be a major barrier to effective global knowledge flows for the foreseeable future. In fact, even within the United States, increasing populations, particularly in border states, do not speak English. This trend creates an increasingly urgent need for finding the "Rosetta Stone" necessary to ensure common understanding, whether across a global knowledge network or in every-day encounters in a shopping center.

One way to bridge the gap might be to have educators teach Standard English terms in English courses internationally. Another might be to have television programs world-wide begin to use Standard English so that the international form of the language becomes familiar to individuals globally.

# CREATING A STRATEGIC CAPABILITY

The second issue is the creation of a strategic capability that global knowledge flows are beginning to enable. Current literature emphasizes open systems that include customers and vendors for knowledge flows. This emphasis is beneficial in that it adds value to the end product or service by creating a lean organization. However, it ignores the internal network and the means to enhance the capabilities of those elements. As a result, precious planning resources are spent on external resources, which are much more difficult to influence and control than internal resources.

## Pulling information

Open knowledge flows provide data that suppliers and customers can "pull" from a server. This server is equipped with a security system permitting only "authenticated" vendors and customers to access the data about their accounts with the firm. Finding a means to increase the access of external parties who have a business relationship with the source firm and a need to know the posted data is the subject of many current research efforts.

As customers and vendors penetrate further and further into the transactional data of a firm, the ability to control and manage the account becomes more and more problematic. The external party does not need guides or enablers, as it is able to access what it needs to do business with the firm with minimal human intervention. While this may drive down costs, it also loosens the ties that bind customers to the firm.

## Electronic intermediary

In a strict e-commerce model, both the supplier and the customer interact through an electronic intermediary. Relationship marketing is impossible in such an environment.

Customer reaction to the product or service cannot be assessed in the subtle and nonexplicit reactions that indicate whether a continued relationship can be expected.

Instead, only the grossest reactions, a returned product or complaint, provide feedback. Frustration at any point in the process of doing business with the firm usually results in lost business, which is simply not recorded or responded to. The ability to delight the customer cannot be adequately observed or determined. The purpose of a global knowledge network is to obtain information and to interact with it in some fashion to create knowledge and understanding.

The network itself is a medium that enables knowledge creation by making information ubiquitous. Not only must the firm enable ever-present information, it must be in such a context that it has the same meaning to a person regardless of her or his culture or native language. This problem is both addressed and exacerbated by training and employee selection procedures.

## Training opportunities

Training has the opportunity to create common understandings among the workers of a global company. However, training must address commonality while being sensitive to differences. Training increases organizational capability. Training may also be strategic in that it may create entirely new capability over time.

Training produces strategic skills, knowledge, and experience within the workforce. This is best done at points that will address anticipated new products or service delivery. In doing so, the firm creates competitive advantage. The same situation occurs in new employee selection. The skills, knowledge, and experience of the new employee add capability to the distributed system of the firm by adding a knowledge "node."

All too often, the skills, knowledge, and experience of the new employee ("node") are brought in to address an immediate need of the firm and that is all. The firm does not anticipate how the other skills, knowledge, or experiences that the "node" already has may lead to new products or services. Yet it is this strategic component of new hires that creates the ability of the organization to maintain competitiveness over the longer term.

## Strategic capability migration mapping

Strategic capability migration mapping is a method to address the issue of how a firm moves from where it is today to where it needs to be in the future to be competitive in its chosen marketplace. Such mapping examines the distributed knowledge network nodes and determines the relationships among and between them. The weaknesses in the network are noted and evaluated. The most appropriate means of creating the capability that the firm needs in order to successfully compete are selected from internal development, consultants, and new hires. Then a "roadmap" that spells out the means of reaching the desired level of capability is detailed. Elements are built into outsourcing, hiring, and individual employee training plans.

Few firms evaluate the knowledge flows of the organization from the aspect of the network. Regarding individuals as knowledge "nodes" creates a new framework to evaluate how the network as a whole performs. Weaknesses in capability can be evaluated across the whole company. Interventions are targeted to increase capability and strengthen the entire organization.

Managing the firm from a "knowledge flows" perspective removes the traditional silos, stovepipes, and islands, and focuses on enabling the "nodes" on the network to access information. This provides opportunities to interact with that information in such a manner as to create knowledge while adding value to company products and services.

## SUMMARY

The more U.S.-based multinational firms increase their global efforts, the greater the efforts required to overcome barriers to successful knowledge sharing, knowledge creation, and customer satisfaction. While diversity training and awareness are on the increase in U.S. firms, language training and cultural sharing are not. The modern multinational corporation is suffering from the "Tower of Babel" syndrome. Employees in different parts of the organization may be able to use Standard English or software tools that help to translate standard words from one language to another, but lack the ability to understand each other at more complex levels. In most organizations this has not been adequately addressed or resolved, which limits organizational effectiveness.

In the ideal world, a "Rosetta Stone" would be found (or invented) that could serve as both translator (language) and bridge (culture) for global knowledge networks. Such a "universal translator" could unlock the knowledge in the "nodes" and leverage the ingenuity and insights of the entire work force.

Until that happens, training is one of the best means any multinational organization has to maximize its global knowledge flow. Training promotes understanding of and sensitivity to different languages and cultures, and helps Americans, in particular, to better embrace cultural or language differences.

# 22

# Mapping a Migration Path for the Workforce

SIX SIGMA IS EFFECTIVE WHEN APPLIED TO KNOWLEDGE PROCESSES AND
END PRODUCTS; HOWEVER, THE TEAMS NEED TO FOCUS ON TOOL AND METHOD
APPLICATION ADAPTABILITY.

## INTRODUCTION

The ability to anticipate and respond to changes in business and market environments is what differentiates the market leaders from those out on the sidelines. Market leaders have a Vision that allows them to foresee opportunities and proactively minimize or eliminate threats. Without a clear Vision, companies may stumble and fall or become stragglers in the race for market dominance and profits.

For most companies, the main focus is on inventing or improving their products or services to respond to any anticipated opportunities and threats. For many companies, this is a major undertaking. However, it is only half of the equation that leads to success. Companies with Vision also invest heavily in the developmental (migration) paths for their people, the ones who develop, market, and deliver those innovations.

A company on the winning track periodically takes a critical look at the capabilities of its workforce. Specifically, the company analyzes the gap between what will be needed to meet strategic goals and what is currently lacking in skills, knowledge, and experience to meet those goals. After the gap analysis is complete, a company might create a "roadmap" for corporate education programs that give the workforce the skills and knowledge to successfully execute the business strategy. Corporate education is a powerful tool for attaining and maintaining the competitive edge in the anticipated markets and changing general environment.

For example, in the early 1990s e-commerce skills were virtually unknown. Visionary companies were able to predict how online shopping would revolutionize retailing. Many of these companies sought or taught staff members to develop Internet applications. They were the ones providing maps to take their people from where they were to where they needed to be with the skills and knowledge that would allow them to dominate the market. Companies that missed the opportunity to develop their workforces soon found they were lagging behind in the market and constantly needing to catch up. Often the learning curve to develop the skills and capabilities internally was steep and long. To be competitive, they were forced to acquire these skills from the outside, from other firms that had already taken the initiative. This was a far more costly approach, with the added drawback that new employees still needed time to learn the business and the culture before being able to contribute to development and deployment, which, in turn, prolonged any delay in entering a competitive proposition in the marketplace.

Companies dealing with rapidly changing technology are not the only ones that need to map the current state of the workforce to the anticipated skills and knowledge for the future. When an industry is relatively static, management teams may believe that they do not need to anticipate change or find means to manage it. However, each year static industries are finding more and more competitors from other industries seeking to enter their industry. The new firms generally offer different solutions to the market opportunities than the original firm would normally pursue. Companies slow to respond to this challenge may find themselves fighting for survival rather than deploying assets to exploit market niches and opportunities.

Companies that are proactive in responding to competitive challenges position themselves to be market leaders. Part of this positioning involves creating means to map strategic migration paths to educate the workforce. Experience in this field has led to the identification of a dozen skills, tools, and capabilities that are needed to ensure the effective alignment of business strategy with the maps to follow these future-oriented migration paths. The identified skills, tools, and capabilities are listed in this chapter.

Because cost and schedule drive every training need, the focus is in tools that address the following areas:

- Keeping overall training costs contained, and demonstrating the value-add and return-on-investment for each training opportunity.

- Accelerating the process of building the migration maps and deploying the systems and content.

- Creating a just-in-time capability or laying foundations that permit rapid migration to the knowledge, skills, and experience necessary to lead markets.

- Permitting analysis of the best value for internal or externally sourced training or educational services.

- Using internal resources as much as possible to create specific applications and pathways.

Benchmarking performance against best in class and/or peer groups as reference points to understand the competitive positioning and relative changes in capability creation.

Several core competencies for migration mapping have been identified:

- Developing business cases and strategic business plans to build top-level support for educational and training investments to effect the capability migration.

- Analyzing the current learning system architecture and providing recommendations that will improve effectiveness, including investment plans and requirements.

- Developing new strategic training plans in conjunction with management to accelerate the process, and bringing in outside perspectives to test the logic of internally derived decisions and assumptions.

- Developing consultative selling models and skills among the training organizations to ensure that the training offered meets organizational needs and builds support for further investment in training.

- Determining the organizational cultural barriers to change and developing custom responses that will assist with the culture change requirements to effect capability migration.

- Analyzing current processes, either in the education and training organizations or anywhere in the company, to enhance the training investments through process redesign. This allows the company to optimize performance by deploying more effective processes and providing training specific to the new process needs. This focused approach to performance enhancement leverages the investment in training through ensuring that what is being trained is current, effective, and optimal for business results.

- Reviewing and benchmarking technology applications, platforms, and content for maximum training effectiveness.

- Planning for technology transition by creating roadmaps and investment plans to move the training systems toward technology-enhanced platforms and content such as electronic performance support systems.

- Benchmarking assessment systems and redesigning to ensure immediate application and contribution by those who complete training.

- Assisting in the design of performance-based assessment systems that demonstrate key knowledge acquisition and application ability and/or skill development.

- Planning training systems migration for those organizations seeking to implement strategic, educational, or training systems deployment.

- Analyzing and offering recommendations on governance, organizational structures, and strategic alignment of the educational or training systems deployment.

- Analyzing and offering recommendations on governance, organizational structures, and strategic alignment of the educational and training plans with stated business strategy execution.

Often an independent assessment is required of the organizational needs, capabilities, and relative investment to arrive at the effectiveness standards. These standards may be set by management or determined in cooperation with an outside consultant. Either way, the effectiveness standards are essential to obtain management support for mapping migration paths.

An outside look provides reassurance to management that "experts" have reviewed the business case for making the investment and concur that it will provide the anticipated benefits. Consultants also are able to provide the knowledge transfer necessary to develop the internal capabilities to perform the tasks associated with such a migration mapping.

For example, a Six Sigma team recently responded to a request for assistance in targeted transformation assessments and planning. The firm wished to substantially improve its competitiveness within a single year. After an analysis of eight key processes the Six Sigma team recommended specific changes to improve performance. These changes reduced the new product development process time by more than 40 percent, the machining set-up time by more than 50 percent, and reduced the scrap rate by 50 percent thus saving the firm several billion Lira per year.

Next, specific management metrics and reporting requirements were developed and integrated into an ERP system using BAAN (an ERP system brand name like Oracle). The new system enabled the traceability and selection of specific metrics needed to manage the business and determine who would collect the data, how often, and what transformation of the data was needed to create the metrics needed by management. It provided a validation that the metric would indeed indicate what the requesting manager needed to know. A discussion of the predictive capability of the metric and what movements meant in terms of management response ensured that the metrics were understood and effectively used by the requesting managers. The entire senior management team was briefed as to which managers were reviewing what metrics and for what purpose. This was done to ensure that the entire senior management team understood how the metrics were used to make informed decisions by the entire team.

After the metrics and reporting system was designed and confirmed, the firm's top management team visited the Raytheon Executive Leadership and Experiential Learning Center known as Eurosite near Barcelona, Spain. The first day of a two-day workshop focused on management team communication and teamwork through outdoor activity-based sessions. The next day miniworkshops produced companywide communications plans and set a high-level strategic plan for the following year.

Upon completion of this first phase, a Predictor™ (skill requirements analysis tool set) team conducted a job skills analysis to help the firm establish a training requirements baseline and assist in analyzing reorganizational and staffing requirements to execute the business strategy. The results of this work led to the development of a strategic training plan and deployment of a training management system to monitor and manage the investment in employee knowledge and skill development.

# SUMMARY

A company on the winning track periodically takes a critical look at the capabilities of its workforce. Specifically, the company analyzes the gap between what will be needed to meet strategic goals and what is currently lacking in skills, knowledge, and experience to meet those goals. After the gap analysis is complete, a company might create a "roadmap" for corporate education programs that give the workforce the skills and knowledge to successfully execute the business strategy. Corporate education is a powerful tool for attaining and maintaining the competitive edge in the anticipated markets and changing general environment.

This chapter recounts the experience of one firm in the use of a Six Sigma workshop approach to understanding the capability requirements of the firm from not only a workforce, but also an organizational, point of view. Once the requirements are understood, this same strategic approach permits the development of a migration path, leading the way to having the capabilities in place to reap the rewards of market opportunities.

The firm in this example has been able to evaluate the effectiveness of its investment in the migration path through improved business results. The integration of new processes into the BAAN ERP system has ensured that the process is followed and that reports of the results move immediately to the proper management team members on a routine basis. The Six Sigma team transferred knowledge and skills that have permitted the firm to continue self-analysis, manage continuing improvement efforts, and evaluate the results. This evaluation serves as the basis for replanning and adjusting efforts to lead change rather than react to it.

# 23

# Governance and Governance Transition

DEPLOYMENT OF SIX SIGMA MUST BE GOVERNED BY A TEMPORARY STRUCTURE INCLUDING LEADERSHIP TEAM PARTICIPATION WITH GRADUAL MIGRATION OF SIX SIGMA INTO THE NORMAL COURSE OF BUSINESS RATHER THAN AS A SEPARATE STRUCTURE WITHIN THE FIRM.

Even when thoroughly planned and executed, a Six Sigma transition is a highly complex, costly, and disruptive process to the organization, but the results are well worth the investment. Proper planning is the key. Without it, the transition develops a life of its own, evolving into something counter to the fundamental principles of Six Sigma.

If one believes that Six Sigma is the way to conduct business, then any team exclusively devoted to Six Sigma deployment activities must be considered, by definition, a temporary entity. The transition to Six Sigma is a culture change. Once this culture change is achieved, and the Six Sigma tools, knowledge, and methods become diffused (as standard operating procedure) throughout the organization, then the temporary entity created to accomplish the culture change is no longer required.

## GOVERNANCE

Governance is defined as the function or power to govern. In this chapter the governance organization for a Six Sigma deployment consists of the board of directors, executive council, leadership team, or otherwise named group of executives and business administrators who are responsible for the performance of the organization and the Six Sigma consultant-leaders, with various members of the Six Sigma initiatives brought in as representatives of how the efforts are progressing.

The specific duties of the governance organization are to:

- Establish and share the Vision.

- Provide structure and scope to the initial activity.

- Reward and recognize results.

- Model behaviors for the rest of the organization.

- Share research, information, and sources.

- Keep various constituencies informed of progress and verified results.

- Prioritize and maintain the focus on measured results.

- Set policies.

- Set standards.

- Set goals.

- Appoint personnel.

- Authorize resources.

- Evaluate effectiveness.

- Conduct third party evaluations of program effectiveness.

- Participate in benchmark studies.

- Approve recommendations for changes or modifications.

- Take early appropriate actions in response to deployment developments.

## LEADING BY EXAMPLE

Even before, or concurrent to, creating a temporary entity to deploy Six Sigma, the Leadership Team needs to first create and then share the Vision of what a Six Sigma culture means to the firm, shareholders, customers, employees, and suppliers. The Leadership Team creates incentives for all levels of management to adopt Six Sigma concepts and pursue rapid implementation. Then the Leadership Team leads by example, learning how use Six Sigma to set policies and goals, and demonstrating its use in everyday business decisions.

The Leadership Team charters a team to deploy Six Sigma. Responsibility for changing the corporate culture does not, however, shift to the deployment team. The Leadership Team retains responsibility while simultaneously empowering the deployment team to manage the resources necessary to complete the projects that will lead to organizational success.

Upon the completion of the Six Sigma deployment activity, the deployment team is expected to be absorbed into the Leadership Team of the organization. This elevates the continued use of Six Sigma as a way of leading the organization and conducting business once the initial deployment effort is complete.

## THE DEPLOYMENT TEAM

Six Sigma teams are made up of cross-functional representatives from within the organizational structure, and Six Sigma "consultant-leaders." The consultant-leaders are empowered and specifically authorized to lead the team to gather data, analyze the data, and select optimal opportunities to achieve performance improvements, and then move forward to implement them.

The deployment team has much the same structure. Consultant-leaders are designated by the Leadership Team to select and train others to become consultant-leaders and at the same time begin the process of qualifying large blocks of employees as Six Sigma Green Belts. Green Belts are those individuals who retain their regular positions within the firm, but are trained in the tools, methods, and skills necessary to conduct Six Sigma improvement projects either individually or as part of larger teams.

The analyses and projects are the hands-on training grounds for the newly minted consultant-leaders. While this is a modified train-the-trainer approach, those who are taught on-the-job are more effective more quickly than those who attend classes and conceptual demonstrations but are not charged with conducting activities and evaluated on the results that they achieve in applying toolsets, methods, and the new skills that the company is investing in them.

The governance council established to oversee the deployment must consist of the key executive officers along with the deployment team leadership and several representatives of the Black Belt and Green Belt community.

The key executive officers are there for the purpose of learning what is going on with Six Sigma throughout the organization, and not just their part of it. They are there to commit resources and to break down barriers to implementation. They are there to practice being a Six Sigma Leader, using the tools, methods, and skills in the decision-making process of deploying Six Sigma.

There is also a competitive element to the participation of the key executive members. The CEO can gauge the effectiveness of individual leadership team members in rolling out Six Sigma efforts in their organizations and can also observe their individual use of Six Sigma. Discussions and demonstrations about Six Sigma increase the whole team's overall knowledge of what is possible, as well as what they are capable of actually achieving individually.

Black Belt and Green Belt representatives bring the voice of those attempting to make the transition to the council table. Their involvement needs to be short term so that input from different parts of the organization can be heard and a balanced picture be allowed to emerge regarding the effectiveness of the deployment effort. If any of these

Black Belt or Green Belt representatives remain too long, it becomes more about power than about representation and objectivity.

At least one "outside" member, not a consultant but rather a business leader from an outside company familiar with Six Sigma, can serve as the "voice of reason." Even better are outside members from suppliers or customers who are applying Six Sigma in their organizations. They can offer an objective perspective of those already familiar with what it takes to deploy Six Sigma with realistic stories about the results to expect. Such outside voices tend to bring objectivity to what rapidly becomes a "political" environment as new empires are being established at the very moment that others are being destroyed.

The deployment team consultant-leaders are able to use the council forum as an opportunity to train the business leadership team in the Six Sigma tools, methods, and skill sets. This training is in preparation for the time at which the Leadership Team will be given sole responsibility for leading using Six Sigma, not only in the council, but also as leaders of the company or organization.

For organizationwide credibility, the leadership must use Six Sigma tools and methods in conducting its business. Each action the Leadership Team takes must be accompanied by the analysis of data collected. No major action should be taken without a reasonable amount of data upon which to base the decision.

In the real world, however, the leadership is often required to take actions based on preliminary or incomplete data. This is acceptable as long as the probable implications to using the limited data are explored. Then the additional required data needs to be gathered and analyzed; if the subsequent data imply that a change of course from the original decision is needed, then the new action should happen without waiting for the next governance council meeting.

## TRANSFORMING THE TRANSITION

In many organizations the Six Sigma deployment comes as a result of the acquisition of a business unit or company or a major restructuring effort. In such cases, the integration aspects of Six Sigma become extremely important and must be carefully considered and planned.

When talking about restructuring an organization, the discussions are not restricted to moving boxes around on the organization chart. They often include such radical actions as discontinuing products or whole product lines, adopting new strategies within a market such as moving from a high-priced, high-quality product manufacturer to a global multichannel marketer of a range of products that are not only made by the company, but also by competitors and companies not even in the market space yet. Through these discussions and negotiations, the governance council has the responsibility to set policy and direction, including how the Six Sigma deployment will be used toward creating a unified culture.

When merging organizations are put on the common turf of Six Sigma and are provided the tools to look at how they are performing their work and measure the results of these efforts, barriers begin to fall. Rivalries are set aside and a common sense of leadership emerges. The cross-functional teams know they are being evaluated in how well they can perform as an integrated team. Failure becomes a career-limiting situation for all involved.

That is not to say that everyone in the organization can be aligned on implementation teams. Clearly there will be competition to show results, hoping that this will lead to the senior spots in the integrated business unit management teams. In the end it all comes back to leadership. Those who quickly learn the Six Sigma tools, methods, and skills will be those most prepared to lead in ambiguous situations and therefore rise to the leadership of the business unit.

## ORGANIZING THE REINVENTION

Remaining competitive requires organizations to continually reinvent themselves. Those that are most successful remain leaders in their markets much longer than those that do not, unless the markets are regulated and competition not a factor. However, even regulated industries have come under the legislative knife in recent years and are opening up to competition.

Six Sigma provides a structured, organized approach to such reinvention efforts, changing the way decisions are made, and forcing them to be based on data and analysis rather than precedent, increment, and "windage" factors.

The governance council has the tools to gather data, analyze, and make decisions about the reinvention of the company, the integration of new organizations, and restructuring organizations within the larger whole.

While the senior business leadership conducts the normal analysis of the numbers indicating operating results, the council has the ability to use other data gathered and analyzed as a result of the Six Sigma efforts to delve deeper than the control systems and illustrate the issues that surround the traditionally reported results. Once a more complete picture comes into view it is possible to determine the root causes of the current results and from there identify and implement opportunities that lead to performance improvement.

## GOVERNANCE TRANSITION

Once the deployment has been undertaken, and increasing numbers of Black Belts and Green Belts are reporting significant improvements in business operations and customer satisfaction, what happens to the governance structure? The original charter was time limited. The expectation was that the governance council would begin to lead the organization as Six Sigma business leaders. However, one thing essential for the governance council to verify before the structure is dismantled is the validity of the results that are being reported.

## Validity of Six Sigma reported results

Verifying the validity of results can be tricky because cost avoidance is extremely difficult to measure. Estimates of "potential" results are appropriate when a project has not yet been conducted and a decision must be made in terms of prioritizing resources to conduct the work. However, many firms do not take the extra step of validating and verifying that the estimated results can actually be accounted for in the operating results of the organization. If it cannot be measured, it generally does not achieve what is hoped for. Only that which can be measured should be reported. What is reported must go into the financial reporting systems of the organization and be visible within the results because Six Sigma results become the yardstick of long-term corporate performance improvement, especially for the external financial community.

Yet measuring Six Sigma success is considered difficult, inaccurate, and unreliable by the internal financial leadership in many of the firms that employ Six Sigma teams. They often report that they have difficulty reconciling the financial claims resulting from Six Sigma efforts with the performance data reported by their financial accounting systems. This happens when Six Sigma teams are focused on "cost avoidance" efforts rather than the actual hard-dollar savings that are measured by the accounting systems.

It is not possible to accurately measure what is avoided. The core of the problem is that the costs that were avoided are "potential" costs and not real costs. Would normal program management activity have eliminated the costs that were thus reported? How does one know that such costs would even have been incurred if they were only possible or potential costs?

Basing results solely on cost avoidance is totally inconsistent with the concept of data-driven decision-making and should be anathema to Six Sigma practitioners.

The crux of verifying the validity of results is to know what was measured and how it was reported. Whether it is time or money, cost avoidance is, at best, an estimated impact that is based on a "reasonableness factor." However, with no precise starting or ending points, the margin of error is infinity.

Understating the cost and inflating the results through a "reasonableness factor" permits Six Sigma organizations to use "cost avoidance" to build bureaucracies that add little or no value to the overall improvement effort. In fact, these bureaucracies have exactly the opposite effect by introducing waste into the very system that was originally put into place to eliminate waste.

The most accurate and desirable approach is to measure the initial cycle-time and/or cost and the final cycle-time and/or cost of a process or system and determine the difference as impacted by the Six Sigma activity. This can be reported as "hard" improvements. However, the desire for immediate reporting often drives Six Sigma teams to estimate the changes and report the estimates rather than wait for the real data.

Estimation is appropriate, but only if a means to capture the actual data and report the estimate versus the actual is implemented at some future point in time. Unfortunately, in the author's observation, this loop is rarely closed and estimates are often the only reporting that reaches the managers and analysts. Thus, it is up to the governance council to verify the validity of reported results before transitioning the Six Sigma effort.

## Avoid creating parallel structures

Governance councils must make every effort not to develop parallel structures that operate outside the normal business organization. Black Belts and Green Belts need to be part of the organizations they serve. The leadership needs to be the leadership of the organization they serve. Deployment consultant-leaders need to return to their respective organizations or take on new leadership assignments when the deployment task is completed.

The reason for the new leadership assignment is the need to reward and recognize the efforts of these emerging leaders. Making Six Sigma-dedicated activity a route to promotion and increasing leadership responsibility is one means of ensuring a rapid and successful deployment. Publishing and sharing the research and independent thought of Black Belts and Green Belts across the organization is another means of reward and recognition. Whether it is in the form of a published journal of Six Sigma research for the firm, or a shared Web page, the results can be the same. In some firms a printed document carries much more weight than a Web summary or even a copy of the entire research piece, because a hard-copy document carries with it a sense of permanence that is not available from a Web page that may be changed at any time and is only a short-term sharing tool.

The rewards and recognition needs to not be limited to Black Belts and Green Belts, but also be given to the Leadership Team members who personally demonstrate their use of Six Sigma tools, methods, and skills in the decisions made and the results that are achieved. When the Leadership Team members lead through modeling behaviors then the whole organization is aligned with an initiative much more rapidly. This demonstrated commitment and personal use is a strong message to the organization that what they are asked to do is something the leadership team embraces, believes in, and is personally doing in their everyday activity.

Once the organization has transitioned to a point where Six Sigma is stable and producing the anticipated improvement in performance, what then is the role of the governance council? Is Six Sigma the only initiative that the organization will ever embrace in the quest for improvements? As long as customers learn about different tool sets and methodologies that enhance performance and results, it is unlikely. Therefore, there will probably be a continuing need to have an organization that performs the same governance oversight for such additional activity.

Some examples of other performance improvement efforts are the movement to higher levels of the SEI-CMM. For some firms it might even be related to obtaining ISO certifications. For aircraft manufacturers it may be certifications for the various certifying bodies such as the FAA or the CAA or others.

Making the transition to assuming oversight of other improvement activities begins with the need to add or change some of the personnel. However, it remains important to continue to invite outside personnel who can provide an objective perspective to participate. These outsiders can provide the "voice of reason" that often gets lost in political bodies, especially those in transition.

# LEVERAGING THE SIX SIGMA INITIATIVE

The rest of this chapter reviews the current strategic situation of various initiatives, needs, and systemic issues that have a relationship to the strategic capability creation and coordination mission of the training organization.

In addition, a discussion is included of the opportunity that the proposal for a Six Sigma council could provide for migration, evaluation, and analytical and coordination reviews to encompass not only Six Sigma, but also the wider role of the training organization in respect to other initiatives and within the company as a whole.

## Needs Assessment

The company identified that it needed to create a vehicle for the systematic evaluation and adjustment of the Six Sigma initiative to ensure that it continually met the needs of the company as a whole. One "gap" was the lack of coordination between the various business segments and units to ensure that individual Six Sigma efforts yielded the greatest total company payback.

Thus, a key role for the proposed council was to leverage companywide assets to achieve the greatest payback for the investment in the Six Sigma effort. An important early adopter in the Six Sigma effort was the training organization, which had a companion mission to achieve the greatest return on the investment in the workforce. With both roles in mind, the Advance Planning and Strategic Integration Council was created to make the transition, at an appropriate point after completing the deployment of the Six Sigma, to play a similar role for all of the initiatives across the company, becoming the strategy development, alignment, and coordination body for the training organization.

Thus, the council was created to coordinate the various initiatives, evaluate the effectiveness of the enterprise capability creation investments, and provide insight and direction on how to continuously improve and target the investments in the areas of greatest payback leverage.

## The charter of operations

A model concept of operations (ConOps) is included in Appendix H for reference. This document details the creation and operation of such an *Advanced Planning and Strategic Integration Council*. Although the format as presented is used primarily in military organizations, a similar structured approach can easily be adapted to nonmilitary organizations.

In this example, the council was the temporary organization chartered by leadership to deploy Six Sigma across the organization. The ConOps document is the framework and operating "charter" provided by the leadership.

Although the specifics of the operating "charter" may vary from organization to organization, it is crucial that the "charter" be provided in writing and sufficiently detailed for the leadership to be able to define and direct how the Six Sigma deployment team will operate. In addition to the charter, the leadership needs to prepare a detailed budget and schedule prior to commencing Six Sigma operations. In large organizations, or instances where members of the Six Sigma deployment team are new to the company, resumes of the deployment team may also need to be provided to allow the Leadership Team to become comfortable with the qualifications of those recommended to transition into the leadership of the organization.

## COUNCIL ROLES

Through membership in the council, the training organization became authorized to rapidly expand its operations to meet a more significant and strategic requirement of the company. This newly defined role made the training organization a prominent leader in the development of internal capability to:

- Enter new markets.
- Win a greater percentage of the business opportunities the company chooses to pursue.
- Train the right people, in the right skills, knowledge, and experience to provide the desired products and services at the right price when the customer wants them.

Building this type of internal capability required a clear picture of how the leadership, at all levels, perceives threats and opportunities to the company:

- In the global marketplace
- Internally in our operations
- Among the workforce
- In the technologies we develop and apply to our products

Creating this clear picture required time and the involvement of leadership in working with the training organization staff to develop an understanding of what was needed, and in creating and reviewing roadmaps that the training organization would use to transition the company capability to align with the expected operating realities, both in the near- and long-term anticipated future.

## CURRENT INITIATIVES

Significant initiatives were pervasive across the company. Among them:

- *The Engineering Restructuring Program*—creating and deploying an entirely new approach to the PDP.

- *The Enterprise Resource Planning*—deploying the SAP business management and reporting tool sets. The objective of this initiative was to bring all business units together through a common business management and reporting tool set, which is neither a short-term nor an inexpensive process.

- *Six Sigma*—reducing cost and cycle-time while improving product quality through systematic reduction or elimination of defects and application of innovative business processes that result in breakthrough change in how we approach our customers, and develop and manufacture or deliver our products and services.

- *Leadership Training and Development*—defining the specific training leadership needs in order to effect the changes resulting from the other initiatives, and lead the way to superior market performance for each individual company operation and the company as a whole.

## Other Needs

In addition to the formal initiatives already listed, there are many other needs for assistance from the training organization that were identified:

- Consistent and dynamic training for program management.

- Innovative training for new business pursuit personnel and teams.

- Best-practice reinforced process-oriented training for capture teams.

- Consistent and integrated training for each engineering discipline.

- Programs that encourage higher-level knowledge, experience, and skill attainment among support personnel in all areas to increase expertise and flexibility.

- Supervisor/manager training. A critical element is to select integration efforts that help individuals identify with the Vision, mission, and goals of the company. This effort is oriented such that employees identify with the company rather than their legacy organizations and can visualize their role and future with the company. The elimination of disidentification (not understanding the individual's role in the future of the organization) reduces employee turnover and increases employee morale.

## Systemic Issues

At the same time, there were systemic issues that needed to be addressed to ensure the effectiveness and leverage the return on the investment being made in capability creation. Among them were:

*Knowledge management, sharing, and reuse:* Systems were under study to break down the geographical and time barriers to knowledge capture, management, and dissemination across the organization. Targeted knowledge needed to be ubiquitous for company personnel to leverage investments made in developing knowledge, skills, and experience in one area to profitable applications in others. Such efforts needed to be encouraged, but they also needed to be coordinated and integrated as research and learning facilitation channels and tools, which is a natural role for the training organization.

*Application of new learning technology platforms:* Systems such as Electronic Performance Support Systems (EPSS) provide just-in-time training and reference capability for employees right at their workstations. This was broken down into Web-based instruction for knowledge component requirements paired with instructor-led experiential and application-based instruction for skill development. Investment in the research, design, and development of such tools was essential to reduce on-going workforce capability creation costs. Assessment needed to be integrated and performance-based. This was a significant change from the way most organizations conduct evaluations. The training organization was the natural entity to take the lead in developing such performance-based assessment tools and capabilities along with rational means of understanding what such assessments mean. The company could no longer accept a check-the-box approach to accountability and expect to achieve world-class capabilities and performance.

*Level 4/5 accountability:* A system was needed to understand the most efficient and effective investments. As seen at Dell Computer and other companies, such systems provide management with the information needed to target the investments and reposition training and experiences to maximize the value-add that is realized from each component of the overall training objective being addressed. Such systems are also needed to track the effectiveness of the investment over time to understand the true value-add.

*The need for a Company Press:* The company took the opportunity to recognize employee contributions to knowledge creation and technology development through the publication of employee technical papers, success stories, and outstanding achievements. A company business journal with some technical papers interspersed with success stories and articles about unique products, capabilities, or services not only helped create a positive image of the company amongst the workforce, but also became a business development tool when provided to customers and prospective customers. Very few people in the company had been aware of the full range of capabilities the company possessed or the successes that it routinely achieved. The Company Press featured articles from employees and experts in business, including an internal business journal, and also published technical papers on technology and related topics that were presented at conferences both internal and external.

## THE MIGRATION

At the point in time when the Six Sigma deployment efforts were considered complete and the responsibility of the council broadened, it was appropriate to rename it to the Advance Planning Council. At that point in time, the council membership was reconstituted to remove some of the Six Sigma-specific participants and add members from some of the other initiatives to more adequately reflect the breadth of activity for which the council was responsible.

The sponsor for this council was the vice president of companywide training organization. The vice president had an enterprisewide responsibility and therefore legitimacy to request the participation of the key individuals needed.

# SUMMARY

When Six Sigma is new to a company, temporary structures are created to manage that deployment. Governance of that effort becomes critical to the success and effectiveness of the resulting change in organizational structure, behavior, and commitment of organizational resources.

If one believes that Six Sigma is the way to conduct business, then any team exclusively devoted to Six Sigma deployment activities must be considered, by definition, a temporary entity. The transition to Six Sigma is a culture change. Once this culture change is achieved, and the Six Sigma tools, knowledge, and methods become diffused (as standard operating procedure) throughout the organization, then the temporary entity created to accomplish the culture change is no longer required.

The overarching organization that leads a company and also governs the Six Sigma operations within an organization evolves once the Six Sigma deployment efforts are complete. At that time, the deployment team is often absorbed into the leadership team of the organization. This elevates the continued use of Six Sigma as a way of leading the organization and conducting business.

Six Sigma is all about deriving the maximum value from corporate investments to add to the annual operating results. The investment in deploying Six Sigma is not small. To simply discard the infrastructure created to manage and govern the deployment is waste as defined by any Six Sigma analysis. So what is the alternative? Transition the assets and capabilities to provide value for other "initiatives."

This chapter overviews governance approaches and issues. It reviews the transitions that might occur when success has been achieved. Finally, it provides ideas and concepts on how to extract additional value from the investment made in deployment capability that has been established.

# 24

# The Myth of Measuring
# Cost Avoidance

Measuring the results of Six Sigma efforts must meet the Six Sigma
test for data that leads to facts and must be integrated as part of the
normal business accounting procedures and methods.

This chapter precedes the book's conclusion as a cautionary note about using cost avoidance as a measure of Six Sigma effectiveness.

## COST AVOIDANCE IN PROGRAM MANAGEMENT

The first question that comes to mind when discussing cost avoidance is, "Why is cost avoidance a Six Sigma activity in the first place?" The responsibility and bulk of the activity undertaken to avoid cost overruns are traditional engineering and program management tasks.

The issue stems from the sheer number of programs that have been unable to effectively manage risks and deliver the profits expected when the programs are initially bid.

This has caused many to speculate that the training and experience of engineering and program managers in many firms is not sufficient to control large-scale program risks. Deferring the responsibility for managing program risk to Six Sigma Black Belts is an admission that new tools are needed to achieve the expected results.

Raytheon has undertaken such a front-end optimization of processes and training on a recent large-scale multinational effort. While program management estimated that approximately $50 million in savings are expected over the life of the program, it will be seven years before anyone knows whether the investment will yield the expected results. Unless there is a dedicated follow-through, the measurement of those results will not be accurate. Even then, unless there are objective criteria established now that will still be in effect in seven years, the results will be open to interpretation.

Long program life puts the tracking and observation of results over the time horizon. This causes most program managers to decide not to fund those activities that could have a beneficial long-term impact on the program results. The rationale is that the payback is achieved far into the future while the investment is immediate. Program managers often do not have reason to believe that they will still be with a program when it concludes. Thus, even if results are tracked, the consequences fall to another program management team, while criticism for immediate investments without immediate returns fall to them.

## MEASUREMENT, REPORTING, AND ADMINISTRATION

Most large companies are organized around programs or products. As such, a dedicated management team works to maximize profitability through development and installation of control systems that produce predictable results. The area where Six Sigma appears to have the greatest opportunity to impact those profitability and predictability factors is in program/product management. While traditionally Six Sigma has been an engineering discipline, a singular engineering focus limits the overall impact that Six Sigma can bring to bear on organizational performance.

Six Sigma is most effective when the customer is involved in the design, development, and implementation of the Six Sigma projects. In an example cited earlier, Raytheon involved its international customer throughout the process definition phase. Thus, the customer teams were "in sync" with the contractor teams as to how the program would be commenced, managed, and controlled to ensure the expected results.

Program management also has a total effort vision that includes all of the support services, including those that interface directly with the customer such as billing and collections, supply chain, legal, contracts, and quality. The management of these areas will impress the customer either positively or negatively. Each of these areas contributes to a firm's overall cost basis and provides opportunities to achieve the expected profitability.

Thus programs and program management should be the focal point for all Six Sigma activity. Programs should fund the cost of all Six Sigma efforts and supply the expertise. Programs have the ultimate responsibility to report results to management and, if Six Sigma is an extension of the program, the reporting is also integrated.

This proposal goes further than just suggesting that each program have a Six Sigma Black Belt assigned. The individual responsible for Six Sigma should not only be trained and experienced in the tools and methodologies, but within the program should have responsibility for the following areas:

- Risk reduction to protect anticipated profits

- Winning new business to ensure future profit opportunities

- Performance and productivity improvements to realize immediate profit gains

*Program risk* is the greatest potential threat to "making the numbers." Six Sigma tools and methods are particularly effective in reducing program risk because they focus on actual and verifiable data to base decisions upon. The data may readily be captured on the program or may result from designed experiments. Thus, resulting risk mitigation efforts can be focused, tailored, and data-driven. This has the greatest chance for successful mitigation.

Program risk reduction translates into ensuring expected profit and is measurable through the risk evaluation methodologies used in program performance reporting. Program performance becomes the measure of Six Sigma impact in that risk factors do not come into play and the program margins are realized or exceeded.

*New business acquisition* becomes a Six Sigma effort in that application of Six Sigma tools to the conceptual product design effort identifies early the areas where cost and schedule have the greatest probability of being improved. This leads to more aggressive bids, technology enhancements or breakthroughs, and increased success in program acquisition.

New business acquisition translates into additional bookings and backlog leading to new and additional profit opportunities and, therefore, a more secure future for the program team and the corporation. Six Sigma impact is measurable in that the basis is the factored forecast and the improvement over that forecast resulting from improved proposals and bids.

*Productivity improvements* are the traditional activities that one thinks of in conjunction with Six Sigma; however, they probably afford the lowest overall continuing results of the three areas over the length of the program itself. Low-hanging fruit provides the initial gains in cost and schedule improvements. However, when the low-hanging fruit is gone, the increasing efforts to achieve results become ever more costly to achieve until breakthrough opportunities are identified. Diminishing productivity results divert attention from other areas where more substantial gains can be achieved.

When DFSS becomes a core element of the PDP, the designs are more capable of being manufactured, and much of the schedule and cost overrun issues are dramatically reduced. Thus, DFSS reduces even further the need for activity focused on productivity gains as the factors that limit productivity have been removed with the initial design.

Productivity improvements translate into varied immediate profit results. Reduced cost increases the margin for fixed price contracts; however, it reduces the margin on cost plus contracts. The opportunity created by reduced cost on cost plus contracts is improved competitiveness and opportunities to sell enhancements or additional products to the customer. This may lead to further new business opportunities, although frequently not within the current budget or fiscal year. Thus, for cost plus programs, Six Sigma improvements must be factored against goals and results to provide the incentive to give up today's bookings, sales, and profits to gain greater bookings, sales, and profits in future years.

# COST PLUS ENVIRONMENTS

Where cost plus contracts are concerned, program managers have a tendency to push back indicating that Six Sigma efforts undermine their current results. The effect is a lowering of projected sales and profits by taking cost out of the program effort. This observation is accurate, but the logic fails for two reasons. When a program has a cost plus effort and does not attempt to find opportunities to take cost out of the effort, the customer will eventually move the program to a firm that proposes opportunities to save money.

The second logic failing is that if a program cost can be reduced, money should be sent back to the customer. If the Six Sigma team is focused on new business, however, a proposal for enhancements or new functionality should be presented that will keep the program within budget, but add desirable features/functionality. This approach will have a beneficial result in locking competition out through keeping the offering cost competitive and at the same time providing the customer with greater functionality/features than originally expected. The intent is to delight the customer and build loyalty.

As stated earlier, management must be willing to provide offsetting relief from goals and objectives for the organization to "defer" sales and profits from this quarter or year into future years through the Six Sigma efforts. Thus, to maximize Six Sigma improvement, management must factor Six Sigma reductions against goals and objectives to provide increased incentives toward the efforts that lead to next year's improving results. If Six Sigma is truly an investment in organizational performance, the incentives must align with an investment and deferred returns.

# REPORTING AND TRACKING

Large programs have periodic business reviews. This is the forum in which Six Sigma results are most logically reported. Reporting specific improvements in risk reduction, new business acquisition, and productivity improvements all focus on bottom-line performance. Six Sigma is most effective when it is the way in which programs/product lines are managed. It is the application of data-driven decision-making that leads to overall performance improvement.

The results that are reported must be able to be taken to the bank. The results should reflect hard dollars that drop to the bottom line. Anything less is not real savings, is illusory, and misleads management into creating waste, sustaining waste, and supporting less-than-optimal program performance.

# A TRAINING PERSPECTIVE

One perception mentioned earlier is that many program and engineering managers do not have the tools to effectively manage large-scale programs. If, in fact, Six Sigma provides additional tools to aid this effort, then the proposal offered herein creates an exceptional training ground for lead program and engineering managers. The focus on bottom-line results and the application of data-driven tools and decision-making approaches creates the right focus for effective engineering and program management.

## SUMMARY

When program managers begin to use Six Sigma tools and processes to systematically reduce and eliminate the risks and barriers, they will be able to consistently help their organization reach program goals and profitability. When applied across the organization, tools such as DFSS and others that result in highly competitive product or service offerings increase the probability of winning new business. The ability to better analyze and restructure work processes and approaches result in improved cycle-times, and therefore lower the cost to perform or increase capacity and throughput, which increases bottom-line results.

When the program manager can delegate the measurement of Six Sigma efforts to the financial organization and integrate the results into monthly or periodic business reviews, the action follows the lean principles of Six Sigma, and thus eliminates non-value-added cost to program administration. Actual cost based on accurate data is the desired result. While projects may have an effect that helps the program avoid costs that it might experience otherwise, this is not the focus and should not be included in the results, because those effects are not accurately or consistently measurable. They are also normal program management responsibilities that should be tracked through established program reporting procedures, and force the Six Sigma community to focus on real bottom-line improvements.

# 25

# The Six Sigma Journey Continues...

LEADERSHIP EFFECTIVENESS IS THE MOST IMPORTANT ASPECT OF ORGANIZA-
TIONAL TRANSFORMATION THAT OCCURS WHEN SIX SIGMA IS DEPLOYED.

The premise of this book is that Six Sigma is a journey of leadership development. Six Sigma as a model for leadership training provides practical, hands-on experience in how to achieve dramatic results through the application of specific tools and methodologies on a consistent basis, while working with cross-functional teams.

Every reader has a different starting point, yet every individual in an organization that embraces Six Sigma has a tremendous opportunity to develop leadership skills that will help the organization successfully weather the storms of rapidly changing competitive environments.

The conclusion the author draws from the observations he has reported in this book is that Six Sigma is the most powerful tool set he has used in working with organizational management and Leadership Teams to enhance or improve performance and results. The key is in getting the Leadership Team to model the behaviors. Only then will the organization adopt and learn to adapt Six Sigma to obtain optimal performance.

Nothing is static. No tool set is ever complete. No methodology, even one as robust as Six Sigma, is impervious to improvement. The author describes many adaptations to the "classic" Six Sigma methodologies. Their effectiveness is recounted in the various chapters of this book. What the reader does not see is the constant adjustment in methods that were made. Every process, tool set, and approach to Six Sigma teams was a customization of the classic method. Recognition must always be given to the uniqueness of the organization and team members working the business analysis or projects.

The most successful teams were those that willingly invented as they went. Those who were willing to try something new usually achieved much more than those who wanted only to follow the prescribed steps and continually check to see if they were doing it right.

Six Sigma requires significant planning, data gathering, and analysis even before the team activities start. The more structured and prepared the Six Sigma Black Belts and Green Belts, the more effective the time spent and the higher quality the results. While this may seem contradictory to the assertion that the most successful teams were the most inventive and willing to try something new, creativity is essential to learn the boundaries of tools and methodology effectiveness and application. Once inside the project or analysis, the drive for facts must be unrelenting. The methods of finding those facts must be well understood and agreed upon by all participants, or they will not trust the results.

All business leaders and members of a corporate or organizational leadership team should, in the author's opinion, become a Six Sigma Leader. If they were, there would be no need for the government to set accounting standards or legislate penalties for shredding documents or for not fulfilling their fiduciary responsibilities.

## SUMMARY

Every business leader should strive to become a Quantum Leader, using Six Sigma as the methodology for gathering and assessing the data that support fact-based decisions (see Figure 25.1).

*At the end of the day,* Six Sigma can lead the way if individuals will take the initiative to invest in themselves, set aside learned behaviors and predispositions, and embrace a rational fact-based approach to Quantum Leadership.

Do you:

|  | Yes | No |
|---|---|---|
| ☐ Study the marketplace and environment | | |
| ☐ Envision an alternative future | | |
| ☐ Map a course that leads to that future state | | |
| ☐ Build a consensus around the Vision and the course | | |
| ☐ Create the capability to create that future | | |
| ☐ Plunge ahead without hesitation or regret | | |
| ☐ Learn from mistakes and rapidly implement lessons learned | | |
| ☐ Engage external organizations as if they were internal | | |
| ☐ Learn continuously and teach others | | |
| ☐ Perpetuate forward momentum | | |
| ☐ Communicate and build consensus on the Vision | | |
| ☐ Change the measurements | | |
| ☐ Perform "blood" transfusions | | |
| ☐ Engage people who make the organization uncomfortable | | |
| ☐ Find the doers and liberate them | | |
| ☐ Manage the status quo people | | |
| ☐ Put change in context | | |
| ☐ Serve as a lightning rod | | |
| ☐ Just do it | | |
| ☐ Not linger – move on | | |

**Figure 25.1** The Quantum Leader* checklist.

*Quantum Leaders lead change through interpreting data and modeling behavior.

# Glossary

*Acceptance Test Analysis*—An evaluation of supplier acceptance test data to identify test reduction opportunities and parameters, which drive yields.

*ADA*—A programming language named after Lady Ada Lovelace, who is considered to be the world's first programmer. ADA was used on the NASA Space Station Training Facility (SSTF).

*Affinitization*—The grouping or arranging of like issues or solutions into a set to draw out commonality. This technique is used to examine observations, issues, and solutions and to narrow the list to a single or few opportunities to improve.

*Agile Manufacturing*—A method of determining methods that permit rapid redeployment of assets in response to changing product or process requirements.

*Agreement Continuum*—An agreement based on long-term relationships with suppliers through mutually beneficial goals, trust, and benefits.

*AICPA*—American Institute of Certified Public Accountants

*Alliance Agreement*—An agreement that supports the supply chain Vision.

*Barriers*—Anything that prevents an organization from achieving the desired state. When identifying barriers it is crucial to be brutal and honest because the most obvious barriers are seldom the real barriers. Getting to the root cause of barriers is necessary to achieve the transformation to the desired state.

*BAAN*—An enterprise resource planning (ERP) software application.

*Black Belt*—Individuals trained in Six Sigma methodologies including data-driven decision-making. Responsibilities include completing process improvement projects, reducing defects and waste, and training Green Belts.

*Blitz*—A short-term, limited objective team effort with the objective of improving the performance of an underperforming process. Also known as Kaizen Blitz.

*Bold Long-Term Goal*—The long-term state of the organization envisioned by the Leadership Team. This should be the mother of all stretch goals; something so bold that the team should almost be embarrassed to set it as the overall goal. However, a bold goal is exactly what is needed to galvanize the Leadership Team and the team members of the organization into action.

*Capstone Project*—A project conducted at the end of formal training or an apprenticeship to demonstrate competency and contribute to the overall body of knowledge.

*CASE*—Computer-aided software engineering

*CE*—Concurrent engineering

*Champion*—An individual who selects and mentors Black Belts.

*CMM*—Capability Maturity Model (by the Software Engineering Institute)

*Concurrent Engineering*—A systematic approach to the integrated, concurrent design of products and their related processes, including manufacture and support.

*Continuous Flow Manufacturing*—Planning for consistent operational performance by improved product and information flow through the manufacturing cycle.

*Continuous Measurable Improvement*—A work regime that employs statistical tools to measure and track the performance improvement that occurs through planned and specific efforts on an ongoing basis.

*Control Activities*—The policies and control procedures to address risks and accomplish management objectives. Control activities include: (1) segregation of duties, (2) information processing, such as checking accuracy and completeness or authorization over transactions, (3) performance reviews comparing actual with expected performance, and (4) physical controls, such as limiting access to computer systems, independent reconciliation of accounting records, and safeguarding assets.

*Control Environment*—The overall attitude, awareness, and actions of the board of directors, management, owners, and others concerning the importance of control and its emphasis in the entity. Seven factors affect the control environment: (1) integrity and ethical values, (2) audit committee and board of directors, (3) philosophy of management and operating style, (4) assignment of authority and responsibility, (5) commitment to competence, (6) human resource policies and procedures, and (7) organizational structure.

*Core Purpose*—The reason the organization exists, which drives the organization toward its desired (future) state.

*Core Values*—The fundamental principles or bedrock of the organization's culture. In order to change the organization's performance, actions taken must be consistent with the core values so the members of the organization will embrace the changes that are sought.

***Corporate Project Office for Internal Controls***—A group of people carefully selected to have the right blend of controls expertise, audit and compliance focus, along with Six Sigma and project management experience.

***COSO Framework***—Committee of Signatory Organizations report of the Treadway Commission on Internal Controls, in response to the Sarbanes-Oxley Act of 2002 to strengthen the public reporting requirements of firms who publicly trade their stock in the United States.

***CTQ***—Critical to quality.

***Cultural Integration***—Methods to bridge the differences between groups that happen when companies acquire other businesses or merge activities with other organizations.

***Current State***—The "as is" condition of the organization. The current state should encompass both the problems that the firm encounters in executing its strategy and the basic areas of strength that the firm exploits (otherwise, the desired state simply becomes the inverse of the current state).

***Default Processes***—The result of procedures and processes that evolve without direction due to changing personnel or being applied to new situations without being adequately tailored to the new situation.

***Design for Assembly***—Methods used to identify design features that increase the labor time required to assemble a final product and identify lower cost alternatives.

***Design for Manufacturability***—Methods used to identify alternative design solutions to reduce design complexity, reduce design cost to build, and increase the ease of manufacturing.

***Design for Manufacturing and/or Assembly Workshop***—A workshop format targeted for DMFA hardware manufacturing processes.

***Design of Experiments***—Methods used to optimize product designs or manufacturing processes through experimentation changing variables to determine optimal performance outputs.

***Design Quality Scorecards***—A quality tool used to display data on quality performance to provide ongoing and historical visibility to the analyst.

***Design to Cost***—Methods used to set and achieve product cost goals through design trade-off analysis.

***Design/Part Failure Modes and Effects Analysis***—Methods used to identify the elements of design or parts used in a design that have the greatest statistical probability of failure and the conditions under which failure is most likely to occur.

***Desired State***—A measurable statement of what the collective Leadership Team wishes to achieve within a set period of time that becomes the focal point of all activity undertaken to reach it. The desired state needs to be built from the strengths that the organization possesses today, unless the strategy is to acquire a new business.

*Deterministic*—Empirically determined.

*DFA*—Design for Assembly.

*DFM*—Design for Manufacturing.

*DFMAS*—Design for Manufacturing and/or Assembly. Using a designated set of tools within a facilitated workshop to create a best-value product design that minimizes cost and cycle-time to produce while ensuring that performance and quality targets are reached.

*DFMEA*—Design failure modes and effects analysis.

*DFSS*—Design for Six Sigma.

*Disclosure Committee*—A committee for Sarbane-Oxley Act of 2002, section 302 and 404 assessments and management assertions that reviews work plans and schedules, and monitors progress made against schedules and budgets. They report back to the corporate board audit committee.

*Disidentification*—Apathy about the Vision.

*E-commerce Linkage*—One of the drivers for total cost/best value.

*Electron Stage*—The point in the product development process where the design is still on the computer "drawing board." This is the best time and place to make changes to a design.

*ERP*—Enterprise resource planning (software system).

*Essential Performance*—Each firm has several areas that are so important to the performance of the firm that they should be considered areas of essential performance.

*Executive Dashboard*—A tool to manage the implementation of tasks. The purpose of the dashboard is to provide a summary view of the status of each major task. Subtasks are not identified on the dashboard, but they are specified on the individual task statements and the individual responsible for a particular effort has the ability to drill down to the status on each subtask as necessary.

*Functional Silos*—Separate organizations and reporting structures within an organization.

*Governance*—The body that governs or has authority in an organization.

*Governing Council*—The council that assists in the transition at the end of Six Sigma efforts.

*Green Belt*—An individual who retains his or her regular position within the firm, but is trained in the tools, methods, and skills necessary to conduct Six Sigma improvement projects either individually or as part of larger teams.

*IDA*—Institute for Defense Analyses.

*Information System and Communication*—An internal control that establishes an information system to manage and communicate the organization's activities and prepare financial statements. This system includes the accounting system, which consists of the methods and documents established to record, process, summarize, and report an entity's transactions and to maintain accountability for related assets and liabilities.

*Innovation Workshop*—A workshop format where the focus is on inventing a totally different approach to doing the work.

*Internal Control*—Based on the Sarbane-Oxley Act of 2002, the Committee of Sponsoring Organizations of the Treadway Commission defines internal control as a process, effected by an entity's board of directors, management, and other personnel, designed to provide reasonable assurance regarding the achievement of objectives in the categories of: (1) reliability of financial reporting, (2) operational effectiveness and efficiency, (3) compliance with applicable laws and regulations.

*IPD*—Integrated product development.

*IPT*—Integrated product team.

*ISO*—International Organization for Standardization.

*Just-in-time*—Removal of buffer stocks to organize production around delivery of raw materials or subsystems at the point in time at which they are going to be incorporated in production.

*Kaizen*—"Think common."

*Kaizen Blitz*—A short-term, limited objective team effort with the objective of improving the performance of an underperforming process.

*Kickoff Meeting*—A planned event to get everyone on the same page at the beginning. It allows all participants to see the same demonstrations, ask questions in a manner that everyone hears the answers at the same time, and obtains the same guidance.

*Lean and Agile Manufacturing Principles*—A combination of minimizing waste to create value and incorporation of responsiveness to change in responding to market opportunities.

*Lean Manufacturing*—A method of determining a production flow that eliminates waste and derives maximum value-add to the product.

*Lean Thinking*—The dynamic, knowledge-driven, and customer-focused process through which all people in a defined enterprise continuously eliminate waste with the goal of creating value.

*Low-Hanging Fruit*—The obvious problems. Finding and fixing these problems provides a measure of immediate results, but often only fixes symptoms and not root causes.

*Ministry of Defence (MoD)*—The United Kingdom counterpart to the U.S. Department of Defense (DoD).

*Monitoring*—An internal control that establishes mechanisms to provide feedback on whether the internal controls are operating as intended. Monitoring includes ongoing activities or separate evaluations, such as: (1) internal auditors,

(2) continual management review of exception and operation reports, (3) periodic independent audit, (4) regulators' suggestions for improvement, (5) response to customer complaints.

*Monte Carlo Analysis*—The probability of various scenarios essential to the identification of failure points.

*MRB*—Material Review Board.

*Organizational Integration Workshop*—A workshop format used to define the best methods of transitioning from the current state to one that is built upon the strengths of the new players. This is used after acquisitions or divestitures occur, or significant reorganizations change the responsibilities in the organization.

*Ownership and Analysis Capability for Processes*—The outcome of a workshop or process in which there is an enhanced sense of responsibility in those involved. This frequently happens after an intensive effort to look at how a process is conducted and a new process is created that improves upon the old. With team members putting their name on the process, they want to make sure that it works.

*Part Selection Process*—A method to standardize on fewer parts and suppliers, reduce part count, and improve part producibility/reliability; strategies to reduce obsolescence risk; and identify and develop strategies to minimize problem suppliers and parts.

*Performance-Based Specifications*—A shift in requirements. The new requirement includes a performance specification for a part rather than providing the supplier with a part number to supply.

*Performance Improvement Workshop*—A workshop format where the focus is on looking for root causes and opportunities for improvement in a facilitated cross-functional team where open and direct feedback on observations, concerns, and ideas lead to a new depth of understanding of cross-organizational discontinuities and opportunities. Most often used when organizations perform suboptimally or behind plan/schedule.

*Picos*—A workshop format targeted for hardware manufacturing processes.

*PIT*—Process improvement team.

*Predictor*™—An application that helps managers evaluate skill gaps against validated job families from a variety of world-class companies.

*Prereading*—A method for starting a strategic planning or positioning event by having Leadership Team members describe the key "take away" from books and articles on how organizations transform themselves and studies of firms that have successfully achieved high levels of continuing success. This allows members to share a conceptual understanding of how some firms progress from a current state to a desired state and the level of effort and commitment required to achieve this.

*Prime Contractor*—The program manager and project coordinator.

*Prioritization*—The process of establishing priorities for action or importance.

***Probabilistic***—The relationship between cause and effect using the tools of probability theory.

***Probabilistic Fracture Mechanics***—The engineering application of fracture mechanics specifically as applied to reliability.

***Process Documentation Workshop***—A workshop format used to capture and validate the processes that exist in an organization and determine how the work is actually being done. Essential for knowledge capture and sustained organizational improvement results.

***Process Improvement Workshop***—A workshop format used to determine means of improving a process, bringing together process actors and redesigning to speed process flow and efficiency. It involves determining how a process can be improved or replaced by inventing a totally different approach to doing the work.

***Process Optimization Workshop***—A workshop format used to work through the issues within the process to determine the optimal method of doing the work required.

***Prototype Stage***—The point in a product development process where the detailed design is complete and a first attempt is made to make a working model of the intended final product.

***QFD***—Quality function deployment. (See www.qfdi.org for more information.)

***Quality Circles***—A group that meets regularly to discuss quality-related work problems so that they may examine and generate solutions to these. The circle is empowered to promote and bring the quality improvements through to fruition.

***Quantum Results***—The ability to take an organization to dramatically higher levels of performance.

***Rapid Prototyping***—Software development methodology.

***Reduction in Cost***—Time is money. The leaner the process, the faster it may be performed. However, a reduction in cost is not automatically a reduction in headcount. Often, in growth organizations, the result of a Six Sigma project workshop is for existing staff to be able to process increasing volumes of work, which eliminates the need to add to staff. Thus, the efficiency does not result in the elimination of existing personnel, but rather the ability to contain cost increases while managing substantial increases in business activity.

***Reduction in Cycle-Time***—A method for reducing the amount of time that it takes to execute a process or build a specific product. It is accomplished by placing a task where it is performed with highest efficiency. Elimination of duplicate or unnecessary tasks also reduces the time that is necessary to execute a process. Improving hand-offs, which tend to be points of substantial discontinuity, also eliminates rework or duplicate efforts.

***Reduction in Space Requirements***—Most organizations do not engineer their workflow. Functional organizations may not be collocated with other organizations with which they conduct the most business. Workshops are often able to identify opportunities to rearrange the workflow to make it more efficient. In so doing they often identify opportunities to reduce space requirements.

*Relationship Focus*—One of the drivers for total cost/best value.

*Risk Assessment*　An internal control that involves identification, analysis, and management of risks affecting the organization. Management may initiate plans, programs, or actions to address specific risks or it may decide to accept a risk because of cost or other considerations.

*ROI*—Return on investment.

*Root Cause Analysis*—Diagnose and resolve critical problems through analysis of the presenting symptoms to determine the common causes rather than attacking individual symptoms.

*Rosetta Stone*—A device used to decipher an unknown language, set of circumstances, or presenting problems.

*SAP*—An enterprise resource planning (ERP) software application.

*Sarbanes-Oxley Act of 2002*—A Federal law, applying to all publicly traded companies regulated by the Securities and Exchange Commission, that is intended to bring about a new level of attention to corporate governance and to strengthen the public reporting requirements.

*Schedule/Plan Validation/Verification Workshop*—A workshop format for bringing together cross-functional teams to determine whether a schedule or plan can be met and what actions can be taken to improve upon the current plan/schedule.

*SEI*—Software Engineering Institute (at Carnegie Mellon University) best known for the Capability Maturity Model (CMM).

*Six Sigma*—A concurrent process that brings the customer, supplier, and company personnel together to change and/or integrate cultures, using development tools and a methodology to collectively invent best value process/product solutions. A major benefit is that it is an intense, disciplined activity that quickly and decisively improves processes or designs while reducing cycle time and/or cost, and increasing performance and/or quality.

*Smart Procurement Process*—A U.K. Ministry of Defence (MoD) process that closely parallels Six Sigma.

*Software Development Workshop*—A workshop format that harnesses the power of cross-functional teams, which include customers and vendors to optimize the development process. This process creates a consistent approach by the development team and minimizes steps and tasks, thereby reducing cycle-time and cost while reaching quality and consistency targets of the final products.

*Software Innovation Workshop*—A workshop format in which a diverse team of experts work together in a structured process to discover means and methods of dramatically improving how software is developed for a defined application, moving beyond the traditional processes and structures. The goal is to standardize cost efficient software processes tailored to design goals and system requirements.

*SPICE*—Software Process Improvement Capability dEtermination.

*SPO*—System program office.

*SSTF*—Space Station Training Facility (NASA).

*Statistical Analysis and Process Control*—The use of statistical sampling to determine whether a manufacturing process is operating within specific control limits to maintain final product quality.

*Strategic Planning*—The process of gathering information about the larger environment in which an organization operates and through a structured process selecting a course of actions that will result in desired business objectives over a defined period of time.

*Strategy/Capability Alignment Workshop*—A workshop format used to determine what is needed for the organizational capabilities to support the corporate strategy, and then create a roadmap that defines the transition to alignment.

*Subcontractors*—Suppliers that provide components for the main project.

*Sun Tzu*—A group of Chinese authors during the period 500-320 BC who produced a treatise on philosophy, logistics, espionage, strategy, and tactics known as The Art of War.

*Supplier Day Activity*—A way to develop partnership with suppliers.

*Supplier Development Workshop*—A workshop format that brings together cross-organizational teams to clearly express expectations to vendors and determine methods and means that will permit the vendor to meet those expectations. May apply tools such as those used in design for manufacturing depending upon the product or service to be acquired.

*Supply Chain*—The entire set of suppliers to an organization.

*SWOT Analysis*—An analysis of the organization's strengths, weaknesses, opportunities, and threats.

*Synchronous*—A workshop format targeted for hardware manufacturing processes.

*Synchronous Engineering*—A methodology bringing together cross-functional teams to maximize concurrence in the processes used to produce or deliver services to customers.

*Synchronous Workflow Analysis Workshop*—A workshop format that brings together cross-functional teams to maximize concurrence in the processes used to produce or deliver services to customers.

*Task Statement of Work*—The detailed planning of each task by the Champion that has been selected. The task and expected result is clearly defined and reviewed by the sponsor, and resources required to complete the task are identified. Then the task is assigned to a task lead and team with due dates.

*Top-Five Tasks*—A method to narrow the tasks to achieve any kind of performance improvement effort. Twenty percent of the actions achieve 80 percent of the solution, so the top-five tasks list is an attempt to identify that 20 percent, give them focused attention with adequate resources, and ensure that these actions are completed expeditiously.

*Total Cost/Best Value*—A collaboration driven by collaborative planning, continuous product improvement, relationship focus, and E-commerce linkage.

*Training Requirements Analysis Workshop*—A workshop format used to accelerate the process of defining the organizational requirements for training and maintaining a highly skilled workforce.

*Vision*—A conceptualization of a different or future state that an organization aspires to achieve.

*WORKOUT*—A General Electric program of town meetings focused on empowerment and bureaucracy busting started in the late 1980s.

# Bibliography
# and Further Reading

Akers, Michael D., and Frank A. Wiebe. 1991. Accountants as change agents. *Woman CPA* 53, no. 4 (Fall): 22-25.

Armenakis, Achilles A., and Arthur G. Bedeian. 1992. The roles of metaphors in organizational change: Change agent and change target perspectives. *Group & Organization Management* 17, no. 3 (September): 242-248.

Belasco, James A. 1990. Enlist champion change agents. *Executive Excellence* 7, no. 8 (August): 9-10.

Bennis, Warren G. 1993. *Beyond bureaucracy: Essays on the development and evolution of human organization.* San Francisco: Jossey-Bass.

Bennis, Warren. 1993a. Change agents. *Executive Excellence* 10, no. 9 (September): 18-19.

Breyfogle III, Forest W., James M. Cupello, and Becky Meadows. 2001. *Managing Six Sigma: A practical guide to understanding, assessing and implementing the strategy that yields bottom-line success.* New York: John Wiley.

Carr, David K. 1996. *Managing the change process: A field book for change agents, consultants, team leaders and reengineering managers.* New York: McGraw Hill.

Cripe, Edward J. 1993. How to get top-notch change agents. *Training & Development* 47, no. 12 (December): 52-58.

Currid, Cheryl. 1993. Test yourself for the seven traits of 'change agent syndrome.' *InforWorld* 15, no. 11 (15 March): 69.

Dinsmore, Paul C. 1995. Revisiting change management. *PM Network* 9, no. 6 (June): 28-31.

Eckes, George, 2001. *The Six Sigma Revolution: How General Electric and others turned process into profits.* New York: John Wiley.

Fougere, Kenneth T. 1991. The future role of the systems analyst as a change agent. *Journal of Systems Management* 42, no. 11 (November): 6-9.

Freed, David H. 1998. Please don't shoot me: I'm only the change agent. *Health Care Supervisor* 17, no. 1 (September): 56-61.

General Electric Company. 2001. What is Six Sigma? The roadmap to customer impact. Available on the GE website: www.ge.com/sixsigma/

Grant, Robert M., and Renato Cibin. 1996. The chief executive as change agent. *Planning Review* 24, no. 1 (January/February): 9-11.

Guaspari, John. 1996. If you want your people to buy-in to change. *Across the Board* 33, no. 5 (May): 32-36.

Harry, Mikel, and Richard Schroeder. 2000. *Six Sigma: The breakthrough management strategy revolutionizing the world's top corporations.* New York: Currency.

Hitt, William D. 1988. The leader as change agent. [2] *The leader-manager: Guidelines for action.* Columbus, OH: Battelle Press.

Hutton, David W. 1994. *The change agent's handbook: A survival guide to quality improvement champions.* Milwaukee: ASQC Quality Press.

Kennedy, Arnold. 1996. Attila the Hun: Leadership as a change agent. *Hospital Materiel Management* 17, no. 3 (February): 29-37.

Kumar, Kamalesh, and Mary S. Thibodeaux. 1990. Organizational politics and planned organizational change: A pragmatic approach. *Group & Organization Studies* 15, no. 4 (December): 357-365.

London, Manuel. 1997. *Change agents: New roles and innovation strategies for human resource professionals.* San Francisco: Jossey-Bass.

Marshall, Jeffrey. A change agent looks back. *US Banke.* 107, no. 6 (June): 39-42.

Maurer, Rick. 1996. Put resistance to work for you. *HR Magazine* 41, no. 4 (April): 75+.

Murman, Earll et. al. 2002. *Lean enterprise value: Insights from MIT's lean aerospace initiative.* London: Palgrave.

Pande, Peter S., Robert P. Neuman, and Roland R. Cavanagh. 2000. *The Six Sigma way: How GE, Motorola, and other top companies are honing their performance.* New York: McGraw Hill.

Pickering, John W., and Robert E. Matson. 1992. Why executive development programs (alone) don't work. *Training & Development* 46, no. 5 (May): 91-95.

Potter, Christopher C. 1989. What is culture: And can it be useful for organizational change agents? *Leadership & Organization Development Journal* 10, no. 3: 17-24.

Recardo, Ronald J. 1995. Overcoming resistance to change. *National Productivity Review* 14, no. 2 (Spring): 5-12.

Scharf, Alan. 1987. Improving your personal effectiveness as a change agent. *Industrial Management* 29, no. 5 (September/October): 17-21.

Sicker, Ronald. 2002. *Driving Six Sigma.* Rochester, NY: TCM Books.

Stebel, Paul. 1996. Why do employees resist change? *Harvard Business Review* 74, no. 3 (May/June): 86-92.

Thompson, James. 1996. Rogue workers and change agents. *Government Executive* 28, no. 4 (April): 46-49.

Tribus, Myron. 1989. Changing the corporate culture – A roadmap for the change agent." *Human Systems Management* 8, no.1: 11-22.

Von Dran, Gisela M. et al. 1996. Arizona State University's lesson in creating public-sector change agents. *National Productivity Review* 15, no. 2 (Spring): 17-22.

# Index